Mastering Flask Web Development

Development
Second Edition

Build enterprise-grade, scalable Python web applications

Daniel Gaspar
Jack Stouffer

BIRMINGHAM - MUMBAI

Mastering Flask Web Development
Second Edition

Commissioning Editor: Amarabha Banerjee
Acquisition Editor: Devanshi Doshi
Content Development Editor: Onkar Wani
Technical Editor: Diksha Wakode
Copy Editor: Safis Editing
Project Coordinator: Sheejal Shah
Proofreader: Safis Editing
Indexer: Rekha Nair
Graphics: Alishon Mendonsa
Production Coordinator: Aparna Bhagat

First published: September 2015
Second Edition: October 2018

Production reference: 1301018

Published by Packt Publishing Ltd.
Livery Place
35 Livery Street
Birmingham
B3 2PB, UK.

ISBN 978-1-78899-540-5

www.packtpub.com

`mapt.io`

Mapt is an online digital library that gives you full access to over 5,000 books and videos, as well as industry leading tools to help you plan your personal development and advance your career. For more information, please visit our website.

Why subscribe?

- Spend less time learning and more time coding with practical eBooks and Videos from over 4,000 industry professionals

- Improve your learning with Skill Plans built especially for you

- Get a free eBook or video every month

- Mapt is fully searchable

- Copy and paste, print, and bookmark content

Packt.com

Did you know that Packt offers eBook versions of every book published, with PDF and ePub files available? You can upgrade to the eBook version at `www.packt.com` and as a print book customer, you are entitled to a discount on the eBook copy. Get in touch with us at `customercare@packtpub.com` for more details.

At `www.packt.com`, you can also read a collection of free technical articles, sign up for a range of free newsletters, and receive exclusive discounts and offers on Packt books and eBooks.

Contributors

About the authors

Daniel Gaspar is a programmer and DevOps engineer with more than 20 years' experience. He has worked in a wide range of sectors, including government and finance. He is currently working at Miniclip (the global leader in digital games). He uses a wide range of tools in his daily work, but Flask caught his attention because of its excellently designed API and simplicity. Daniel is an OSS and Python enthusiast, and has developed a widely used extension/framework named Flask-AppBuilder, used by Airbnb on Superset and AirFlow.

> *First, I would like to thank my wife, Susana, and my beautiful children, Mariana and Pedro, for their amazing support, enthusiasm, and patience. Also, a big thank you to everyone at Packt Publishing, especially to Onkar Wani, with whom it was a pleasure to work.*

Jack Stouffer is a programmer who has several years of experience in designing web applications. He switched to Flask two years ago for all his projects. He currently works for Apollo America in Auburn Hills, Michigan and writes internal business tools and software using Python, Flask, and JavaScript. Jack is a believer and supporter of open source technology. When he released his Flask examples with the recommended best practices on GitHub, it became one of the most popular Flask repositories on the site. Jack has also worked as a reviewer for Flask Framework Cookbook, Packt.

About the reviewer

Damyan Bogoev is based in Bulgaria, where he currently works at Gtmhub as a software engineer. Prior to Gtmhub, Damyan worked at Telerik.

His background is in developing backend server applications and tools for infrastructure automation, management, and monitoring.

Damyan is also technical reviewer for the *Web API Development with Flask* video course.

Packt is searching for authors like you

If you're interested in becoming an author for Packt, please visit `authors.packtpub.com` and apply today. We have worked with thousands of developers and tech professionals, just like you, to help them share their insight with the global tech community. You can make a general application, apply for a specific hot topic that we are recruiting an author for, or submit your own idea.

Table of Contents

Preface

Flask is a microframework with a very well designed API, designed to provide the minimum amount of functionality that is needed to create web applications. It does what it's designed to do really well. Unlike other web frameworks, Flask does not have an entire ecosystem bundled with it, no out-of-the-box features to handle databases, cache, security or form handling.

The goal of this concept is to allow programmers to design their applications or tools any way they want, no structure or design is imposed. However, because Flask community is rather large, you can find a wide range of extensions that will help you leverage Flask with a huge set of technologies. One of the main focuses of this book is to introduce these extensions and find out how they can help to avoid reinventing the wheel. The best part about these extensions is that if you don't need their extra functionalities, you don't need to include them and your app will remain small.

This book will help you structure your application to easily scale up to any size. Using packages and a simple and predictable namespace is paramount to keep maintainability and boost team productivity. This is why the other main focus of this book is how to create a **Model View Controller** (**MVC**) architecture with Flask apps.

Modern applications must go beyond well-structured code. Security, dependency isolation, environment configuration, development/production parity and ability to scale on load are factors that must not be neglected. Throughout this book, you will learn how to address these issues, identify possible risks and think ahead of time.

A large amount of research and a lot of first-hand experience of what can go wrong when developing and deploying web applications has been poured into this book. I sincerely hope you will enjoy reading it.

Who this book is for

The ideal target audience for this book is Python developers who want to use Flask and its advanced features to create enterprise grade and lightweight applications. The book is for those who have had some exposure of Flask and want of take their skills from introductory to master level.

What this book covers

Chapter 1, *Getting Started*, helps readers set up a Flask environment for development using the best practices for Python projects. You are given a very basic skeleton Flask app that is built throughout the book.

Chapter 2, *Creating Models with SQLAlchemy*, shows how to use the Python database library SQLAlchemy in conjunction with Flask to create an object-oriented API for your database.

Chapter 3, *Creating Views with Templates*, shows how to use Flask's templating system, Jinja, to dynamically create HTML by leveraging your SQLAlchemy models.

Chapter 4, *Creating Controllers with Blueprints*, covers how to use Flask's blueprints feature in order to organize your view code while also avoiding repeating yourself.

Chapter 5, *Advanced Application Structure*, uses the knowledge gained in the last four chapters, explains how to reorganize the code files in order to create a more maintainable and testable application structure.

Chapter 6, *Securing Your App*, explains how to use various Flask extensions in order to add a login system with permissions-based access to each view.

Chapter 7, *Using NoSQL with Flask*, shows what a NoSQL database is and how to integrate one into your application when it allows more powerful features.

Chapter 8, *Building RESTful APIs*, shows how to provide the data stored in the application's database to third parties in a secure and easy-to-use manner.

Chapter 9, *Creating Asynchronous Tasks with Celery*, explains how to move expensive or time-consuming programs to the background so the application does not slow down.

Chapter 10, *Useful Flask Extensions*, explains how to leverage popular Flask extensions in order to make your app faster, add more features, and make debugging easier.

Chapter 11, *Building Your Own Extension*, teaches you how Flask extensions work and how to create your own.

Chapter 12, *Testing Flask Apps*, explains how to add unit tests and user interface tests to your app for quality assurance and reducing the amount of buggy code.

Chapter 13, *Deploying Flask Apps*, explains how to take your completed app from development to being hosted on a live server.

To get the most out of this book

To get started with this book, all you will need is a text editor of your choice, a web browser, and Python installed on your machine.
Windows, Mac OS X, and Linux users should all be able to easily follow along with the content of this book.

Download the example code files

You can download the example code files for this book from your account at `www.packt.com`. If you purchased this book elsewhere, you can visit `www.packt.com/support` and register to have the files emailed directly to you.

You can download the code files by following these steps:

1. Log in or register at `www.packt.com`.
2. Select the **SUPPORT** tab.
3. Click on **Code Downloads & Errata**.
4. Enter the name of the book in the **Search** box and follow the onscreen instructions.

Once the file is downloaded, please make sure that you unzip or extract the folder using the latest version of:

- WinRAR/7-Zip for Windows
- Zipeg/iZip/UnRarX for Mac
- 7-Zip/PeaZip for Linux

The code bundle for the book is also hosted on GitHub at `https://github.com/PacktPublishing/Mastering-Flask-Web-Development-Second-Edition`. In case there's an update to the code, it will be updated on the existing GitHub repository.

We also have other code bundles from our rich catalog of books and videos available at `https://github.com/PacktPublishing/`. Check them out!

Conventions used

There are a number of text conventions used throughout this book.

`CodeInText`: Indicates code words in text, database table names, folder names, filenames, file extensions, pathnames, dummy URLs, user input, and Twitter handles. Here is an example: "Mount the downloaded `WebStorm-10*.dmg` disk image file as another disk in your system."

A block of code is set as follows:

```
from flask import g
....
# Set some key with some value on a request context
g.some_key = "some_value"
# Get a key
v = g.some_key
# Get and remove a key
v = g.pop('some_key', "default_if_not_present")
```

When we wish to draw your attention to a particular part of a code block, the relevant lines or items are set in bold:

```
from flask import Flask, render_template
from flask_sqlalchemy import SQLAlchemy
from flask_migrate import Migrate

db = SQLAlchemy()
migrate = Migrate()
```

Any command-line input or output is written as follows:

```
$ source env/bin/activate
$ pip install -r requirements.txt
```

Bold: Indicates a new term, an important word, or words that you see onscreen. For example, words in menus or dialog boxes appear in the text like this. Here is an example: "Select **System info** from the **Administration** panel."

 Warnings or important notes appear like this.

Tips and tricks appear like this.

Get in touch

Feedback from our readers is always welcome.

General feedback: If you have questions about any aspect of this book, mention the book title in the subject of your message and email us at customercare@packtpub.com.

Errata: Although we have taken every care to ensure the accuracy of our content, mistakes do happen. If you have found a mistake in this book, we would be grateful if you would report this to us. Please visit www.packt.com/submit-errata, selecting your book, clicking on the Errata Submission Form link, and entering the details.

Piracy: If you come across any illegal copies of our works in any form on the Internet, we would be grateful if you would provide us with the location address or website name. Please contact us at copyright@packt.com with a link to the material.

If you are interested in becoming an author: If there is a topic that you have expertise in and you are interested in either writing or contributing to a book, please visit authors.packtpub.com.

Reviews

Please leave a review. Once you have read and used this book, why not leave a review on the site that you purchased it from? Potential readers can then see and use your unbiased opinion to make purchase decisions, we at Packt can understand what you think about our products, and our authors can see your feedback on their book. Thank you!

For more information about Packt, please visit packt.com.

Getting Started

1

Over the course of this book, you will be introduced to multiple concepts that will enable you to build a complete modern web application. You will progress from a "Hello world" web page to a complete web application that uses databases, caches, asynchronous task processing, authentication, role-based access, a REST API, and internationalization. You will learn a comprehensive way of structuring your application so that it can grow effortlessly. To choose between SQL and NoSQL technologies, you will learn how to use the most common Flask extensions to help you leverage multiple technologies, from sending emails to authentication using social media accounts. Toward the end, you will learn how to write tests, build a modern continuous integration/delivery pipeline with Docker and Jenkins, deploy your application to multiple cloud services, and know how to deal with high availability and scaling. We will tackle all of these topics with a simple and practical approach.

Flask is the Python web framework that we are going to use. It has a very well-designed API, is very easy to learn, and makes no assumptions whatsoever as to what technology stack you are going to use, so it won't get in your way. Flask has a micro footprint, but leverages an extension system that contains hundreds of packages from a very active and vibrant community.

In this first chapter, you will learn how to set up your development environment and build your first Flask application. We will be covering the following topics:

- Setting up and learning how to use Git, a powerful version control system
- Learning pip, the Python management system, and how to create virtual environments with different setups
- Setting up and learning the basic facts about Docker
- Building a first simple Flask application

Version control with Git

Using Python or any other language requires you to use a version control system. A version control system is a tool that records changes in files over time. This allows a programmer to revert to an earlier version of the file and identify bugs more easily. You can test new ideas without fear of breaking your current code, and your team can work using a predefined workflow without stepping on each others' toes. Git was developed by Linus Torvalds, the father of Linux. It's decentralized, light, and has great features that get the job done the right way.

Installing Git

Installing Git is very simple. Simply go to http://www.git-scm.com/downloads and click on the **operating system (OS)** that is being run. A program will begin to download will walk you through the basic installation process.

Git on Windows

Git was originally solely developed for Unix OSes (for example, Linux and macOS X). Consequently, using Git on Windows is not seamless. During the installation, the installer will ask whether you want to install Git alongside the normal Windows Command Prompt. Do not pick this option. Choose the default option that will install a new type of command processor on your system named **Bash** (**Bourne-again shell**), which is the same command processor that the Unix systems use. Bash is much more powerful than the default Windows command line, and this is what we will be using for all the examples in this book.

 A good introduction to Bash for beginners can be found at http://linuxcommand.org.

Git basics

Git is a very complex tool; only the basics that are needed for this book will be covered in this section.

To learn more, refer to the Git documentation at
http://www.git-scm.com/doc.

Git does not track your changes automatically. In order for Git to run properly, we have to give it the following information:

- Which folders to track
- When to save the state of the code
- What to track and what not to track

Before we can do anything, we have to tell Git to initialize a new git repository in our directory. Run the following code on your Terminal:

```
$ git init
```

Git will now start to track changes in our project. As git tracks our files, we can see the status of our tracked files and any files that are not tracked by typing the following command:

```
$ git status
```

Now we can save our first commit, which is a snapshot of our code at the time that we run the commit command:

```
# In Bash, comments are marked with a #, just like Python
# Add any files that have changes and you wish to save in this
# commit
$ git add main.py
# Commit the changes, add in your commit message with -m
$ git commit -m "Our first commit"
```

Now, at any point in the future, we can return to this point in our project. Adding files that are to be committed is called **staging** files in Git. Remember that you should only add stage files if you are ready to commit them. Once the files are staged, any further changes will not be staged. For an example of more advanced Git usage, add any text to your main.py file with your text editor and then run the following:

```
# To see the changes from the last commit
$ git diff
# To see the history of your changes
$ git log
# As an example, we will stage main.py
# and then remove any added files from the stage
```

```
$ git add main.py
$ git status
$ git reset HEAD main.py
# After any complicated changes, be sure to run status
# to make sure everything went well
$ git status
# lets delete the changes to main.py, reverting to its state at the
# last commit # This can only be run on files that aren't staged
$ git checkout -- main.py
```

Your terminal should look something like the following:

Note that in the preceding example I have modified the `main.py` file by adding the comment `# Changed to show the git diff command`.

One important step to include in every Git repository is a `.gitignore` file. This file tells Git what files to ignore. This way you can safely commit and add all your files. The following are some common files that you can ignore:

- Python's byte code files (`*.pyc`)
- Databases (specially for our examples using SQLLite database files) (`*.db`)
- Secrets (never push secrets (password, keys, and so on) to your repositories)
- IDE metadata files (`.idea`)
- The `Virtualenv` directory (env or venv)

Here's a simple example of a `gitignore` file:

```
*.pyc
*.pem
*.pub
*.tar.gz
*.zip
*.sql
*.db
secrets.txt
./tmp
./build/*
.idea/*
.idea
env
venv
```

Now we can safely add all the files to `git` and commit them:

```
$ git add --all
$ git status
$ git commit -a -m "Added gitignore and all the projects missing
  files"
```

The Git system's `checkout` command is rather advanced for this simple introduction, but it is used to change the current status of the Git system's HEAD pointer, which refers to the current location of our code in the history of our project. This will be shown in the next example.

Now, if we wish to see the code in a previous commit, we should first run the following command:

```
$ git log
commit cd88be37f12fb596be743ccba7e8283dd567ac05 (HEAD -> master)
Author: Daniel Gaspar
Date: Sun May 6 16:59:46 2018 +0100

    Added gitignore and all the projects missing files
commit beb471198369e64a8ee8f6e602acc97250dce3cd
Author: Daniel Gaspar
Date: Fri May 4 19:06:57 2018 +0100

    Our first commit
```

The string of characters next to our `commit` message, `beb4711`, is called the **hash** of our commit. It is the unique identifier of the commit that we can use to return to the saved state. Now, to take the project back to the previous state, run the following command:

```
$ git checkout beb4711
```

Your Git project is now in a special state where any changes or commits will neither be saved nor affect any commits that were made after the one you checked out. This state is just for viewing old code. To return to the normal mode of Git, run the following command:

```
$ git checkout master
```

Git branches and flow

Source control branches are an important feature that works great in team projects. A developer can create a new line of code from a specific point in time, revision, or tag. In this way, developing new features, creating releases, and making bugfixes or hotfixes can be done safely and subjected to team revision, and/or automatic integration tools (such as tests, code coverage, lint tools). A branch can be merged with other branches until it finally reaches the main line of code, called the *master branch*.

But let's get our hands on a practical exercise. Let's say that we want to develop a new feature. Our first chapter example displays the traditional "Hello World" message, but we want it to say "good morning" to the users. First, we create a branch from a special branch called the `feature/good-morning` that for now is a copy of the master branch, as shown in the following code:

```
# Display our branches
$ git branch
* master
# Create a branch called feature/good-morning from master
$ git branch feature/good-morning
# Display our branches again
$ git branch
  feature/good-morning
* master
# Check out the new feature/good-morning branch
$ git checkout feature/good-morning
```

This could be resumed to the following:

```
$ git checkout -b feature/good-morning master
```

Now let's change our code to display **good morning** to the visitors of a certain URL, along with their names. To do this, we change `main.py`, which looks like the following code:

```
@app.route('/')
def home():
    return '<h1>Hello world</h1>'
```

We change `main.py` to the following:

```
@app.route('/username')
def home():
    return '<h1>Good Morning %s</h1>' % username
```

Let's look at what we have done:

```
$ git diff
diff --git a/main.py b/main.py
index 3e0aacc..1a930d9 100755
--- a/main.py
+++ b/main.py
@@ -5,9 +5,9 @@ app = Flask(__name__)
 app.config.from_object(DevConfig)

 # Changed to show the git diff command
-@app.route('/')
-def home():
```

```
- return '<h1>Hello World!</h1>'
+@app.route('/<username>')
+def home(username):
+ return '<h1>Good Morning %s</h1>' % username

 if __name__ == '__main__':
     app.run()
```

Looks good. Let's commit, as shown in the following code:

```
$ git commit -m "Display good morning because its nice"
[feature/good-morning d4f7fb8] Display good morning because its nice
 1 file changed, 3 insertions(+), 3 deletions(-)
```

Now, if we were working as part of a team, or if our work was open source (or if we just wanted to back up our work), we should upload (push) our code to a centralized remote origin. One way of doing this is to push our code to a version control system, such as **Bitbucket** or **GitHub**, and then open a **pull request** to the master branch. This pull request will show our changes. As such, it may need approval from other team members, and many other features that these systems can provide.

 One example of a pull request on the Flask project can be found at https://github.com/pallets/flask/pull/1767.

For our example, let's just merge to the master, as shown in the following code:

```
# Get back to the master branch
$ git checkout master
Switched to branch 'master'
bash-3.2$ git log
commit 139d121d6ecc7508e1017f364e6eb2e4c5f57d83 (HEAD -> master)
Author: Daniel Gaspar
Date: Fri May 4 23:32:42 2018 +0100

    Our first commit
# Merge our feature into the master branch
$ git merge feature/good-morning
Updating 139d121..5d44a43
Fast-forward
 main.py | 6 +++---
 1 file changed, 3 insertions(+), 3 deletions(-)
bash-3.2$ git log
commit 5d44a4380200f374c879ec1f7bda055f31243263 (HEAD -> master,
feature/good-morning)
Author: Daniel Gaspar
```

```
Date: Fri May 4 23:34:06 2018 +0100

Display good morning because its nice

commit 139d121d6ecc7508e1017f364e6eb2e4c5f57d83
Author: Daniel Gaspar <daniel.gaspar@miniclip.com>
Date: Fri May 4 23:32:42 2018 +0100

Our first commit
```

As you can see from the output, Git uses the fast-forward strategy by default. If we wanted to keep an extra commit log message that mentions the merge itself, then we could have used the `--no-ff` flag on the `git merge` command. This flag will disable the fast-forward merging strategy.

 For more details, go to `https://git-scm.com/book/en/v2/Git-Branching-Basic-Branching-and-Merging`.

Now imagine that we regret our change and want to revert the feature that we have just created back to an earlier version. To do this, we can use the following code:

```
$ git revert
```

With Git, you can actually delete your commits, but this is considered a really bad practice. Note that the `revert` command did not delete our merge, but created a new commit with the reverted changes. It's considered a good practice not to rewrite the past.

What was shown is a feature branch simple workflow. With big teams or projects, the use of more complex workflows is normally adopted to better isolate features, fixes, and releases, and to keep a stable line of code. This is what is proposed when using the git-flow process.

Now that we have a version control system, we are ready to cover Python's package management system.

Python package management with pip

In Python, programmers can download libraries from other programmers that extend the functionality of the standard Python library. As you already know from using Flask, a lot of Python's power comes from its large number of community-created libraries.

However, installing third-party libraries can be a huge pain to do correctly. Say that you want to install package X. Simple enough: download the ZIP file and run `setup.py`, right? Not quite. Package X relies on package Y, which in turn relies on Z and Q. None of this information was listed on package X's website, but these packages need to be installed for X to work at all. You then have to find all of the packages one by one and install them, and then hope that the packages you are installing don't require any extra packages themselves.

In order to automate this process, we use **pip**, the Python package manager.

Installing the Python package manager on Windows

If you are using Windows, and your previously installed version of Python is the current version, then you already have pip! If your Python installation is not the most recent version, then the easiest thing to do is to simply reinstall it. Download the Python Windows installer at `https://www.python.org/downloads/`.

In Windows, the variable that controls which programs are accessible from the command line is the `path`. To modify our `path` to include Python and pip, we have to add `C:\Python27` and `C:\Python27\Tools`. Edit the Windows `path` by opening the Windows menu, right-clicking on **Computer**, and clicking on **Properties**. Under **Advanced system settings**, click **Environment Variables...**. Scroll down until you find **Path**, double-click on it, and add `;C:\Python27;C:\Python27\Tools` to the end.

To make sure that you have modified your path correctly, close and reopen your Terminal and type the following into the command line:

```
pip --help
```

Pip should have printed its usage message, as shown in the following screenshot:

```
MINGW32:/c/dashboard                                            _ □ X

jstouffer@PULSAR /c/dashboard (master)
$ pip --help

Usage:
  pip <command> [options]

Commands:
  install                    Install packages.
  uninstall                  Uninstall packages.
  freeze                     Output installed packages in requirements format.
  list                       List installed packages.
  show                       Show information about installed packages.
  search                     Search PyPI for packages.
  wheel                      Build wheels from your requirements.
  zip                        DEPRECATED. Zip individual packages.
  unzip                      DEPRECATED. Unzip individual packages.
  help                       Show help for commands.

General Options:
  -h, --help                 Show help.
  --isolated                 Run pip in an isolated mode, ignoring
                             environment variables and user configuration.
  -v, --verbose              Give more output. Option is additive, and can be
                             used up to 3 times.
```

Installing pip Python package manager on macOS X and Linux

Some Python installations of Linux do not come with pip, and Mac OS X's installations doesn't come with pip by default. If you are using Python 2.7, then you may need to install pip, but pip is already included in Python 3.4, and in later versions. You can check this using the following:

```
$ python3 -m pip list
```

If you need to install it, download the get-pip.py file from https://bootstrap.pypa.io/get-pip.py.

Once you have downloaded it, run it with elevated privileges using the following code:

```
# Download and install pip
$ wget https://bootstrap.pypa.io/get-pip.py
$ sudo python get-pip.py
```

Once this has been entered, pip will be installed automatically.

Pip basics

We are now going to learn the basic commands for using Python package manager. To install a package with `pip`, enter the following code:

```
$ pip install [package-name]
```

On Mac and Linux, because you are installing programs outside of the user-owned folders, you might have to prepend `sudo` to the `install` commands. To install Flask, simply run the following:

```
$ pip install flask
```

Once you have done this, all of the requirements that you need for using Flask will be installed for you.

If you want to remove a package that you are no longer using, run the following:

```
$ pip uninstall [package-name]
```

If you wish to explore or find a package, but don't know its exact name, you can use the `search` command:

```
$ pip search [search-term]
```

Now that we have a couple of packages installed, it is common courtesy in the Python community to create a list of packages that are required to run the project so that others can quickly install every necessary package. This also has the added benefit that any new member of your project will be able to run your code quickly.

This list can be created with pip by running the following command:

```
$ pip freeze > requirements.txt
```

What exactly did this command do? The `pip freeze` command automatically prints out a list of the installed packages and their versions. For our example, it prints the following:

```
click==6.7
Flask==0.12.4
itsdangerous==0.24
Jinja2==2.10
MarkupSafe==1.0
Werkzeug==0.14.1
```

The > operator tells Bash to take everything printed by the last command and write it to this file. If you look in your project directory, you can see a new file named `requirements.txt` that contains the output of `pip freeze`.

To install all the packages from this file, a new project maintainer would have to run this, as shown in the following code. Normally, this will also be used to deploy the production environment of your project:

```
$ pip install -r requirements.txt
```

The preceding code tells `pip` to read all the packages listed in `requirements.txt` and install them.

Dependency sandboxing with virtualenv

So you have installed all the packages that you want for your new project. Great! But what happens when we develop a second project some time later that will use newer versions of the same packages? And what happens when a library that you wish to use depends on a library that you installed for the first project, but which uses an older version of these packages? When newer versions of packages contain breaking changes, upgrading them would require extra development work on an older project that you may not be able to afford. So in our system, we could have clashing Python packages between projects.

We should also consider automated build environments, such as **Jenkins**, where we want to run tests. These builds may run on the same system on which other projects are being built, so it's essential that during the build jobs we create a contained Python package environment that is not shared between jobs. This environment is created from the information in the `requirements.txt` file that we created earlier. This way, multiple Python applications can be built and tested on the same system without clashing with each other.

Thankfully, there is **virtualenv**, a tool that sandboxes your Python projects. The secret to virtualenv is in tricking your computer to look for and install packages in the project directory rather than in the main Python directory, which allows you to keep them completely separate.

If you're using Python 3—and I recommend that you do, because Python 2 support will end in 2020—then you don't have to install virtualenv; you can use it just by running it like a package, as shown in the following code:

```
# Create a python 3 virtualenv
$ python3 -m venv env
```

Now that we have pip, if we need to install `virtualenv`, then we can just run the following command:

```
$ pip install virtualenv
```

Virtualenv basics

Let's initialize `virtualenv` for our project, as follows:

```
$ virtualenv env
```

The extra `env` tells virtualenv to store all the packages in a folder named `env`. Virtualenv requires you to start it before it will sandbox your project. You can do this using the following code:

```
$ source env/bin/activate
# Your prompt should now look like
(env) $
```

The `source` command tells Bash to run the `env/bin/activate` script in the context of the current directory. Let's reinstall Flask in our new sandbox, as follows:

```
# you won't need sudo anymore
(env) $ pip install flask
# To return to the global Python
(env) $ deactivate
```

Setting up Docker

Your development projects normally need more then a web server application layer; you will most definitely need some kind of database system. You might be using a cache, **redis**, workers with **Celery**, a messaging queuing system, or something else. Normally, all of the systems that are needed for your application to work are collectively referred to as **stack**. One simple way to easily define and quickly spawn all these components is to use **Docker** containers. With Docker, you define all of your application components and how to install and configure them, and you can then share your stack with your team, and send it to production with the exact same specification.

You can download and install Docker from `https://docs.docker.com/install/`.

First, let's create a very simple **Dockerfile**. This file defines how to set up your application. Each line will serve as a container layer for very fast rebuilds. A very simple Dockerfile will look like the following:

```
FROM python:3.6.5
# Set the working directory to /app
WORKDIR /app
# Copy local contents into the container
ADD . /app
# Install all required dependencies
RUN pip install -r requirements.txt
EXPOSE 5000
CMD ["python", "main.py"]
```

Next, let's build out first container image. We will tag it as `chapter_1` for further ease of use, as shown in the following code:

```
$ docker build -t chapter_1 .
```

Then we will run it, as shown in the following code:

```
$ docker run -p 5000:5000 chapter_1
# List all the running containers
$ docker container list
```

Docker is easy, but it's a complex tool with lots of options for configuring and deploying containers. We will look at Docker in more detail in `Chapter 13`, *Deploying Flask Apps*.

The beginning of our project

Finally, we can get to our first Flask project. In order to build a complex project at the end of this book, we will need a simple Flask project to start us off.

Simple application

Flask is very powerful, but will most definitely not get in your way. You can use it to create a simple web application using a single file. Our aim is to create a project that is structured in a way that it can scale and be easy to understand. For now, we will create a `config` file first. In the file named `config.py`, add the following:

```
class Config(object):
    pass

class ProdConfig(Config):
    pass

class DevConfig(Config):
    DEBUG = True
```

Now, in another file named `main.py`, add the following:

```
from flask import Flask
from config import DevConfig

app = Flask(__name__)
app.config.from_object(DevConfig)

@app.route('/')
def home():
    return '<h1>Hello World!</h1>'

if __name__ == '__main__':
    app.run()
```

For anyone who is familiar with the base Flask API, this program is very basic. It will simply show `Hello World!` on the browser if we navigate to `http://127.0.0.1:5000`. One point that may be unfamiliar to Flask users is the use of the phrase `config.from_object` rather than `app.config['DEBUG']`. We use `from_object` because in future, multiple configurations will be used, and manually changing every variable when we need to switch between configurations is time consuming.

Project structure

We have created a very simple project structure, but can it serve as the base skeleton for any Python project. In Chapter 5, *Advanced Application Structure*, we will get our hands on a more scalable structure, but for now, let's go back to our environment, as shown in the following code:

```
Dockerfile # Instructions to configure and run our application on a
container
requirements.txt # All the dependencies needed to run our application
/venv # We will not add this folder to our Git repo, our virtualenv
.gitignore # Instruction for Git to ignore files
main.py # Our main Flask application
config.py # Our configuration file
```

Remember to commit these changes in Git, as shown in the following code:

```
# The --all flag will tell git to stage all changes you have made
# including deletions and new files
$ git add --all
$ git commit -m" ""created the base application"
```

 You will no longer be reminded of when to commit your changes to Git. It is up to you to develop the habit of committing whenever you reach a stopping point. It is also assumed that you will be operating inside the virtual environment, so all command-line prompts will not be prefixed with (env).

Using Flask's command-line interface

In order to make the next chapters easier for the reader, we will look at how to use the Flask CLI (using version 0.11 onward). The CLI allows programmers to create commands that act within the **application context** of Flask—that is, the state in Flask that allows the modification of the Flask object. The Flask CLI comes with some default commands to run the server and a Python shell in the application context.

Let's take a look at the Flask CLI and how to initialize it. First, we must tell it how to discover our application using the following code:

```
$ export FLASK_APP=main.py
```

Then, we will use the Flask CLI to run our application using the following code:

```
$ flask run
```

Now, let's enter the shell on the application context and see how to get all the defined URL routes, using the following code:

```
$ flask shell
Python 3.6.5 (v3.6.5:f59c0932b4, Mar 28 2018, 03:03:55)
[GCC 4.2.1 (Apple Inc. build 5666) (dot 3)] on darwin
App: main [debug]
Instance: /chapter_1/instance
>>> app.url_map
Map([<Rule '/' (OPTIONS, GET, HEAD) -> home>,
 <Rule '/static/<filename>' (OPTIONS, GET, HEAD) -> static>])
```

As you can see, we already have two routes defined: the / where we display the "Hello World" sentence and the static default route created by Flask. Some other useful information shows where Flask thinks our templates and static folders are, as shown in the following code:

```
>>> app.static_folder
/chapter_1/static'
>>> app.template_folder
'templates'
```

Flask CLI, uses the `click` library from the creator of Flask itself. It was designed to be easily extensible so that the Flask extensions can extend it and implement new commands that are available when you use them. We should indeed extend it—it makes it more useful to extend it ourselves. This is the right way to create management commands for our applications. Think about commands that you can use to migrate database schemas, create users, prune data, and so on.

Summary

Now that we have set up our development environment, we can move on to implementing advanced application features in Flask. Before we can do anything visual, we need content to display. This content will be kept on a database. In the next chapter, you will be introduced to working with databases in Flask, and you will learn how master them.

2
Creating Models with SQLAlchemy

As we saw in the last chapter, models are a means of abstracting and providing a common interface to access data. In most web applications, data is stored and retrieved from a **relational database management system (RDBMS)**, which is a database that holds data in a tabular format with rows and columns and is able to implement a relational model with data across tables. Some examples include MySQL, Postgres, Oracle, and MSSQL.

In order to create models on top of our database, we will use a Python package named **SQLAlchemy**. SQLAlchemy is a database API at its lowest level, and performs **object relational mapping** at its highest level. An **ORM (object relational mapper)** is a tool that allows developers to store and retrieve data using object-oriented approaches and solve object-relational mismatches—a set of conceptual and technical difficulties that are often encountered when a relational database management system is being used by a program that is written in an object-oriented programming language. Relational and object-oriented models are so different that additional code and functionalities are required to make them work together efficiently. This creates a virtual object database and converts data between the large number of types in databases into the mix of types and objects in Python. Also, a programming language, such as Python, allows you to have different objects that hold references to each other, and to get and set their attributes. An ORM, such as SQLAlchemy, helps translate these when inserting them into a traditional database.

In order to tie SQLAlchemy into our application context, we will use **Flask SQLAlchemy**. Flask SQLAlchemy is a convenience layer on top of SQLAlchemy that provides useful defaults and Flask-specific functions. If you are already familiar with SQLAlchemy, then you are free to use it without Flask SQLAlchemy.

By the end of this chapter, we will have a full database schema of our blogging application, as well as models that interact with that schema.

In this chapter, we'll cover the following topics:

- Designing database tables and relationships using SQLAlchemy
- Creating, reading, updating, and deleting models
- Learning to define model relationships, constraints, and indexes
- Creating automatic database migrations

Setting up SQLAlchemy

In order to go through the exercises in this chapter, you will need a running database, if you do not already have one. If you have never installed a database, or you do not have a preference, then **SQLite** is the best option for beginners, or if you want to quickly bootstrap a proof of concept.

SQLite is an SQL-embedded database engine that is fast, works without a server, and is entirely contained in one file. SQLite is also natively supported in Python, so if you choose to go with SQLite, an SQLite database will be automatically created for you during the exercise in the *Our first model* section.

Python packages

Flask SQLAlchemy can be used with multiple database engines, such as ORACLE, MSSQL, MySQL, PostgreSQL, SQLite, and Sybase, but we need to install additional specific packages for these engines. Now it is time to bootstrap our project by creating a new virtual environment for all our application's dependencies. This virtual environment will be used for our blogging application. Enter the following code:

```
$ virtualenv env
```

Then, in `requirements.txt`, add the following code to install the package:

```
flask-sqlalchemy
```

You will also need to install specific packages for your chosen database that will act as the connector for SQLAlchemy, so add the specific packages for your engine in `requirements.txt`, as shown in the following code. SQLite users can skip this step:

```
# MySQL
PyMySQL
# Postgres
psycopg2
```

```
# MSSQL
pyodbc
# Oracle
cx_Oracle
```

Finally, activate and install the dependencies using the following code:

```
$ source env/bin/activate
$ pip install -r requirements.txt
```

Flask SQLAlchemy

Before we can abstract our data, we need to set up Flask SQLAlchemy. SQLAlchemy creates its database connection through a special database URI. This is a string that looks like a URL that contains all the information that SQLAlchemy needs to connect. It takes the general form of the following code:

```
databasetype+driver://user:password@host:port/db_name
```

For each driver that you installed previously, the URI would be as follows:

```
# SQLite connection string/uri is a path to the database file - relative or
absolute.
sqlite:///database.db
# MySQL
mysql+pymysql://user:password@ip:port/db_name
# Postgres
postgresql+psycopg2://user:password@ip:port/db_name
# MSSQL
mssql+pyodbc://user:password@dsn_name
# Oracle
oracle+cx_oracle://user:password@ip:port/db_name
```

In our `config.py` file, add the URI to the `DevConfig` file with the following:

```
class DevConfig(Config):
  debug = True
  SQLALCHEMY_DATABASE_URI = "YOUR URI"
```

Our first model

You may have noticed that we did not actually create any tables in our database to abstract from. This is because SQLAlchemy allows us to create either models from tables or tables from our models. We will look at this after we have created the first model.

In our `main.py` file, SQLAlchemy must first be initialized with our app as follows:

```
from flask import Flask
from flask_sqlalchemy import SQLAlchemy
from config import DevConfig

app = Flask(__name__)
app.config.from_object(DevConfig)
db = SQLAlchemy(app)
```

SQLAlchemy will read our app's configuration and automatically connect to our database. Let's create a `User` model to interact with a user table in the `main.py` file, as follows:

```
class User(db.Model):
    id = db.Column(db.Integer(), primary_key=True)
    username = db.Column(db.String(255))
    password = db.Column(db.String(255))

    def __init__(self, username):
        self.username = username

    def __repr__(self):
        return "<User '{}'>".format(self.username)
```

What have we accomplished? We now have a model that is based on a user table with three columns. When we inherit from `db.Model`, the entire connection and communication with the database will already be handled for us.

Each class variable that is the `db.Column` instance represents a column in the database. There is an optional first argument in the `db.Column` instance that allows us to specify the name of the column in the database. Without it, SQLAlchemy will assume that the name of the variable is the same as the name of the column. Using this, optional variable would look like the following:

```
username = db.Column('user_name', db.String(255))
```

The second argument to `db.Column` tells SQLAlchemy what type the column should be treated as. The main types that we will work with in this book are as follows:

- `db.String`
- `db.Text`
- `db.Integer`

- db.Float
- db.Boolean
- db.Date
- db.DateTime
- db.Time

What each type represents is rather simple, as shown in the following list:

- The String and Text types take Python strings and translate them to the varchar and text type columns, respectively.
- The Integer and Float types take any Python number and translates it into the correct type before inserting it into the database.
- Boolean takes Python True or False statements and, if the database has a boolean type, inserts a Boolean into the database. If there is no boolean type in the database, SQLAlchemy automatically translates between Python Booleans and a 0 or a 1 in the database.
- The Date, DateTime, and Time types use the Python types of the same names from the datetime native library and translates them into the database.

The String, Integer, and Float types take an extra argument that tells SQLAlchemy the length limit of our column.

 If you wish to truly understand how SQLAlchemy translates your code into SQL queries, add the following to the DevConfig file, SQLALCHEMY_ECHO = True.
This will print out the created queries to the Terminal. You may wish to turn this feature off as you get further along in the book, as dozens of queries could be printed to the terminal with every page load.

The primary_key argument tells SQLAlchemy that this column has the **primary key index** on it. Each SQLAlchemy model requires a primary key to function. All object-relationally mapped objects are linked to their database rows within the session via an identity map, a pattern central to the unit of work mechanism implemented in SQLAlchemy. That's why we need primary keys to be declared in the model.

SQLAlchemy will assume that the name of your table is the lowercase version of your model class name. However, what if we want our table to be called something other than user? To tell SQLAlchemy what name to use, add the __tablename__ class variable.

This is also how you connect to tables that already exist in your database. Just place the name of the table in the following string:

```
class User(db.Model):
    __tablename__ = 'user_table_name'

    id = db.Column(db.Integer(), primary_key=True)
    username = db.Column(db.String(255))
    password = db.Column(db.String(255))
```

We don't have to include the __init__ or __repr__ functions. If we don't, then SQLAlchemy will automatically create an __init__ function that accepts the names and values of your columns as keyword arguments.

 Naming a table user using an ORM may lead to problems, since in MySQL, user is a reserved word. One of the advantages of using an ORM is that you can easily migrate your engine from SQLite to MySQL and then to ORACLE, for example. One very easy fix would be to prefix your schema and use.

Creating the user table

Using SQLAlchemy to do the heavy lifting, we will now create the user table in our database. Update manage.py to the following:

```
from main import app, db, User

@app.shell_context_processor
def make_shell_context():
    return dict(app=app, db=db, User=User)
```

 From now on, whenever we create a new model, we will import it and add it to the returned dict.

This will allow us to work with our models in the Flask shell, because we are injecting. Run the shell now and use db.create_all() to create all of the tables, as shown in the following code:

```
# Tell Flask where to load our shell context
$ export FLASK_APP=manage.py
$ flask shell
>>> db.create_all()
```

In your database, you should now see a table called `users` with the columns specified. Also, if you are using SQLite, you should now see a file named `database.db` in your file structure, as shown in the following code:

```
$ sqlite3 database.db .tables
user
```

CRUD

In every storage mechanism for data, there are four basic types of functions: **create**, **read**, **update**, and **delete** (**CRUD**). These allow us to perform all the basic ways of manipulating and viewing the data that is needed for our web apps. To use these functions, we will use an object in the database named a **session**. Sessions will be explained later in the chapter, but for now, think of them as a storage location for all of our changes to the database.

Creating models

To create a new row in your database using our models, add the model to the `session` and `commit` objects. Adding an object to the session marks its changes for saving. Committing is when the session is saved to the database, as follows:

```
>>> user = User(username='fake_name')
>>> db.session.add(user)
>>> db.session.commit()
```

As you can see, adding a new row to our table is simple.

Reading models

After we have added data to our database, data can be queried using `Model.query`. For those who use SQLAlchemy, this is shorthand for `db.session.query(Model)`.

For our first example, use `all()` to get all rows from the user table as a list, as follows:

```
>>> users = User.query.all()
>>> users
[<User 'fake_name'>]
```

When the number of items in the database increases, this query process becomes slower. In SQLAlchemy, as in SQL, we have the `limit` function to specify the total number of rows we wish to work with:

```
>>> users = User.query.limit(10).all()
```

By default, SQLAlchemy returns the records ordered by their primary keys. To control this, we have the `order_by` function, which is given as follows:

```
# ascending
>>> users = User.query.order_by(User.username).all()
# descending
>>> users = User.query.order_by(User.username.desc()).all()
```

To return just one record, we use `first()` instead of `all()`, as follows:

```
>>> user = User.query.first()
>>> user.username
fake_name
```

To return one model by its primary key, use `query.get()`, as follows:

```
>>> user = User.query.get(1)
>>> user.username
fake_name
```

All these functions are chainable, which means that they can be appended onto each other to modify the returned result. Those of you who are fluent in JavaScript will find the following syntax familiar:

```
>>> users = User.query.order_by(
            User.username.desc()
        ).limit(10).first()
```

The `first()` and `all()` methods return a value, and therefore end the chain.

There is also a Flask-SQLAlchemy-specific method, called **pagination**, that can be used rather than `first()` or `all()`. This is a convenient method that is designed to enable the pagination feature that most websites use while displaying a long list of items. The first parameter defines which page the query should return to and the second parameter defines the number of items per page. So, if we passed 1 and 10 as the parameters, the first 10 objects would be returned.

If we instead passed 2 and 10, then objects 11–20 would be returned, and so on. The pagination method is different from the `first()` and `all()` methods because it returns a pagination object rather than a list of models. For example, if we want to get the first 10 items of a fictional `Post` object for the first page in our blog, we would use the following:

```
>>> User.query.paginate(1, 10)
<flask_sqlalchemy.Pagination at 0x105118f50>
```

This object has several useful properties, as follows:

```
>>> page = User.query.paginate(1, 10)
# returns the entities in the page
>>> page.items
[<User 'fake_name'>]
# what page does this object represent
>>> page.page
1
# How many pages are there
>>> page.pages
1
# are there enough models to make the next or previous page
>>> page.has_prev, page.has_next
(False, False)
# return the next or previous page pagination object
# if one does not exist returns the current page
>>> page.prev(), page.next()
(<flask_sqlalchemy.Pagination at 0x10812da50>,
 <flask_sqlalchemy.Pagination at 0x1081985d0>)
```

Filtering queries

Now we get to the actual power of SQL—that is, filtering results by a set of rules. To get a list of models that satisfy a set of qualities, we use the `query.filter_by` filter. The `query.filter_by` filter takes named arguments that represent the values we are looking for in each column in the database. To get a list of all users with a username of `fake_name`, we would use the following:

```
>>> users = User.query.filter_by(username='fake_name').all()
```

This example is filtering on one value, but multiple values can be passed to the `filter_by` filter. Just like our previous functions, `filter_by` is chainable, as shown in the following code:

```
>>> users = User.query.order_by(User.username.desc())
        .filter_by(username='fake_name')
        .limit(2)
        .all()
```

The `query.filter_by` phrase only works if you know the exact values that you are looking for. This is avoided by passing Python comparison statements to the query with `query.filter`, as follows:

```
>>> user = User.query.filter(
        User.id > 1
    ).all()
```

This is a simple example, but `query.filter` accepts any Python comparison. With common Python types, such as `integers`, `strings`, and `dates`, the == operator can be used for equality comparisons. If you had an `integer`, `float`, or `date` column, an inequality statement could also be passed with the >, <, <=, and >= operators.

We can also translate complex SQL queries with SQLAlchemy functions. For example, to use IN, OR, or NOT SQL comparisons, we would use the following:

```
>>> from sqlalchemy.sql.expression import not_, or_
>>> user = User.query.filter(
    User.username.in_(['fake_name']),
    User.password == None
).first()
# find all of the users with a password
>>> user = User.query.filter(
    not_(User.password == None)
).first()
# all of these methods are able to be combined
>>> user = User.query.filter(
    or_(not_(User.password == None), User.id >= 1)
).first()
```

In SQLAlchemy, comparisons to None are translated to comparisons to NULL.

Updating models

To update the values of models that already exist, apply the `update` method to a query object—that is, before you return the models with a method such as `first()` or `all()`, as shown in the following code:

```
>>> User.query.filter_by(username='fake_name').update({
    'password': 'test'
})
# The updated models have already been added to the session
>>> db.session.commit()
```

Deleting models

If we wish to remove a model from the database, we would use the following code:

```
>>> user = User.query.filter_by(username='fake_name').first()
>>> db.session.delete(user)
>>> db.session.commit()
```

Relationships between models

Relationships between models in SQLAlchemy are links between two or more models that allow models to reference each other automatically. This allows naturally related data, such as comments on posts, to be easily retrieved from the database with its related data. This is where the R in RDBMS comes from, and it gives this type of database a large amount of power.

Let's create our first relation. Our blogging website is going to need some blog posts. Each blog post is going to be written by one user, so it makes sense to link posts back to the user who wrote them so that we can easily get all the posts by a user. This is an example of a **one-to-many** relationship, as shown in the following code:

 SQLite and MySQL/MyISAM engines do not enforce relationship constraints. This might cause problems if you are using SQLite on your development environment and a different engine on production (MySQL with innodb), but you can tell SQLite to enforce foreign key constraints (with a performance penalty).

```
@event.listens_for(Engine, "connect")
def set_sqlite_pragma(dbapi_connection, connection_record):
    cursor = dbapi_connection.cursor()
```

```
cursor.execute("PRAGMA foreign_keys=ON")
cursor.close()
```

One-to-many relationship

Let's add a model to represent the blog posts on our website:

```
class Post(db.Model):
  id = db.Column(db.Integer(), primary_key=True)
  title = db.Column(db.String(255))
  text = db.Column(db.Text())
  publish_date = db.Column(db.DateTime())
  user_id = db.Column(db.Integer(), db.ForeignKey('user.id'))

  def __init__(self, title):
    self.title = title

  def __repr__(self):
    return "<Post '{}'>".format(self.title)
```

Note the `user_id` column. Those who are familiar with RDBMSes will know that this represents a **foreign key constraint**. A foreign key constraint is a rule in the database that forces the value of `user_id` to exist in the `id` column in the user table. This is a check in the database to make sure that `Post` will always refer to an existing user. The parameter to `db.ForeignKey` is a string representation of the user ID field. If you have decided to call your user table with `__table_name__`, then you must change this string. This string is used instead of a direct reference with `User.id` because during initialization of SQLAlchemy, the `User` object might not exist yet.

The `user_id` column itself is not enough to tell SQLAlchemy that we have a relationship. We must modify our `User` model as follows:

```
class User(db.Model):
  id = db.Column(db.Integer(), primary_key=True)
  username = db.Column(db.String(255))
  password = db.Column(db.String(255))
  posts = db.relationship(
    'Post',
    backref='user',
    lazy='dynamic'
  )
```

The db.relationship function creates an attribute in SQLAlchemy that connects with db.ForeignKey in our Post model. The first parameter is the name of the class that we are referencing. We will cover what backref does soon, but what is the lazy parameter? The lazy parameter controls how SQLAlchemy will load our related objects.

The subquery phrase would load our relations as soon as our Post object is loaded. This cuts down the number of queries, but will slow down when the number of returned items grows larger. In contrast, with the dynamic option, the related objects will be loaded upon access and can be filtered down before returning. This is best if the number of returned objects is or will become large.

We may now access the User.posts variable that will return a list of all the posts whose user_id field equals our User.id. Let's try this now in our shell, as follows:

```
>>> user = User.query.get(1)
>>> new_post = Post('Post Title')
>>> new_post.user_id = user.id
>>> user.posts
[]
>>> db.session.add(new_post)
>>> db.session.commit()
>>> user.posts
[<Post 'Post Title'>]
```

Note that we were not able to access our post from our relationship without committing our changes to the database.

The backref parameter gives us the ability to access and set our User class via Post.user. This is given by the following code:

```
>>> second_post = Post('Second Title')
>>> second_post.user = user
>>> db.session.add(second_post)
>>> db.session.commit()
>>> user.posts
[<Post 'Post Title'>, <Post 'Second Title'>]
```

Because user.posts is a list, we could have also added our Post model to the list to save it automatically, as follows:

```
>>> second_post = Post('Second Title')
>>> user.posts.append(second_post)
>>> db.session.add(user)
>>> db.session.commit()
>>> user.posts
[<Post 'Post Title'>, <Post 'Second Title'>]
```

With the `backref` option as dynamic, we can treat our relation column as a query as well as a list, as follows:

```
>>> user.posts
[<Post 'Post Title'>, <Post 'Second Title'>]
>>> user.posts.order_by(Post.publish_date.desc()).all()
[<Post 'Second Title'>, <Post 'Post Title'>]
```

Before we move on to our next relationship type, let's add another model for user comments with a one-to-many relationship, which will be used in the book later on. We can do this using the following code:

```
class Post(db.Model):
    id = db.Column(db.Integer(), primary_key=True)
    title = db.Column(db.String(255))
    text = db.Column(db.Text())
    publish_date = db.Column(db.DateTime())
    comments = db.relationship(
      'Comment',
      backref='post',
      lazy='dynamic'
    )
    user_id = db.Column(db.Integer(), db.ForeignKey('user.id'))
    def __init__(self, title):
        self.title = title
    def __repr__(self):
        return "<Post '{}'>".format(self.title)
```

Note the __repr__ method signature in the preceding code. This is a built-in function in Python that is used to return the string representation of the object. Next is the `Comment` model, as shown in the following code:

```
class Comment(db.Model):
    id = db.Column(db.Integer(), primary_key=True)
    name = db.Column(db.String(255))
    text = db.Column(db.Text())
    date = db.Column(db.DateTime())
    post_id = db.Column(db.Integer(), db.ForeignKey('post.id'))
    def __repr__(self):
        return "<Comment '{}'>".format(self.text[:15])
```

Many-to-many relationship

What if we have two models that can reference each other, but each model needs to reference more than one of each type? In our example, our blog posts will need tags in order for our users to easily group similar posts. Each tag can refer to many posts, but each post can have multiple tags. This type of relationship is called a **many-to-many** relationship. Consider the following example:

```python
tags = db.Table('post_tags',
    db.Column('post_id', db.Integer, db.ForeignKey('post.id')),
    db.Column('tag_id', db.Integer, db.ForeignKey('tag.id'))
)

class Post(db.Model):
    id = db.Column(db.Integer(), primary_key=True)
    title = db.Column(db.String(255))
    text = db.Column(db.Text())
    publish_date = db.Column(db.DateTime())
    comments = db.relationship(
      'Comment',
      backref='post',
      lazy='dynamic'
    )
    user_id = db.Column(db.Integer(), db.ForeignKey('user.id'))
    tags = db.relationship(
        'Tag',
        secondary=tags,
        backref=db.backref('posts', lazy='dynamic')
    )

    def __init__(self, title):
        self.title = title
    def __repr__(self):
        return "<Post '{}'>".format(self.title)

class Tag(db.Model):
    id = db.Column(db.Integer(), primary_key=True)
    title = db.Column(db.String(255))
    def __init__(self, title):
        self.title = title
    def __repr__(self):
        return "<Tag '{}'>".format(self.title)
```

The db.Table object is a lower-level access to the database than the abstraction of db.Model. The db.Model object rests on top of db.Table and provides a representation of specific rows in the table. The db.Table object is used because there is no need to access the individual rows of the table.

The tags variable is used to represent the post_tags table, which contains two rows: one that represents an ID of a post, and another that represents the ID of a tag. To illustrate how this works, let's look at an example. Say that the table had the following data:

```
post_id   tag_id
1         1
1         3
2         3
2         4
2         5
3         1
3         2
```

SQLAlchemy would translate this to the following:

- A post with an ID of 1 has the tags with the IDs of 1 and 3
- A post with an ID of 2 has the tags with the IDs of 3, 4, and 5
- A post with an ID of 3 has the tags with the IDs of 1 and 2

You may describe this data as easily as tags being related to posts.

Before the db.relationship function sets up our relationship, this time it has the secondary parameter. The secondary parameter tells SQLAlchemy that this relationship is stored in the tags table, as shown in the following code:

```
>>> post_one = Post.query.filter_by(title='Post Title').first()
>>> post_two = Post.query.filter_by(title='Second Title').first()
>>> tag_one = Tag('Python')
>>> tag_two = Tag('SQLAlchemy')
>>> tag_three = Tag('Flask')
>>> post_one.tags = [tag_two]
>>> post_two.tags = [tag_one, tag_two, tag_three]
>>> tag_two.posts
[<Post 'Post Title'>, <Post 'Second Title'>]
>>> db.session.add(post_one)
>>> db.session.add(post_two)
>>> db.session.commit()
```

As given in the one-to-many relationship, the main relationship column is just a list, the main difference being that the `backref` option is now also a list. Because it's a list, we may add posts to tags from the `tag` object, as follows:

```
>>> tag_one.posts.append(post_one)
[<Post 'Post Title'>, <Post 'Second Title'>]
>>> post_one.tags
[<Tag 'SQLAlchemy'>, <Tag 'Python'>]
>>> db.session.add(tag_one)
>>> db.session.commit()
```

Constraints and indexing

Using constraints is considered a good practice. This way, you can restrict the domain of a certain model attribute and ensure data integrity and quality. There are many types of constraints that you can use; primary key and foreign key constraints were already covered in the previous sections. The other kinds of constraints that are supported by SQLAlchemy are shown in the following list:

- Not NULL (ensures that a certain attribute contains data)
- UNIQUE (ensures that a certain attribute value is always unique in the database table, which contains the model data)
- DEFAULT (sets a default value for the attribute when no values were provided)
- CHECK (used to specify range of values)

Using SQLAlchemy, you can ensure that your data's domain restrictions are explicit and all in the same place, not spread across your application code.

Let's improve our models by setting some constraints on the data. First, we should not accept NULL values for usernames on the user model, and ensure that a username is always unique. We do this using the following code:

```
...
class User(db.Model):
    id = db.Column(db.Integer(), primary_key=True)
    username = db.Column(db.String(255), nullable=False, unique=True)
...
```

The same principle applies to the rest of our models: A `Post` must always have a title, a `Comment` is always made by someone, and a `Tag` always has a title, and this title value is unique. We put these constraints in place using the following code:

```
...
class Post(db.Model):
    id = db.Column(db.Integer(), primary_key=True)
    title = db.Column(db.String(255), nullable=False)
...
class Comment(db.Model):
    id = db.Column(db.Integer(), primary_key=True)
    name = db.Column(db.String(255), nullable=False)
...
class Tag(db.Model):
    id = db.Column(db.Integer(), primary_key=True)
    title = db.Column(db.String(255), nullable=True, unique=True)
...
```

Default values are really nice; they ensure data quality, and make your code shorter. We can let SQLAlchemy handle the date timestamp of when a comment or post was made using the following code:

```
class Comment(db.Model):
    id = db.Column(db.Integer(), primary_key=True)
...
    date = db.Column(db.DateTime(), default=datetime.datetime.now)
...

class Post(db.Model):
    id = db.Column(db.Integer(), primary_key=True)
...
    publish_date = db.Column(db.DateTime(), default=datetime.datetime.now)
```

Note how SQLAlchemy handles the default definitions. This is a powerful feature. We are passing a reference to a Python function, so we can use any Python function we want as long as no parameters are required (except for partials). This function will be called upon the creation of a record or an update, and its return value is used for the column's value. Of course, SQLAlchemy also supports simple scalar values on default definitions.

RDBMS indexes are used to improve query performance, yet you should be careful about using them as this comes at a cost of additional writes on INSERT, UPDATE, and DELETE functions, as well as an increase in storage. Careful index choice and configuration is out of the scope of this book, but take into account the fact that an index is used to reduce the O(N) lookup on certain table columns that may be frequently used, or that are in tables with a huge number of rows where a linear lookup is simply not possible in production. Index query performance can go from logarithmic to O(1). This is possible at a cost of additional writes and checks.

An example of creating an index using Flask SQLAlchemy, can be seen in the following code:

```
...
class User(db.Model):
    id = db.Column(db.Integer(), primary_key=True)
    username = db.Column(db.String(255), nullable=False, index=True,
unique=True)
...
```

The following code shows an example of using an index for multiple columns:

```
db.Index('idx_col_example', User.username, User.password)
```

The convenience of SQLAlchemy sessions

Now you understand the power of SQLAlchemy and what the SQLAlchemy session object is, and why web apps should never be made without them. As stated before, the session can be simply described as an object that tracks the changes in our models and commits them to the database when we tell it to. However, there is a bit more to it than this.

First, the session is also the handler for **transactions**. Transactions are sets of changes that are flushed to the database on commit. Transactions provide a lot of hidden functionality. For example, transactions automatically determine which objects are to be saved first when objects have relations. You might have noted this when we were saving tags in the previous section. When we added tags to the posts, the session automatically knew to save the tags first despite the fact that we did not add them to be committed. If we are working with raw SQL queries and a database connection, we will have to keep track of which rows are related to which other rows to avoid saving a foreign key reference to an object that does not exist.

Transactions also automatically mark data as stale when changes to an object are saved to the database. The next time we access the object, a query is made to the database to update the data, but all of this happens behind the scenes. If we are not using SQLAlchemy, we will also need to manually track which rows need to be updated. If we want to be resource efficient, we only need to query and update those rows.

Second, the session makes it impossible for there to be two different references to the same row in the database. This is accomplished by ensuring that all queries go through the session (`Model.query` is actually `db.session.query(Model)`), and if the row has already been queried in this transaction, that the pointer to that object will be returned and not a new object. If this check did not exist, two objects that represent the same row could be saved to the database with different changes. This creates subtle bugs that might not be caught instantly.

Keep in mind that Flask SQLAlchemy creates a new session for every request and discards any changes that were not committed at the end of the request, so always remember to save your work.

 For an in-depth look at sessions, the creator of SQLAlchemy, Mike Bayer, gave a talk at PyCon Canada 2012. Refer to *The SQLAlchemy Session - In Depth*, at `https://www.youtube.com/watch?v=PKAdehPHOMo`.

Database migrations with Alembic

The functionality of web apps changes all the time, and with every new functionality, we need to change the structure of our database. Whether it's adding or dropping new columns or creating new tables, our models will change throughout the life cycle of our app. However, problems quickly arise when the database changes often. When moving our changes from development to production, how can you be sure that you carried over every change without manually comparing each model and its corresponding table? Let's say that you want to go back into your Git history to see whether an earlier version of your app had the same bug that you are now encountering in production. How will you change your database back to the correct schema without a lot of extra work?

As programmers, we hate extra work. Thankfully, there is a tool called **Alembic**, which automatically creates and tracks database migrations from the changes in our SQLAlchemy models. **Database migrations** are records of all the changes of our schema. Alembic allows us to upgrade or downgrade our database to a specific saved version. Upgrading or downgrading by several versions will execute all the files between the two selected versions. The best thing about Alembic is that its history files are only Python files. When we create our first migration, we can see how simple the Alembic syntax is.

 Alembic does not capture every possible change—for example, it does not record changes on the SQL indexes. After every migration, the reader is encouraged to review the migration file and make any necessary corrections.

We won't work directly with Alembic. Instead, we will use **Flask-Migrate**, which is an extension created specifically for SQLAlchemy, and which works with the Flask CLI. You will find it in the requirements.txt file, as shown in the following code:

```
Flask-Migrate
```

To get started, we don't need to add anything to our manage.py file since Flask-Migrate already extends the Flask CLI with its own CLI options, as shown in the following code:

```
from main import app, db, User, Post, Tag, migrate


@app.shell_context_processor
def make_shell_context():
    return dict(app=app, db=db, User=User, Post=Post, Tag=Tag,
migrate=migrate)
```

And on our main.py:

```
import datetime

from flask import Flask
from flask_sqlalchemy import SQLAlchemy
from flask_migrate import Migrate
from config import DevConfig

app = Flask(__name__)
app.config.from_object(DevConfig)

db = SQLAlchemy(app)
migrate = Migrate(app, db)
```

To initialize the `Migrate` object with our app and our SQLAlchemy instance, run the following code:

```
# Tell Flask where is our app
$ export FLASK_APP=main.py
$ flask db
```

To start tracking our changes, we use the `init` command, as follows:

```
$ flask db init
```

This will create a new folder in our directory named `migrations` that will hold all of our history. Now we start with our first migration, as shown in the following code:

```
$ flask db migrate -m"initial migration"
```

This command will cause Alembic to scan our SQLAlchemy object and find all the tables and columns that did not exist before this commit. As this is our first commit, the migration file will be rather long. Be sure to specify the migration message with −m, as it's the easiest way to identify what each migration is doing. Each migration file is stored in the `migrations/versions/` folder.

To apply the migration to your database and change your schema, run the following code:

```
$ flask db upgrade
```

If we want to check out all the SQLAlchemy generated DDL code, then we use the following code:

```
$ flask db upgrade --sql
```

To return to the previous version, find the version number with the `history` command and pass it to the `downgrade` command, as follows:

```
$ flask db history
<base> -> 7ded34bc4fb (head), initial migration
$ flask db downgrade 7ded34bc4fb
```

Like Git, a hash marks each migration. This is the main functionality of Alembic, but it is only surface level. Try to align your migrations with your Git commits in order to make it easier to downgrade or upgrade when reverting commits.

In the code for this book, you will find in each chapter an initialization script that will create a Python virtual environment, install all declared dependencies, and initialize the database. Take a look at the `init.sh` Bash script.

Summary

Now that we have mastered data control, we may move on to displaying our data in our application. The next chapter, Chapter 3, *Creating Views with Templates*, will dynamically cover creating HTML based on our models and adding models from our web interface.

Creating Views with Templates 3

Now that we have our data in an easily accessible format, displaying the information in a web page becomes much easier. In this chapter, we will learn how to do the following:

- Use the included templating language for Flask, Jinja, to dynamically create HTML for our SQLAlchemy models
- Use Jinja's methods to automate the creation of HTML and modify data for presentation inside a template
- Automatically create and validate HTML forms with Jinja

Jinja's syntax

Jinja is a templating language written in Python. A **templating language** is a simple format that is designed to help automate the creation of documents. In any templating language, variables passed to the template replace predefined elements in the template. In Jinja, variable substitutions are defined by `{{ }}`. The `{{ }}` syntax is called a **variable block**. There are also **control blocks** defined by `{% %}` that declare language functions, such as **loops** or `if` statements. For example, when the `Post` model from Chapter 2, *Creating Models with SQLAlchemy*, is passed to it, we get the following Jinja code:

```
<h1>{{ post.title }}</h1>
```

This produces the following:

```
<h1>First Post</h1>
```

The variables displayed in a Jinja template can be any Python type or object as long as they can be converted into a string via the Python function `str()`. For example, a dictionary or a list passed to a template can have its attributes displayed via the following code:

```
{{ your_dict['key'] }}
{{ your_list[0] }}
```

Many programmers prefer to use JavaScript to template and dynamically create their HTML documents to take the HTML rendering load off the server. This will not be covered in this chapter as it is an advanced JavaScript topic. However, many JavaScript templating engines use the {{ }} syntax as well. If you choose to combine Jinja and your JavaScript templates that are defined in your HTML files, then wrap the JavaScript templates in the raw control block to tell Jinja to ignore them, as follows:

```
{% raw %}
<script id="template" type="text/x-handlebars-template">
  <h1>{{title}}</h1>
  <div class="body">
    {{body}}
  </div>
</script>
{% endraw %}
```

Filters

It's a common mistake to believe that Jinja and Python's syntax are the same because of their similarity. However, there is a lot of difference between the two. As you will see in this section, normal Python functions do not really exist. Instead, in Jinja, variables can be passed to built-in functions that modify the variables for display purposes. These functions, called filters, are called in the variable block with the pipe character, |, as shown in the following code:

```
{{ variable | filter_name(*args) }}
```

Otherwise, if no arguments are passed to the filter, the parentheses can be omitted as follows:

```
{{ variable | filter_name }}
```

Filters called control blocks can also be applied to blocks of text, as follows:

```
{% filter filter_name %}
  A bunch of text
{% endfilter %}
```

There are many filters in Jinja; this book will cover only the most useful filters. For the sake of brevity, in each example, the output of each filter will be listed directly beneath the filter itself.

For a full list of all the default filters in Jinja, visit
`http://jinja.pocoo.org/docs/dev/templates/#list-of-builtin-filters`.

The default filter

If the passed variable is `None`, then replace it with a `default` value as follows:

```
{{ post.date | default('2015-01-01') }}
2015-01-01
```

If you wish to replace the variable with the `default` value, and if the variable evaluates to `False`, then pass `True` to the optional second parameter, as follows:

```
{{ '' | default('An empty string', True) }}
An empty string
```

The escape filter

If the passed variable is a string of HTML, then the &, <, >, ', and " characters will be printed as HTML `escape` sequences:

```
{{ "<h1>Title</h1>" | escape }}
<h1>Title</h1>
```

The float filter

The `float` filter converts the passed value to a floating point number with the Python `float()` function as follows:

```
{{ 75 | float }}
75.0
```

The int filter

The `int` filter converts the passed value to an integer with the Python `int()` function as follows:

```
{{ 75.7 | int }}
75
```

The join filter

The `join` filter joins elements of a list with a string, and works in exactly the same way as the `list` method of the same name. It is given as follows:

```
{{ ['Python', 'SQLAlchemy'] | join(',') }}
Python, SQLAlchemy
```

The length filter

The `length` filter fills the same role as the Python `len()` function. It is used as follows:

```
Tag Count: {{ post.tags | length }}
Tag Count: 2
```

The round filter

The `round` filter rounds off a float to the specified precision, as follows:

```
{{ 3.14159265358979323846 | round(1) }}
3.1
```

You can also specify how you want the number to be rounded off, as shown in the following code:

```
{{ 4.7 | round(1, "common") }}
5
{{ 4.2 | round(1, "common") }}
4
{{ 4.7 | round(1, "floor") }}
4
{{ 4.2 | round(1, "ceil") }}
5
```

The `common` option rounds such figures in the same way that a person would: Any number at or above 0.5 is rounded up, and any number lower than 0.5 is rounded down. The `floor` option always rounds the number down and the `ceil` option always rounds up, regardless of the decimal value.

The safe filter

If you try to insert HTML into your page from a variable—for example, when you wish to display a blog post—Jinja will automatically try to add HTML escape sequences to the output. Look at the following example:

```
{{ "<h1>Post Title</h1>" }}
<h1>Post Title</h1>
```

This is a necessary security feature. When an application has inputs that allow users to submit arbitrary text, it creates a vulnerability that a malicious user can use to input HTML code. For example, if a user were to submit a script tag as a comment and Jinja didn't have this feature, the script would be executed on all the browsers that visited the page.

However, we still need a way to display HTML that we know is safe to show, such as the HTML of our blog posts. We can achieve this using the safe filter as follows:

```
{{ "<h1>Post Title</h1>" | safe }}
<h1>Post Title</h1>
```

The title filter

The title filter enables us to capitalize a string using the title case format as follows:

```
{{ "post title" | title }}
Post Title
```

The tojson filter

We use the tojson filter to pass the variable to the Python json.dumps function, as shown in the following code. Remember that your passed object must be serializable by the json module:

```
{{ {'key': False, 'key2': None, 'key3': 45} | tojson }}
{key: false, key2: null, key3: 45}
```

This feature is most commonly used to pass SQLAlchemy models to JavaScript MVC frameworks upon the loading of the page load than waiting for an AJAX request. If you use `tojson` in this way, remember to pass the result to the `safe` filter as well to make sure that you don't get HTML `escape` sequences in your JavaScript. Here is an example with a collection of models from `Backbone.js`, a popular JavaScript MVC framework:

```
var collection = new PostCollection({{ posts | tojson | safe }});
```

The truncate filter

The `truncate` filter takes a long string, returns a string cutoff at the specified length in characters, and appends an ellipsis, as shown in the following code:

```
{{ "A Longer Post Body Than We Want" | truncate(10) }}
A Longer...
```

By default, any words that are cut in the middle are discarded. To disable this, pass `True` as an extra parameter as follows:

```
{{ "A Longer Post Body Than We Want" | truncate(10, True) }}
A Longer P...
```

Custom filters

Adding your own filter into Jinja is as simple as writing a Python function. To understand custom filters, we will look at an example. Our simple filter will count the number of occurrences of a substring in a string and return this figure. Look at the following call:

```
{{ variable | count_substring("string") }}
```

We need to write a new Python function with the following signature, where the first argument is the *piped* variable:

```
def count_substring(variable, sub_string)
```

We can define our filter as the following:

```
@app.template_filter
def count_substring(string, sub_string): return string.count(sub_string)
```

To add this function to the list of available filters on **Jinja2**, we have to register it and add it to the `filters` dictionary of the `jinja_env` object in our `main.py` file. To do this, we can simply use a decorator that will handle this procedure for us—`@app.template_filter`.

Comments

Comments in the template are defined by `{# #}`, as shown in the following code. They will be ignored by Jinja, and will not be in the returned HTML code:

```
{# Note to the maintainers of this code #}
```

Using if statements

Using `if` statements in Jinja is similar to using them in Python. Anything that returns, or is, a Boolean determines the flow of the code, as shown in the following code:

```
{%if user.is_logged_in() %}
  <a href='/logout'>Logout</a>
{% else %}
  <a href='/login'>Login</a>
{% endif %}
```

Filters can also be used in `if` statements, as follows:

```
{% if comments | length > 0 %}
  There are {{ comments | length }} comments
{% else %}
  There are no comments
{% endif %}
```

Loops

We can use loops in Jinja to iterate over any list or generator function, as follows:

```
{% for post in posts %}
  <div>
    <h1>{{ post.title }}</h1>
    <p>{{ post.text | safe }}</p>
  </div>
{% endfor %}
```

Loops and `if` statements can be combined to mimic the `break` functionality in Python loops. In this example, the loop will only use the post if `post.text` is not None:

```
{% for post in posts if post.text %}
  <div>
    <h1>{{ post.title }}</h1>
    <p>{{ post.text | safe }}</p>
  </div>
{% endfor %}
```

Inside the loop, you have access to a special variable called `loop`, which gives you access to information about the `for` loop. For example, if we want to know the current index of the current loop to emulate the `enumerate` function in Python, we can use the index variable of the `loop` variable as follows:

```
{% for post in posts %}
  {{ loop.index }}. {{ post.title }}
{% endfor %}
```

This will produce the following output:

```
1. Post Title
2. Second Post
```

All the variables and functions that the `loop` object exposes are listed in the following table:

Variable	Description
`loop.index`	The current iteration of the loop (1 indexed)
`loop.index0`	The current iteration of the loop (0 indexed)
`loop.revindex`	The number of iterations from the end of the loop (1 indexed)
`loop.revindex0`	The number of iterations from the end of the loop (0 indexed)
`loop.first`	True if the current item is first in the iterator
`loop.last`	True if the current item is last in the iterator
`loop.length`	The number of items in the iterator
`loop.cycle`	The `helper` function to cycle between the items in the iterator (this is explained later)
`loop.depth`	Indicates how deep in a recursive loop the loop currently is (starts at level 1)
`loop.depth0`	Indicates how deep in a recursive loop the loop currently is (starts at level 0)

The `cycle` function is a function that goes through an iterator one item at a time in every loop. We can use the previous example to demonstrate, as shown in the following code:

```
{% for post in posts %}
  {{ loop.cycle('odd', 'even') }} {{ post.title }}
{% endfor %}
```

This will output the following:

```
odd Post Title
even Second Post
```

Macros

A **macro** is best understood as a function in Jinja that returns a template or HTML string. This is used to avoid reproducing code that is repeated over and over again and reduce it to one function call. For example, the following is a macro to add a Bootstrap CSS input and a label to your template:

```
{% macro input(name, label, value='', type='text') %}
  <div class="form-group">
    <label for"{{ name }}">{{ label }}</label>
    <input type="{{ type }}" name="{{ name }}"
      value="{{ value | escape }}" class="form-control">
  </div>
{% endmacro %}
```

Now, to quickly add an input to a form in any template, call your macro using the following:

```
{{ input('name', 'Name') }}
```

This will output the following:

```
<div class="form-group">
  <label for"name">Name</label>
  <input type="text" name="name" value="" class="form-control">
</div>
```

Flask-specific variables and functions

Flask makes several functions and objects available to you by default in your template.

The config object

Flask makes the current `config` object available in templates as follows:

```
{{ config.SQLALCHEMY_DATABASE_URI }}
sqlite:///database.db
```

The request object

The Flask `request` object refers to the current request:

```
{{ request.url }}
http://127.0.0.1/
```

The session object

The Flask `session` object is as follows:

```
{{ session.new }}
True
```

The url_for() function

The `url_for` function returns the URL of a route by giving the route function name as a parameter, as shown in the following code. This allows URLs to be changed without worrying about where links will break:

```
{{ url_for('home') }}
/
```

Here, `home` is the name of a function that is registered as an endpoint on Flask, and the relative URL root associated with it, so on our `main.py`, we must define a function to deal with the HTTP request and register it on Flask using the decorator `app.route(rule, **options)`, as shown in the following code:

```
@app.route('/')
def home():
    ...
```

If we had a route that had positional arguments in the URL, we pass them as kwargs. They will be filled in for us in the resultant URL as follows:

```
{{ url_for('post', post_id=1) }}
/post/1
```

With the respective function that we use to handle the request, we restrict this method to handle only GET and POST HTTP requests, as follows:

```
@app.route('/post/<int:post_id>', methods=('GET', 'POST'))
def post(post_id):
    . . .
```

The get_flashed_messages() function

The get_flashed_messages() function returns a list of all the messages passed through the flash() function in Flask. The flash function is a simple function that queues messages—which consist of Python tuples of (category, message) phrases—for the get_flashed_messages function to consume, as shown in the following code:

```
{% with messages = get_flashed_messages(with_categories=true) %}
    {% if messages %}
        {% for category, message in messages %}
        <div class="alert alert-{{ category }} alert-dismissible"
        role="alert">
            <button type="button" class="close" data-dismiss="alert" aria-
    label="Close"><span aria-hidden="true">&times;</span></button>
                {{ message }}
        </div>
        {% endfor %}
    {% endif %}
{% endwith %}
```

Proper feedback to the user is very important, and Flask makes it very simple to implement—for example, when handling a new post entry, we want to let the user know that his/her post was saved correctly. The flash() function accepts three different categories: info, error, and warning. Refer to the following code snippet:

```
@app.route('/post/<int:post_id>', methods=('GET', 'POST'))
def post(post_id):
    . . .
    db.session.commit()
    flash("New post added.", 'info')
    . . .
```

Creating our views

To get started, we need to create a new folder named `templates` in our project directory. This folder will store all of our Jinja files, which are just HTML files with Jinja syntax mixed in. Our first template will be our home page, which will be a list of the first 10 posts with summaries. There will also be a view for a post that will just show the post content, the comments on the page, links to the author's user page, and links to tag pages. There will also be user and tag pages that show all the posts that have been made by a user and all the posts with a specific tag. Each page will also have a sidebar showing the five most recent posts and the top five most used tags.

The view function

Because each page will have the same sidebar information, we can break that into a separate function to simplify our code. In the `main.py` file, add the following code:

```
from sqlalchemy import func
...
def sidebar_data():
  recent = Post.query.order_by(
    Post.publish_date.desc()
  ).limit(5).all()
  top_tags = db.session.query(
    Tag, func.count(tags.c.post_id).label('total')
  ).join(
    tags
  ).group_by(Tag).order_by('total DESC').limit(5).all()

  return recent, top_tags
```

The most recent posts query is straightforward, but the most popular tags query looks somewhat familiar, but a little odd. This is a bit outside the scope of this book, but using the SQLAlchemy `func` library to return a count on a group by query, we are able to order our tags by the most used tags. The `func` function is explained in detail at http://docs.sqlalchemy.org/en/rel_1_0/core/sqlelement.html#sqlalchemy.sql.expression.func.

The `home` page function in `main.py` will need all the posts ordered by their publish date in a pagination object and the sidebar information, as follows:

```
from flask import Flask, render_template
...
@app.route('/')
```

```
@app.route('/<int:page>')
def home(page=1):
    posts = Post.query.order_by(Post.publish_date.desc()).paginate(page,
app.config['POSTS_PER_PAGE'], False)
    recent, top_tags = sidebar_data()

    return render_template(
        'home.html',
        posts=posts,
        recent=recent,
        top_tags=top_tags
    )
```

Note that using the `app.config['POSTS_PER_PAGE']` phrase gives us the option to configure it without having to change code, which is nice. It's a candidate config key for the main `Config` class, and let all environments inherit its value.

Here, we finally see how Flask and Jinja tie together. The Flask function `render_template` takes the name of a file in the folder `templates` and passes all the `kwargs` to the template as variables. Also, our `home` function now has multiple routes to handle pagination, and will default to the first page if there is nothing after the slash.

Now that you have all the information that you need to write view functions, let's define the first view functions that we need:

- `GET /post/<POST_ID>` to render a specific post by its ID. This also renders all recent posts and tags.
- `GET /posts_by_tag/<TAG_NAME>` to render all posts by a specific tag name. This also renders all recent posts and tags.
- `GET /posts_by_user/<USER_NAME>` to render all posts authored by a specific user. This also renders all recent posts and tags.

This translates to the following view functions:

```
@app.route('/post/<int:post_id>')
def post(post_id)
....

@app.route('/posts_by_tag/<string:tag_name>')
def posts_by_tag(tag_name):
...

@app.route('/posts_by_user/<string:username>')
def posts_by_user(username):
...
```

In Flask SQLAlchemy, there are two convenience functions that return HTTP `404` in the case of a nonexistent entry in the database, `get_or_404` and `first_or_404`, so on our get post by ID, as shown in the following code:

```
@app.route('/post/<int:post_id>')
def post(post_id)
    post = Post.query.get_or_404(post_id)
```

All posts made by a user can be returned using the following code:

```
@app.route('/posts_by_user/<string:username>')
def posts_by_user(username):
    user = User.query.filter_by(username=username).first_or_404()
    posts = user.posts.order_by(Post.publish_date.desc()).all()
    recent, top_tags = sidebar_data()

    return render_template(
      'user.html',
      user=user,
      posts=posts,
      recent=recent,
      top_tags=top_tags
    )
```

However, this doesn't check the `posts_by_tag` function in the `main.py` file (see the provided code for this chapter). After all of your views are written, the only thing left to do is to write the templates.

Writing the templates and inheritance

Because this book does not focus on interface design, we will use the CSS library **Bootstrap** and avoid writing custom CSS. If you have never used it before, Bootstrap is a set of default CSS rules that make your website work well across all browsers and platforms, from desktop to mobile. Bootstrap has tools that allow you to easily control the layout of your website.

We will be downloading Bootstrap, JQuery, and Font Awesome directly from their CDN upon page load, but any extra assets you may need should be included in a project directory named `static`. It's common practice to use `static/css` for CSS, `static/js` for JavaScript, `static/img` for images, and `static/fonts` for fonts. One of the best ways to use Bootstrap is to download its `sass` files and use `sass` to customize it.

For the official documentation about SASS and Bootstrap, visit `https://` `getbootstrap.com/docs/4.0/getting-started/theming/`.

Because every route will have a template assigned to it, each template will need the requisite HTML boilerplate code with our metainformation, style sheets, common JavaScript libraries, and so on. To keep our templates **DRY** (**don't repeat yourself**), we will use one of the most powerful features of Jinja, **template inheritance**. Template inheritance is when a child template can import a base template as a starting point and only replace marked sections in the base. You can also include full sections of Jinja templates from other files; this will allow you to set some rigid default sections.

The base template

We need to outline the base layout for our site, split it into sections, and give each section a specific purpose. The following diagram is an abstract description of the layout:

Navigation bar
Header
messages
body

Left body	right body

Footer

Some of these sections will always get rendered, and you don't want to repeat them on each template. Some possible options for these sections are the navigation bar, header, messages, and footer.

We will use the following include and block structure to maintain our DRY principal and implement the layout:

- **Include navbar**: Jinja2 template: `navbar.html`—Renders a navigation bar.
- **Block head**: The header with the name of the site. Already includes the `head.html` Jinja2 template.
- **Include messages**: Jinja2 template: `messages.html`—Renders alerts for the users with different categories.
- **Block body:**
    - **Block left body**: Normally, templates will override this block.
    - **Block right body**: This will display the most recent posts and tags.
- **Block footer**: Jinja2 template: `footer.html`.

Note how the fixed sections, the ones that will almost always get rendered, already include templates even when inside blocks. The base template will handle these by default. If for some reason you want to override these, you just have to implement/inherit their block on the rendered template. For example, say that you want to render a whole body section on a certain page, taking the space of the right body section that displays the most recent posts and tags. A good candidate for this will be the login page.

To start our base template, we need a basic HTML skeleton and the Jinja2 block structure that we previously outlined (see the highlighted code in the following snippet):

```
<!DOCTYPE html>
<html>
<head>
    <meta charset="utf-8">
    <meta http-equiv="X-UA-Compatible" content="IE=edge">
    <meta name="viewport" content="width=device-width, initial-scale=1,
maximum-scale=1">
    <title>{% block title %}Blog{% endblock %}</title>
    <link rel="stylesheet"
href="https://stackpath.bootstrapcdn.com/bootstrap/4.1.0/css/bootstrap.min.
css"
integrity="sha384-9gVQ4dYFwwWSjIDZnLEWnxCjeSWFphJiwGPXr1jddIhOegiu1FwO5qRGv
FXOdJZ4" crossorigin="anonymous">
    <link rel="stylesheet"
href="https://use.fontawesome.com/releases/v5.0.10/css/all.css"
integrity="sha384-
+d0P83n9kaQMCwj8F4RJB66tzIwOKmrdb46+porD/OvrJ+37WqIM7UoBtwHO6Nlg"
```

```
crossorigin="anonymous">
</head>
<body>
{% include 'navbar.html' %}
<div class="container">
    <div class="row row-lg-4">
        <div class="col">
            {% block head %}
            {% include 'head.html' %}
            {% endblock %}
        </div>
    </div>
    {% include 'messages.html' %}
    {% block body %}
    <div class="row">
        <div class="col-lg-9">
            {% block leftbody %}
            {% endblock %}
        </div>
        <div class="col-lg-3 rounded">
            {% block rightbody %}
            {% include 'rightbody.html' %}
            {% endblock %}
        </div>
    </div>
    {% endblock %}
    {% include 'footer.html' %}
</div>
</body>
<script src="https://code.jquery.com/jquery-3.3.1.slim.min.js"
integrity="sha384-
q8i/X+965DzO0rT7abK41JStQIAqVgRVzpbzo5smXKp4YfRvH+8abtTE1Pi6jizo"
crossorigin="anonymous"></script>
<script
src="https://cdnjs.cloudflare.com/ajax/libs/popper.js/1.14.0/umd/popper.min
.js" integrity="sha384-
cs/chFZiN24E4KMATLdqdvsezGxaGsi4hLGOzlXwp5UZB1LY//20VyM2taTB4QvJ"
crossorigin="anonymous"></script>
<script
src="https://stackpath.bootstrapcdn.com/bootstrap/4.1.0/js/bootstrap.min.js
" integrity="sha384-
uefMccjFJAIv6A+rW+L4AHf99KvxDjWSu1z9VI8SKNVmz4sk7buKt/6v9KI65qnm"
crossorigin="anonymous"></script>    </body>
</html>
```

This is the `base.html` template in the provided code in your `templates` directory. First, we include the Bootstrap and Font Awesome CSS, then implement the HTML body section, and finally include all the necessary JavaScript libraries.

The child templates

Now that we have outlined the base layout, we need to implement all the child pages that will extend the base. Take a look at the way we are implementing the home page and inherit/override the left body block, as shown in the following code:

```
{% extends "base.html" %}
{% import 'macros.html' as macros %}
{% block title %}Home{% endblock %}
{% block leftbody %}
{{ macros.render_posts(posts) }}
{{ macros.render_pagination(posts, 'home') }}
{% endblock %}
```

Surprisingly simple, this template extends the base template has expected, and then overrides the `title` and `leftbody` block sections. Inside, the `leftbody` uses two macros to render the posts and their pagination. The macros help us to reuse Jinja2 code and use it like functions, and also to hide some complexity.

The `render_posts` macro is in the `macros.html` that was imported at the top of the file. We use macros more or less like modules in Python, as shown in the following code:

```
{% macro render_posts(posts, pagination=True) %}
...
{% for post in _posts %}
<div >
    <h1>
        <a class="text-dark" href="{{ url_for('post', post_id=post.id)
}}">{{ post.title }}</a>
    </h1>
</div>
<div class="row">
    <div class="col">
        {{ post.text | truncate(500) | safe }}
        <a href="{{ url_for('post', post_id=post.id) }}">Read More</a>
    </div>
</div>
{% endfor %}
{% endmacro %}
```

The macro iterates on each post, and on each post.title, there is a link to the Flask endpoint post with its respective post ID. As explained, we always use url_for to generate the right URL that references Flask's endpoints.

We are using this macro three times on the templates: to render all posts, all posts by a certain tag, and all posts by a certain user.

The tag.html template renders all posts by a certain tag, as shown in the following code:

```
{% extends "base.html" %}
{% import 'macros.html' as macros %}

{% block title %}{{ tag.title }}{% endblock %}
{% block leftbody %}
<div class="row">
    <div class="col bg-light">
        <h1 class="text-center">Posts With Tag {{ tag.title }}</h1>
    </div>
</div>
{{ macros.render_posts(posts, pagination=False) }}

{% endblock %}
```

If you look at the user.html template in the preceding code, you'll see that they are almost identical. These templates are called by the Flask endpoint functions posts_by_tag and posts_by_user. When rendering the templates, they pass arguments for the tag/user object and a list of posts, as we saw before.

Let's check out how the blog site looks now. In the command line, call init.sh to build a Python virtualenv, and then migrate/create our database and insert some fake data, as follows:

```
$ ./init.sh
. . . .
$ source venv/bin/activate
$ export FLASK_APP=main.py; flask run
```

Open `http://127.0.0.1:5000/` in your browser. You should see the following:

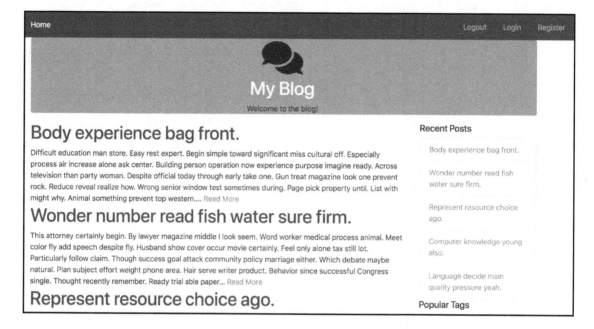

The `init.sh` phrase calls the `test_data.py`, which inserts fake data into the database. This Python module uses the `faker` library to generate data for user names and post text and tags (using color names).

For more details regarding `faker`, you can go to `http://faker.readthedocs.io/en/master/`.

The following code is an example taken from `test_data.py` that inserts users into the database and returns a list of user objects that is reused to insert posts:

```python
import logging
from main import db
from main import User, Post, Tag
from faker import Faker
...

def generate_users(n):
    users = list()
    for i in range(n):
        user = User()
```

```
        user.username = faker.name()
        user.password = "password"
        try:
            db.session.add(user)
            db.session.commit()
            users.append(user)
        except Exception as e:
            log.error("Fail to add user %s: %s" % (str(user), e))
            db.session.rollback()
    return users
```

The `template` folder contains the following templates that are rendered using the aforementioned hierarchy:

- `base.html`: Extended by all the other templates
- `footer.html`: Included by `base.html`
- `head.html`: Included by `base.html`
- `messages.html`: Included by `base.html`
- `navbar.html`: Included by `base.html`
- `rightbody.html`: Included by `base.html`
- `home.html`: Rendered by the `home` Flask endpoint function
- `post.html`: Rendered by the `post` Flask endpoint function
- `tag.html`: Rendered by the `posts_by_tag` endpoint function
- `user.html`: Rendered by the `posts_by_user` endpoint function

Writing the other templates

Now that you know the ins and outs of inheritance, and you know which data is going to go to which template, you can have a clear idea of how to structure your web application to easily scale and maintain the same look and feel on every page. There is one final bit of functionality to add in this chapter—the ability for readers to add comments. For this, we will be using web forms.

Flask WTForms

Adding forms to your application seems to be an easy task, but when you start coding the server-side code, the task of validating user input grows bigger and bigger as the form becomes more complex. Security is paramount, as the data is from an untrustworthy source, and is going to be entered into the database. **WTForms** is a library that handles server form validation for you by checking input against common form types. Flask WTForms is a Flask extension that is built on top of WTForms that adds features, such as Jinja HTML rendering, and protects you against attacks, such as SQL injection and cross-site request forgery. This extension is already installed in your virtualenv, because it's declared in the `requirements.txt` file.

 Protecting yourself against SQL injection and cross-site request forgery is extremely important, as these are the most common forms of attacks that your website will receive. To learn more about these attacks, visit `https://en.wikipedia.org/wiki/SQL_injection` and `https://en.wikipedia.org/wiki/Cross-site_request_forgery` for information on SQL injection and cross-site request forgery, respectively.

To have Flask WTForms' security measures working properly, we will need a **secret key**. A secret key is a random string of characters that will be used to cryptographically sign anything that needs to be tested for its authenticity. This cannot be just any string; it must be randomized and be of a certain length so that brute-force or dictionary attacks won't be able to crack it in any viable amount of time. To generate a random string, enter a Python session and enter the following:

```
$ python
>>> import os
>>> os.urandom(24)
'\xa8\xcc\xeaP+\xb3\xe8|\xad\xdb\xea\xd0\xd4\xe8\xac\xee\xfaW\x072@03'
```

You should generate a different secret key for each environment. Just copy the output from `os.urandom` and paste it into each environment `config` class, as follows:

```
class ProdConfig(object):
  SECRET_KEY = 'Your secret key here'
. . . .

class DevConfig(object):
  SECRET_KEY = 'The other secret key here'
. . . .
```

WTForms basics

There are three main parts of WTForms—**forms**, **fields**, and **validators**. Fields are representations of input fields and perform rudimentary type checking, and validators are functions that are attached to fields that make sure that the data submitted in the form is within our constraints. The form is a class that contains fields and validators, and validates itself on a POST request. Let's see this in action to get a better idea. In the main.py file, add the following:

```
from flask_wtf import FlaskForm as Form
from wtforms import StringField, TextAreaField
from wtforms.validators import DataRequired, Length
...
class CommentForm(Form):
  name = StringField(
    'Name',
    validators=[DataRequired(), Length(max=255)]
  )
  text = TextAreaField(u'Comment', validators=[DataRequired()])
```

Here, we have a class that inherits from Flask WTForm's Form object and defines inputs with class variables that equal WTForm fields. The fields take an optional parameter, validators, which is a list of WTForm validators that will be applied to our data. The most commonly used fields are as follows:

- fields.DateField and fields.DateTimeField: Represents a Python date or datetime object and takes an optional parameter format that takes a stftime format string to translate the data.
- fields.IntegerField: This attempts to coerce passed data to an integer and is rendered in the template as a number input.
- fields.FloatField: This attempts to coerce passed data to a float and is rendered in the template as a number input.
- fields.RadioField: This represents a set of radio inputs and takes a choices parameter , which is a list of tuples that act as the displayed value and the returned value.
- fields.SelectField: Along with SelectMultipleField, this represents a set of radio inputs. It takes a choices parameter, which is a list of tuples that act as the displayed and returned values.
- fields.StringField: This represents a normal text input, and will attempt to coerce the returned data to a string.

For a full list of validators and fields, visit the WTForms documentation at `http://wtforms.readthedocs.org`.

The most common validators are as follows:

- `validators.DataRequired()`
- `validators.Email()`
- `validators.Length(min=-1, max=-1)`
- `validators.NumberRange(min=None, max=None)`
- `validators.Optional()`
- `validators.Regexp(regex)`
- `validators.URL()`

Each of these validations follows the Pythonic naming scheme. Therefore, it is rather straightforward as to what they do. All validators take an optional parameter called `message`, which is the error message that will be returned if the validator fails. If a message is not set, it uses the library defaults.

Custom validations

Writing a custom validation function is very simple. All that is required is to write a function that takes the `form` object and the `field` object as parameters and raises a WTForm. A `ValidationError` is raised if the data does not pass the test. Here is an example of a custom email validator:

```
import re
import wtforms
def custom_email(form, field):
  if not re.match(r"[^@]+@[^@]+.[^@]+", field.data):
    raise wtforms.ValidationError('Field must be a valid email
      address.')
```

To use this function, just add it to the list of validators for your field.

Posting comments

Now that we have our comment form and we understand how to build it, we need to add it to the start of our post view, as follows:

```python
@app.route('/post/<int:post_id>', methods=('GET', 'POST'))
def post(post_id):
    form = CommentForm()
    if form.validate_on_submit():
        new_comment = Comment()
        new_comment.name = form.name.data
        new_comment.text = form.text.data
        new_comment.post_id = post_id
        try:
            db.session.add(new_comment)
            db.session.commit()
        except Exception as e:
            flash('Error adding your comment: %s' % str(e), 'error')
            db.session.rollback()
        else:
            flash('Comment added', 'info')
        return redirect(url_for('post', post_id=post_id))

    post = Post.query.get_or_404(post_id)
    tags = post.tags
    comments = post.comments.order_by(Comment.date.desc()).all()
    recent, top_tags = sidebar_data()

    return render_template(
        'post.html',
        post=post,
        tags=tags,
        comments=comments,
        recent=recent,
        top_tags=top_tags,
        form=form
    )
```

First, we add the POST method to the list of our view's allowed methods. Then, a new instance of our form object is created. The validate_on_submit() method then checks whether the Flask request is a POST request. If it is a POST request, it sends the request form data to the form object. If the data is validated, then validate_on_submit() returns True and adds the data to the form object. We then take the data from each field, populate a new comment, and add it to the database. Note how we don't need to fill in the comment data, because we have set a default value for it in the SQLAlchemy model definition—in this case, the datatime.now function that is going to be evaluated upon the object creation.

It is also important to ensure that we wrap all our database calls with a try/except block, and in the case of an error, roll back the session transaction and send proper feedback to the users.

Note the final redirect Flask call to the same endpoint, this time with an HTTP GET. This means that after a user inserts a new comment, the same page is rendered again with a clean form and shows the newly added comment.

If the form does not validate, or if we are handling an HTTP GET, we fetch the Post object from the database by post_id, collect all the related comments, and finally get all the necessary side-bar data.

The template itself is divided into three main sections. The first renders the post, the second displays the form where the user can submit a new comment about the post, and the third is where we render all the comments related to the post. Let's focus on the third section, as shown in the following code:

```
<div class="p-4 shadow-sm">
    <div class="row">
        <div class="col">
            <h4>New Comment:</h4>
        </div>
    </div>
    <div class="row">
        <div class="col">
            <form method="POST" action="{{ url_for('post',
            post_id=post.id) }}">
                {{ form.hidden_tag() }}
                <div class="form-group">
                    {{ form.name.label }}
                    {% if form.name.errors %}
                        {% for e in form.name.errors %}
                            <p class="help-block">{{ e }}</p>
                        {% endfor %}
                    {% endif %}
                    {{ form.name(class_='form-control') }}
```

```
            </div>
            <div class="form-group">
                {{ form.text.label }}
                {% if form.text.errors %}
                    {% for e in form.text.errors %}
                        <p class="help-block">{{ e }}</p>
                    {% endfor %}
                {% endif %}
                {{ form.text(class_='form-control') }}
            </div>
            <input class="btn btn-primary" type="submit" value="Add
        Comment">
        </form>
        </div>
    </div>
</div>
```

There are several new things happening here. First, we declare an HTML form section and make it submit (using HTTP POST) to our post Flask endpoint function with the current post ID.

Next, the form.hidden_tag() method adds an anticross-site request forgery measure automatically.

Then, when calling field.label, an HTML label will automatically be created for our input. This can be customized when we define our WTForm FlaskForm class; if not, WTForm will pretty print the field name.

Next, we check for any errors using field.errors, and if there are any, we will iterate all of them and render the form validation message to the user. Finally, calling the field itself as a method will render the HTML code of that field.

This third section of the template will display the following:

```
New Comment:
Name

[                                        ]

Comment

[                                        ]

[ Add Comment ]


Comments (2)

    By: user1 on 2018-06-13 15:15:53.373145
    Another comment about it!

    By: Daniel Gaspar on 2018-06-13 15:15:29.443572
    This is just a comment on the post
```

One challenge for the reader is to make a macro that takes a `form` object and an endpoint to send the `POST` request to and autogenerates HTML for the entire form tag. Refer to the WTForms documentation if you get stuck. It's tricky, but not too difficult.

Summary

Now, after only two chapters, you already have a fully functional blog. This is where a lot of books on web development technologies would end. However, there are still 10 more chapters to go to turn your utilitarian blog into something that a user would actually use for their website.

In the next chapter, we will focus on structuring Flask apps to accommodate long-term development and larger scale projects.

4
Creating Controllers with Blueprints

The final piece of the **Model View Controller** (**MVC**) equation is controllers. We have already seen the basic usage of the view functions in our `main.py` file. Now, the more complex and powerful versions will be introduced, and we will turn our disparate view functions into cohesive wholes. We will also discuss the internals of how Flask handles the lifetime of an HTTP request and advanced ways to define Flask views.

Sessions and globals

Sessions are the way Flask will store information across requests; to do this, Flask will use signed cookies using the previously set `SECRET_KEY` config to apply the HMAC-SHA1 default cryptographic method. So, a user can read their session cookie but can't modify it. Flask also sets a default session lifetime that defaults to 31 days to prevent relay attacks; this can be changed by using the configuration key's `PERMANENT_SESSION_LIFETIME` config key.

 Security is paramount in today's modern web applications; read Flask's documentation carefully, where various attacks methods are covered: `http://flask.pocoo.org/docs/security/`.

A Flask session object is a special kind of Python dictionary, but you can use it much like a plain Python dictionary, as follows:

```
from flask import session
...
session['page_loads'] = session.get('page_loads', 0) + 1
...
```

Global is a thread-safe namespace store to keep data during a request's context. At the beginning of each request, a new global object is created, and at the end of the request the object is destroyed. It's the right place to keep a User object or any data that needs to be shared across views, templates, or Python functions that are called within the request context. This is done without the need to pass around any data.

The use of g (global) is very simple, to set a key on a request context:

```
from flask import g
....
# Set some key with some value on a request context
g.some_key = "some_value"
# Get a key
v = g.some_key
# Get and remove a key
v = g.pop('some_key', "default_if_not_present")
```

Request setup and teardown

When your **WSGI** (**Web Server Gateway Interface**) handles a request, Flask creates a request context object that contains all the information about the request itself. This object is pushed into a stack that contains other important information, such as the Flask app , g, session, and flash messages.

The request object is available to any function, view, or template that is currently processing the request; this happens without the need to pass around the request object itself. request contains information such as HTTP headers, URI arguments, URL path, WSGI environment, and whatnot.

> For more detailed information on the Flask request object, see: http://
> flask.pocoo.org/docs/api/#incoming-request-data.

We can easily add more information to the request context by implementing our own hooks on request creation. To achieve this, we can use Flask's decorator function, @app.before_request, and the g object. The @app.before_request function is executed every time, before a new request is made. For example, the following code keeps a global counter for the number of page loads:

```
import random
from flask import session, g

@app.before_request
def before_request():
    session['page_loads'] = session.get('page_loads', 0) + 1
    g.random_key = random.randrange(1, 10)
```

Multiple functions can be decorated with @app.before_request, and they all will be executed before the requested view function is executed. There also exists a decorator, @app.teardown_request, which is called after the end of every request.

Initialize the example code provided for this chapter and watch how the data for g, session, and request changes. Also, note the csrf_token set by WTForm to secure our forms.

Error pages

Displaying a browser's default error pages to the end user is jarring as the user loses all context of your app, and they must hit the back button to return to your site. To display your own templates when an error is returned with the Flask abort() function, use the errorhandler decorator function:

```
@app.errorhandler(404)
def page_not_found(error):
    return render_template('404.html'), 404
```

errorhandler is also useful to translate internal server errors and HTTP 500 codes into user-friendly error pages. The app.errorhandler() function may take either one or many HTTP status codes to define which code it will act on. The returning of a tuple instead of just an HTML string allows you to define the HTTP status code of the Response object. By default, this is set to 200. The recommend method is covered in Chapter 6, *Securing Your App*.

Class-based views

In most Flask apps, views are handled by functions. However, when many views share common functionality or there are pieces of your code that could be broken out into separate functions, it would be useful to implement our views as classes to take advantage of inheritance.

For example, if we have views that render a template, we could create a generic view class that keeps our code *DRY*:

```python
from flask.views import View

class GenericView(View):
    def __init__(self, template):
        self.template = template
        super(GenericView, self).__init__()

    def dispatch_request(self):
        return render_template(self.template)

app.add_url_rule(
    '/', view_func=GenericView.as_view(
        'home', template='home.html'
    )
)
```

The first thing to note about this code is the `dispatch_request()` function in our view class. This is the function in our view that acts as the normal view function and returns an HTML string. The `app.add_url_rule()` function mimics the `app.route()` function as it ties a route to a function call. The first argument defines the route of the function, and the `view_func` parameter defines the function that handles the route. The `View.as_view()` method is passed to the `view_func` parameter because it transforms the `View` class into a view function. The first argument defines the name of the view function, so functions such as `url_for()` can route to it. The remaining parameters are passed to the `__init__` function of the `View` class.

Like the normal view functions, HTTP methods other than GET must be explicitly allowed for the `View` class. To allow other methods, a class variable containing the list of named methods must be added:

```python
class GenericView(View):
    methods = ['GET', 'POST']
    ...
    def dispatch_request(self):
        if request.method == 'GET':
```

```
        return render_template(self.template)
    elif request.method == 'POST':
        ...
```

This can be a very powerful approach. Take for example web pages that render tabular lists from database tables; they are almost identical, so are nice candidates for generic approaches. Although not a trivial task to carry out, the time you take to implement it can save you time in the future. An initial skeleton using class-based views could be this:

```python
from flask.views import View


class GenericListView(View):

    def __init__(self, model, list_template='generic_list.html'):
        self.model = model
        self.list_template = list_template
        self.columns = self.model.__mapper__.columns.keys()
        # Call super python3 style
        super(GenericListView, self).__init__()

    def render_template(self, context):
        return render_template(self.list_template, **context)

    def get_objects(self):
        return self.model.query.all()

    def dispatch_request(self):
        context = {'objects': self.get_objects(),
                   'columns': self.columns}
        return self.render_template(context)


app.add_url_rule(
    '/generic_posts', view_func=GenericListView.as_view(
        'generic_posts', model=Post)
)

app.add_url_rule(
    '/generic_users', view_func=GenericListView.as_view(
        'generic_users', model=User)
)

app.add_url_rule(
    '/generic_comments', view_func=GenericListView.as_view(
        'generic_comments', model=Comment)
)
```

There are some interesting things to notice. First, in the class constructor we initialize the `columns` class property with the SQLAlchemy model columns; we are leveraging the model introspection ability of SQLAlchemy to be able to implement our generic template. So, column names are going to be passed to our generic template so that we can properly render a well formatted tabular list for any model we throw at it.

This is a simple example of how, with a single class view, we handle all list views from all our models.

This is how the template looks like:

```
{% extends "base.html" %}
{% block body %}

<div class="table-responsive">
    <table class="table table-bordered table-hover">
    {% for obj in objects %}
        <tr>
        {% for col in columns %}
        <td>
        {{col}} {{ obj[col] }}
        </td>
        {% endfor %}
        </tr>
    {% endfor %}
    </table>
</div>

{% endblock %}
```

You can access these views by running the example code provided for this chapter, then directly accessing the declared URLs:

- `http://localhost:5000/generic_users`
- `http://localhost:5000/generic_posts`
- `http://localhost:5000/generic_comments`

You may have noticed that our tabular view is missing the table column headers. As an exercise, I challenge you to implement it; you can simply render the provided `columns` class property, or even better, use a label/column mapping to display more user-friendly column names.

Method class views

Often, when functions handle multiple HTTP methods, the code can become difficult to read due to large sections of code nested within `if` statements, as demonstrated in the following:

```
@app.route('/user', methods=['GET', 'POST', 'PUT', 'DELETE'])
def users():
    if request.method == 'GET':
        ...
    elif request.method == 'POST':
        ...
    elif request.method == 'PUT':
        ...
    elif request.method == 'DELETE':
        ...
```

This can be solved with the `MethodView` class. `MethodView` allows each method to be handled by a different class method to separate concerns:

```
from flask.views import MethodView

class UserView(MethodView):
    def get(self):
        ...
    def post(self):
        ...
    def put(self):
        ...
    def delete(self):
        ...

app.add_url_rule(
    '/user',
    view_func=UserView.as_view('user')
)
```

Blueprints

In Flask, a **blueprint** is a method of extending an existing Flask app. They provide a way of combining groups of views with common functionality and allow developers to break their app down into different components. In our architecture, the blueprints will act as our *controllers*.

Views are registered to a blueprint; a separate template and static folder can be defined for it, and when it has all the desired content in it, it can be registered on the main Flask app to add the blueprint's content. A blueprint acts much like a Flask app object, but is not actually a self-contained app. This is how Flask extensions provide view functions. To get an idea of what blueprints are, here is a very simple example:

```
from flask import Blueprint
example = Blueprint(
    'example',
    __name__,
    template_folder='templates/example',
    static_folder='static/example',
    url_prefix="/example"
)

@example.route('/')
def home():
    return render_template('home.html')
```

The blueprint takes two required parameters, the name of the blueprint and the name of the package, which are used internally in Flask, and passing __name__ to it will suffice.

The other parameters are optional and define where the blueprint will look for files. Because `templates_folder` was specified, the blueprint will not look in the default template folder, and the route will render `templates/example/home.html` and not `templates/home.html`. The `url_prefix` option automatically adds the provided URI to the start of every route in the blueprint. So, the URL for the home view is actually `/example/`.

The `url_for()` function will now have to be told which blueprint the requested route is in:

```
{{ url_for('example.home') }}
```

Also, the `url_for()` function will now have to be told whether the view is being rendered from within the same blueprint:

```
{{ url_for('.home') }}
```

The `url_for()` function will also look for static files in the specified `static` folder as well.

Use this to add the blueprint to our app:

```
app.register_blueprint(example)
```

Let's transform our current app to one that uses blueprints. We will first need to define our blueprint before all of our routes:

```
blog_blueprint = Blueprint(
    'blog',
    __name__,
    template_folder='templates/blog',
    url_prefix="/blog"
)
```

Now, because the `templates` folder was defined, we need to move all of our templates into a subfolder of the `templates` folder named `blog`. Next, all of our routes need to have `@app.route` changed to `@blog_blueprint.route`, and any class view assignments now need to be registered to `blog_blueprint`. Remember that the `url_for()` function calls in the templates will also have to be changed to have a period prepended to then to indicate that the route is in the same blueprint.

At the end of the file, right before the `if __name__ == '__main__':` statement, add the following:

```
app.register_blueprint(blog_blueprint)
```

Now, all of our content is back in the app, which is registered under the blueprint. Because our base app no longer has any views, let's add a redirect on the base URL:

```
@app.route('/')
def index():
    return redirect(url_for('blog.home'))
```

Why blog and not `blog_blueprint`? Because blog is the name of the blueprint and the name is what Flask uses internally for routing. `blog_blueprint` is the name of the variable in the Python file.

Summary

In this chapter, we have introduced you to some powerful features of Flask; we have seen how to use sessions to store user data across requests and globals for keeping data during the request context. We have introduced you to the concept of request context and started showing you some new features that will enable us to scale our applications easily to any size, using Blueprints and Method Class views.

We now have our app working inside a blueprint, but what does this give us? Let's say that we wanted to add a photo sharing function to our site, we would be able to group all the view functions into one blueprint with its own templates, static folder, and URL prefix without any fear of disrupting the functionality of the rest of the site.

In the next chapter, blueprints will be made even more powerful by separating them into different files after upgrading our file and code structure.

Advanced Application Structure

5

Our application has gone from a very simple example to an extendable foundation on which powerful features can easily be built. However, having our application entirely reside in one file needlessly clutters our code. This is one of the advantages of Flask; you can write a small REST service or web application on a single file, or a full-blown enterprise application. The framework won't get in your way and won't impose any project layout.

To make the application code clearer and more comprehensible, we will transform the entire code into a Python module and each feature into a module by itself. This modular approach enables you to scale easily and in a predictable way, so new features will have an obvious place and structure. In this chapter, you will learn the best practices for the following:

- Creating a modular application that easily scales
- Application factory pattern

Modular application

Currently, your folder structure should look like the following (take a look at the code provided for the previous chapter):

```
./
  config.py
  database.db
  main.py
  manage.py
  env/
  migrations/
    versions/
  templates/
    blog/
```

To convert our code into a more modular application, our files will be structured as follows:

```
./
  manage.py
  main.py
  config.py
database.db
  webapp/
    __init__.py
    blog/
      __init__.py
      controllers.py
      forms.py
      models.py
    main/
      __init__.py
      controllers.py
    templates/
      blog/
  migrations/
    versions/
```

The first change to make is to create a folder in your application that will hold the module. In this example, it will be called `webapp`.

Next, for each module in our application, we will create a respective Python module. If the module is a classic web application using web templates and forms, we would create the following files:

. /<MODULE_NAME>

```
__init__.py -> Declare a python module
controllers.py -> where our blueprint definition and views are
models.py -> The module database models definitions
forms.py -> All the module's web Forms
```

The idea is to have separation of concerns, so each module will contain all the necessary views (declared and contained inside a Flask blueprint), web forms, and modules. This modular structure will translate into predictable namespaces for URIs, templates, and Python modules. Continuing to reason with an abstract approach, each module will have the following:

- Python module (folder with `__init__.py`) using its name: MODULE_NAME. Inside the module is a `controllers` Python module that declares a blueprint named `<MODULE_NAME>_blueprint` attached to a URL, `prefix /<MODULE_NAME>`.

- Template folder inside `templates` named `<MODULE_NAME>`.

This pattern will make the code very predictable to other team members, and very easy to change and extend. If you want to create a brand new feature, just create a new module using the proposed structure, and all team members will immediately guess the new feature's URI namespace, where all views are declared, and where the database models are defined for this feature. If some bug is identified, you can easily identify where to look for it, and have a much more restricted code base to worry about.

Refactoring the code

At first, it looks like a lot has changed but you will see that, taking into account the previously explained structure, the changes are simple and natural.

First, we have moved our SQLAlchemy code to the `models.py` file inside the `blog` module folder. We just want to move the model definitions, not any database initialization code. All initialization code will be kept in the main application module, `webapp`, inside `__init__.py`. The import section and database-related object creation appear as follows:

```
from flask import Flask, render_template
from flask_sqlalchemy import SQLAlchemy
from flask_migrate import Migrate

db = SQLAlchemy()
migrate = Migrate()


def page_not_found(error):
    return render_template('404.html'), 404

def create_app(config):
    ...
```

The main application module will be responsible for creating the Flask application (factory pattern, explained in the next section) and initializing SQLAlchemy.

The `blog/models.py` file will import the initialized `db` object:

```
from .. import db

...
class User(db.Model):
    ...
class Post(db.Model):
    ...
```

```
class Comment(db.Model):
...
class Tag(db.Model):
...
```

Next, the `CommentForm` object, along with all the WTForms imports, should be moved to the `blog/forms.py` file. The `forms.py` file will hold all the WTForms objects related to the blog feature.

The `forms.py` file should look like this:

```
from flask_wtf import Form
from wtforms import StringField, TextAreaField
from wtforms.validators import DataRequired, Length

class CommentForm(Form):
    ...
```

The `blog_blueprint` object, all its routes, and the `sidebar_data` data function need to be moved to the `blog/controllers.py` file in the `controllers` folder.

The `blog/controllers.py` file should now look like this:

```
from sqlalchemy import func
from flask import render_template, Blueprint, flash, redirect, url_for
from .models import db, Post, Tag, Comment, User, tags
from .forms import CommentForm

blog_blueprint = Blueprint(
    'blog',
    __name__,
    template_folder='../templates/blog',
    url_prefix="/blog"
)


def sidebar_data():
...
```

So, whenever a new feature is needed that is big enough to be a candidate for an application module, a new Python module (folder with an __init__.py file) with the name of the feature is needed with the previously described files. We will be breaking down the application code into logical groups.

Then, we need to import the new feature blueprint into the main __init__.py file and register it in Flask:

```
from .blog.controllers import blog_blueprint
from .main.controllers import main_blueprint

...
app.register_blueprint(main_blueprint)
app.register_blueprint(blog_blueprint)
```

Application factories

Now that we are using blueprints in a modular manner, there is another improvement we can make to our abstraction, which creates a **factory** for our application. The concept of a factory comes from the **object-oriented programming** (OOP) world, and it simply means a function or an object that creates another object. Our application factory will take one of our config objects, which we created at the beginning of the book, and return a Flask application object.

 The object factory design was popularized by the now famous book, *Design Patterns: Elements of Reusable Object-Oriented Software*, by the Gang of Four. To learn more about these design patterns and how they can help simplify a project's code, look at
https://en.wikipedia.org/wiki/Structural_pattern.

Creating a factory function for our application object has several benefits. First, it allows the context of the environment to change the configuration of the application. When your server creates the application object to serve, it can take into account any changes in the server that are necessary, and change the configuration object given to the app accordingly. Second, it makes testing much easier because it allows differently configured applications to be tested quickly. Third, multiple instances of the same application using the same configuration can be created very easily. This is useful for situations where web traffic is balanced across several different servers.

Now that the benefits of application factories are clear, let's modify our __init__.py file to implement one:

```
from flask import Flask, render_template
from flask_sqlalchemy import SQLAlchemy
from flask_migrate import Migrate

db = SQLAlchemy()
migrate = Migrate()
```

```
def page_not_found(error):
    return render_template('404.html'), 404


def create_app(object_name):
    from .blog.controllers import blog_blueprint
    from .main.controllers import main_blueprint

    app = Flask(__name__)
    app.config.from_object(object_name)

    db.init_app(app)
    migrate.init_app(app, db)
    app.register_blueprint(main_blueprint)
    app.register_blueprint(blog_blueprint)
    app.register_error_handler(404, page_not_found)
    return app
```

The change to the file is very simple: we contained our code in a function that takes a config object and returns an application object. To start our application using the right configuration from an environment variable, we need to change main.py:

```
import os
from webapp import create_app

env = os.environ.get('WEBAPP_ENV', 'dev')
app = create_app('config.%sConfig' % env.capitalize())

if __name__ == '__main__':
    app.run()
```

We also need to modify our manage.py file in order to work with the create_app function as follows:

```
import os
from webapp import db, migrate, create_app
from webapp.blog.models import User, Post, Tag

env = os.environ.get('WEBAPP_ENV', 'dev')
app = create_app('config.%sConfig' % env.capitalize())

@app.shell_context_processor
def make_shell_context():
    return dict(app=app, db=db, User=User, Post=Post, Tag=Tag,
migrate=migrate)
```

When we created our configuration objects, it was mentioned that the environment that the application is running in could change the configuration of the application. This code has a very simple example of that functionality, where an environment variable is loaded and determines which `config` object to give to the `create_app` function. Environment variables are dynamic name values that are part of a process environment. These environments can be shared by multiple processes, system-wide, user-wide, or for a single process. They can be set in Bash with the following syntax:

```
$ export WEBAPP_ENV="dev"
```

Use this to read a variable:

```
$ echo $WEBAPP_ENV
dev
```

You can also delete the variable easily, as follows:

```
$ unset $WEBAPP_ENV
$ echo $WEBAPP_ENV
```

On your production server, you would set `WEBAPP_ENV` to `prod`. The true power of this setup will become clearer once you deploy to production in `Chapter 13`, *Deploying Flask Apps*, and when we get to `Chapter 12`, *Testing Flask Apps*, which covers testing our project.

Summary

We have transformed our application into a much more manageable and scalable structure, which will save us a lot of headaches as we move further through the book and add more advanced features. In the next chapter, we will add a login and registration system to our application, and other features to make our site more secure.

6
Securing Your App

We have a mostly functioning blog app, but it is missing some crucial features, such as a user login, registration function, and the ability to add and edit posts from the browser. The user authentication functionality can be achieved in many different ways, so each of the following sections in this chapter will demonstrate a mutually exclusive method to create a login functionality. Each authentication method can have different levels of security, or may be adequate for different kinds of applications, ranging from web exposed to enterprise back office.

In this chapter, we will explore the following topics:

- A brief overview of various authentication methods: basic authentication, remote user, LDAP, database authentication, and OpenID and Oauth
- How to leverage Flask login (database/cookie authentication)
- How to implement **role-based access control (RBAC)** to distinguish functionality and implement granular access to normal blog users

If you haven't already, download the provided code and use the init.sh script to create a virtualenv, database schema, and test data. The test data will create three users, all with their passwords set to password. The users will each have the following permissions respectively:

- user_default with minimal permissions
- user_poster with author permissions
- admin with admin permissions

Let's first explore some very simple authentication methods.

Authentication methods

An authentication method is a process of confirming an identity. In the case of an application, a user is given a username and a secret security token (password) and uses them to verify their identity on the application itself. There are several authentication methods and types, used for different types of applications (such as API, web exposed, intranet, and government). We will be covering the most used type of authentication—single factor.

Basic authentication

As the name suggests, basic authentication is a very simple authentication method implemented by the HTTP protocol itself. It is part of the RFC7617. To use it, we can configure our web servers (IIS, Apache, and NGINX) to implement it, or we can implement it ourselves.

> For details on how to configure NGINX for basic authentication, go to https://docs.nginx.com/nginx/admin-guide/security-controls/ configuring-http-basic-authentication/.

The basic authentication protocol goes through the following general steps:

1. The user requests a protected resource from the server.
2. The server responds with `401` (unauthorized) and the HTTP header `WWW-Authenticate: Basic realm="Login required"`.
3. The browser will display a basic authentication login window for the user to send a username/password back to the server.
4. The username and password provided by the user will be sent to the server on the HTTP header with the form `Authorization: Basic <Username>:<Password>`. The `username:password` will be base64-encoded.

Flask will make it easy for us to implement this protocol, since it will automatically decode the base64 authorization from the HTTP header and place the username and password has properties of the `Request.authorization` object, as shown in the following code:

```
def authenticate(username, password):
    return username == 'admin' and password == 'password'

@app.route('/basic-auth-page')
```

```
def basic_auth_page():
    auth = request.authorization
    if not auth or not authenticate(auth.username, auth.password)
        return Response('Login with username/password', 401, {'WWW-
Authenticate': 'Basic realm="Login Required"'})
    return render_template('some_page.html')
```

This type of authentication is very simple, but not very secure. The username and password will be sent to the server on every request, so make sure that you always use HTTPS to properly encrypt their transmission over the wire. Additionally, as you may have already noticed in the code flow of the preceding example, the authentication method will be invoked on every request, so it is not very efficient. Yet this can be a good option for the internal use of a very simple back-office application, or for rapidly protecting a proof-of-concept application.

Remote-user authentication

We can, with some intranet setups, use single sign-on authentication methods, where the web servers do all the heavy lifting related with security. This can be done using **IIS integrated windows authentication** or **Apache mod_auth_sspi**, **Apache Samba**, or others. The setup is beyond the scope of this book.

 You can check out some examples of how to set up this kind of authentication with Apache Samba at `https://wiki.samba.org/index.php/Authenticating_Apache_against_Active_Directory`.

With this kind of authentication method, the web server will pass the already authenticated username as an environment key to the **WSGI** (**web server gateway interface**), so we just have to fetch it using the following:

```
username = request.environ.get('REMOTE_USER')
```

For our blog application, we could just check whether the user exists on the database, so no password database field is needed. This authentication method can be considered secure if it is properly set up on the server, and can be very convenient on intranet setups since the user, if already authenticated on the domain (for example, Active Directory) will no longer need to fill his/her login/password again (using Kerberos GSSAPI, or Windows SSPI, for example).

LDAP authentication

LDAP (**lightweight directory access protocol**) is an open standard described currently by RFC4511. Its purpose is to implement a distributed information directory over the IP. This directory can contain different types of information normally related to users, groups, and devices. It has a fixed schema describing each object's attributes, but this schema can be changed using LDIF.

 Active Directory is Microsoft's implementation of LDAP. You can take a look at the base-implemented user attributes that are available at `http://www.kouti.com/tables/userattributes.htm`.

An entry (for example, the user) on the directory is identified by a **distinguished name** (**DN**). For example, take a look at the following code:

```
CN=user1,OU=Marketing,DC=example,DC=com
```

The `DC` phrase is the domain component, and it identifies the domain where the user is (an LDAP directory can have trees of domains and subdomains). In our example, the domain is `example.com`. The phrase `OU` refers to the organizational unit where the user is, and `CN` is its common name.

The LDAP implements various operations, such as adding users, searching, deleting and so on. For authentication purposes only, we are interested on the `Bind` and `Search` operations.

To use the LDAP, we will need to install `python-ldap`, so let's do that first using the following code:

```
$ pip install python-ldap
```

The two most commonly used LDAP services nowadays are **OpenLDAP** (open and free) and **Microsoft Active Directory** (commercial). Their implementation differs a bit, mainly regarding their user attributes. The following code is an example of Active Directory. First, we need to define some configuration keys to connect to and authenticate with the service:

```
import ldap

LDAP_SERVER="ldap://example.com:389"
ROOT_DN="dc=example,dc=com"
SERVICE_USER="ServiceAccount"
SERVICE_PASSWORD="SOME_PASSWORD"
UID_FIELD_NAME="userPrincipalName" # specific for AD
USER_DOMAIN="example.com"
```

Note that we are using nonencrypted communication between our application server and the LDAP server; we can turn encryption on by using digital certificates and using LDAPS on our `LDAP_SERVER` configuration key.

If we were to integrate LDAP authentication with our blog application, these values would be good candidates for our configuration on `config.py`.

Next, we will connect to and authenticate with the service as follows:

```
con = ldap.initialize(LDAP_SERVER)
con.set_option(ldap.OPT_REFERRALS, 0)
con.bind_s(SERVICE_USER, SERVICE_PASSWORD)
```

> The `OPT_REFERRALS` is a specific workaround for MSFT AD. Take a look at the FAQ for `python-ldap` for more detailed information at `https://www.python-ldap.org/en/latest/faq.html`.

Now that we have an authenticated connection, we will search for our user to fetch its username, as shown in the following code. In Active Directory, we could bind directly using the user's username and password, yet that method would fail in OpenLDAP. This way, we are following the standard method that will work on both systems:

```
username = username + '@' + USER_DOMAIN
filter_str = "%s=%s" % (UID_FIELD_NAME, username)
user = con.search_s(ROOT_DN,
                    ldap.SCOPE_SUBTREE,
                    filter_str,
                    ["givenName","sn","mail"])
```

A complete authentication function for LDAP could be as follows:

```
def ldap_auth(username, password):
    con = ldap.initialize(LDAP_SERVER)
    con.set_option(ldap.OPT_REFERRALS, 0)
    username = username + '@' + USER_DOMAIN
    con.bind_s(SERVICE_USER, SERVICE_PASSWORD)
    filter_str = "%s=%s" % (UID_FIELD_NAME, username)
    user = con.search_s(ROOT_DN,
                        ldap.SCOPE_SUBTREE,
                        filter_str,
                        ["givenName","sn","mail"])
    if user:
        print("LDAP got User {0}".format(user))
        # username = DN from search
        username = user[0][0]
        try:
```

```
            con.bind_s(username, password)
            return True
        except ldap.INVALID_CREDENTIALS:
            return False
    else:
        return False
```

Finally, with the LDAP username we make a final bind to authenticate our user (the highlighted code).

Database user model authentication

Database authentication is widely used for internet-faced applications. If properly implemented, it can be considered a secure method. It has the advantages of being simple to add new users, and having no dependency on any external services. Security roles, groups, fine-grained access permissions, and extra user attributes are also all kept on the database. These can be easily changed without any external dependencies, and maintained within the scope change of the application.

This authentication method consists of checking the username and password submitted by a user against the stored attributes in our database's user model. But until now, our users had their passwords stored as plain text in the database. This is a major security flaw. If any malicious user were to gain access to the data in the database, they could log in to any account. The fallout of such a breach not be limited to our site. Large numbers of people on the internet use a common password for many sites. If an attacker had access to an email and password combination, it is very likely that this information could be used to log in to a Facebook account, or even a bank account.

To protect our user passwords, they will be encrypted with a one-way encryption method called a **hashing algorithm**. A one-way encryption means that after the information is encrypted, the original information cannot be regained from the result. However, given the same data, the hashing algorithm will always produce the same result. The data given to the hashing algorithm can be anything from a text file to a movie file. In this case, the data is just a string of characters. With this functionality, our passwords can be stored as **hashes** (data that has been hashed). Then, when a user enters their password in the login or registration page, the text entered for the password will be sent through the same hashing algorithm, and the stored hash and the entered hash will be verified.

This is one of the authentication methods we will use; further implementation details are described later in this chapter.

OpenID and OAuth

Integrating alternative login and registration options into your site becomes more important as time goes on. Every month, there is another announcement that passwords have been stolen from a popular website. Implementing the following login options means that our site's database never stores a password for that user. Verification is handled by a large brand-named company that the user already places their trust in. By using social logins, the amount of trust a user has to place in the website they are using is much higher. Your login process also becomes much shorter for the user, decreasing the barrier to entry to your app.

Socially authenticated users act as normal users, and unlike the password-based login methods, they can all be used in tandem.

OpenID is an open-standard authentication protocol that allows users on one site to be authenticated by any third-party site that implements the protocol, which are called **identity providers**. An OpenID login is represented as a URL from one of the identity providers, typically the profile page of the website. The users that wish to use this authentication method need to be already registered on at least one of the OpenID providers.

To see a full list of sites that use OpenID, and to learn how to use each one, go to `https://openid.net/get-an-openid/`.

During the process of authentication, the user is redirected to the OpenID provider, where the user can authenticate—typically using a username/password, but it can be any other method—and is asked if they trust the party (our application). If the user trusts our application and authenticates successfully, then the user is redirected back with a document holding some requested user information (such as the username or email). A final request is made to check whether the data really came from the provider.

OAuth is not an authentication method—it is an access-delegation method. It was mainly designed to enable third-party applications to interact with the OAuth providers (Facebook, Twitter, and so on). With it, we can design an application to interact with a user's Facebook account, performing actions such as posting on his behalf, sending notifications, retrieving their friends list, and so on.

To start using OAuth, we first need to register our application on the OAuth provider and use its consumer key and secret token.

For Facebook, we need to register our application at `http://developers.facebook.com`. Once you create a new app, look for the panel that lists your app's ID and secret key, as shown in the following screenshot:

To create a Twitter app and receive your keys, go to `https://apps.twitter.com/`. Please do so, since we are going to use these keys, tokens and configuration information to set up our blog application for OAuth pseudoauthentication.

The OAuth process is as follows:

1. The application requests access to a user's resources from the OAuth provider.
2. The user is redirected and authorizes the requested access.
3. The application receives an authorization grant, and requests an access token by providing its own credentials (key and token) as well as the received grant.
4. The application receives the access token (this will serve as our authentication method) and can be further used to interact with the provider API on behalf of our user.

For a view of the complete OAuth process, go to `https://flask-dance.readthedocs.io/en/latest/how-oauth-works.html#oauth-2`.

Since we will be using both methods in our application, you will find the implementation details in the following chapters.

Flask-Login overview

Flask-Login is a popular Flask extension for handling the process of logging users in and out, properly handling cookie sessions, and even using basic authentication with HTTP headers. It will set up callbacks for user loading, header authentication, logging in, logging out, unauthorized events, and so on.

To start using Flask-Login, we first need to declare it as a dependency on our `requirements.txt`, as shown in the following code:

```
...
Flask-Login
...
```

Then, we need to update our Python virtual environment as follows:

```
$ source venv/bin/activate
$ pip install -r requirements.txt
```

 If you have executed the provided `init.sh` script, then there is no need to update the `virtualenv`. All the required dependencies for this chapter are already installed.

To use the session and login flow implemented by Flask-Login, we will need to do the following:

- Change the user model and implement the following functions:
  - `is_authenticated`: This checks whether the current user is authenticated
  - `is_active`: This checks whether a user is active
  - `is_anonymous`: This supports anonymous accesses to our blog
  - `get_id`: This fetches the user ID
- Initialize and configure the login manager object, declaring the following:
  - Where our login view is (URL)
  - The type of session
  - The login message (flashed login message)
  - The special user class for anonymous users
  - Register and implement a function to load our authenticated user
  - A function that returns a user object by its ID

Flask-Login is agnostic as to our authentication method, so the authentication system itself needs be implemented.

Setting up

To implement the user authentication system, we will develop a new module in our application by following the rules that were previously proposed in Chapter 5, *Advanced Application Structure*. Our application structure will be as follows:

```
./
  config.py
  manage.py
  main.py
  config.py
  database.db
  webapp/
    __init__.py
    blog/
      __init__.py
      controllers.py
      forms.py
      models.py
    auth/
      __init__.py
      controllers.py
      models.py
      forms.py
    main/
      __init__.py
      controllers.py
    templates/
      blog/
      auth/
  migrations/
    versions/
```

To keep the principle of separation of concerns in our approach to our module's design, we will make a simple change to the way we register each module blueprint. This is a nice thing to have, and it's necessity is more evident now because in this chapter, we will be using lots of new extensions to implement security, and we have to initialize them, register event methods, and configure them. All of these security bootstrapping procedures are best kept in the authentication module itself. To achieve this, we will create a new method in each __init__.py file for each module. Let's take a look at how this is done in our blog and authentication modules:

First, let's look at the code in the `blog/__init__.py` file:

```
def create_module(app, **kwargs):
    from .controllers import blog_blueprint
    app.register_blueprint(blog_blueprint)
```

In the authentication module, we will handle the Flask-Login configuration and initialization as previously described. The main Flask-Login object is the `LoginManager` object.

Let's look at the code in the `auth/__init__.py` file:

```
from flask_login import LoginManager

login_manager = LoginManager()
login_manager.login_view = "auth.login" login_manager.session_protection =
"strong" login_manager.login_message = "Please login to access this page"
login_manager.login_message_category = "info"

@login_manager.user_loader
def load_user(userid):
    from models import User
    return User.query.get(userid)

def create_module(app, **kwargs):
    ...
    login_manager.init_app(app)
    from .controllers import auth_blueprint
    app.register_blueprint(auth_blueprint)
    ...
```

The preceding configuration values define which view should be treated as the login page, and what the message should be to the user after a successful login. Setting the `session_protection` option to `strong` better protects against malicious users tampering with their cookies. When a tampered cookie is identified, the session object for that user is deleted and the user is forced to log back in.

The `load_user` function takes an ID and returns the `User` object. When a cookie is validated, Flask-Login will use our function to fetch the user into the current session.

Finally, in the `create_app` method itself, we just have to call the `create_module` on each module, as follows:

```
    . . .

def create_app(object_name):
    . . .
    app = Flask(__name__)
    app.config.from_object(object_name)

    db.init_app(app)
    migrate.init_app(app, db)

    from .auth import create_module as auth_create_module
    from .blog import create_module as blog_create_module
    from .main import create_module as main_create_module
    auth_create_module(app)
    blog_create_module(app)
    main_create_module(app)

    return app
```

To implement an authentication system, we need a lot of setup code. To run any type of authentication, our app will need the following elements:

- The user models will need proper password hashing
- It will need to implement a system to keep a secure user session context
- A login form and a registration form will be needed to validate user input
- A login view and a registration view (and templates for each) will be needed

Updating the models

There are many hashing algorithms, most of which are not secure because they are easy to **brute force**. With brute-force attacks, hackers continuously try sending data through a hashing algorithm until something matches. To best protect the user passwords, bcrypt will be our hashing algorithm of choice. Bcrypt is purposely designed to be inefficient and slow (milliseconds rather than microseconds) for the computer to process, thereby making it harder to brute force. To add bcrypt to our project, the package flask-bcrypt will need to be installed and added as a dependency on our `requirements.txt`, as follows:

```
. . .
flask-bcrypt
. . .
```

The `flask-bcrypt` package will have to be initialized. This is done in the `auth` module, `auth/__init__.py`, as shown in the following code:

```
. . .
from flask.ext.bcrypt import Bcrypt
bcrypt = Bcrypt()
. . .
def create_module(app, **kwargs):
    bcrypt.init_app(app)
    login_managet.init_app(app)

    from .controllers import auth_blueprint
    app.register_blueprint(auth_blueprint)
. . .
```

Bcrypt is now ready to use. To have our `User` object use bcrypt, we will add two methods that set the password and check whether a string matches the stored hash, as follows:

```
from . import bcrypt

class User(db.Model):
    . . .
    def set_password(self, password):
        self.password = bcrypt.generate_password_hash(password)

    def check_password(self, password):
        return bcrypt.check_password_hash(self.password, password)
. . .
```

Now, our `User` models can store passwords securely. We also need to implement the Flask-Login methods previously described for the session and authentication flow. For this, we first need to define our anonymous user object.

On the `auth/__init__.py`, enter the following:

```
from flask_login import AnonymousUserMixin

class BlogAnonymous(AnonymousUserMixin):
    def __init__(self):
        self.username = 'Guest'
```

Then add our `is_authenticated` property to the user model in `auth/models.py`, as shown in the following code. If the current user is not anonymous, then it is authenticated:

```
class User(db.model):
...

    @property
    def is_authenticated(self):
        if isinstance(self, AnonymousUserMixin):
            return False
        else:
            return True
```

Then we add the `is_active` property; we will not be using it, but it checks whether the user has gone through some sort of activation process, such as an email confirmation. Otherwise, it allows site administrators to ban a user without deleting their data. To implement this, we will create a new Boolean property on our user model schema definition, as follows:

```
class User(db.model):
...

    @property
    def is_active(self):
        return True
```

Finally, we add the following `is_active` property and `get_id` method, which are pretty self explanatory:

```
class User(db.model):
...

    @property
    def is_anonymous(self):
        if isinstance(self, AnonymousUserMixin):
            return True
        else:
            return False

    def get_id(self):
        return unicode(self.id)
```

Next, our login process needs to use these methods to create new users and check passwords, and check whether a user is authenticated.

Creating the forms

Three forms are required: a login form, a registration form, and a form for our **post creation** page. The login form will have username and password fields.

The following is the code for the `auth/forms.py` file:

```
from wtforms import (
  StringField,
  TextAreaField,
  PasswordField,
  BooleanField
)
from wtforms.validators import DataRequired, Length, EqualTo, URL
class LoginForm(Form):
  username = StringField('Username', [
    DataRequired(), Length(max=255)
  ])
  password = PasswordField('Password', [DataRequired()])

  def validate(self):
    check_validate = super(LoginForm, self).validate()
    # if our validators do not pass
    if not check_validate:
      return False
    # Does our user exist
    user = User.query.filter_by(
      username=self.username.data
    ).first()
    if not user:
      self.username.errors.append(
        'Invalid username or password'
      )
      return False
    # Do the passwords match
    if not self.user.check_password(self.password.data):
      self.username.errors.append(
        'Invalid username or password'
      )
      return False
    return True
```

Along with the normal validations, our `LoginForm` method will also check whether the username that was passed exists, and will use the `check_password()` method to check the hashes. This is done by overriding the `validate()` method called on the form `POST` requests. Here, we will first check whether the user exists on the database, and if it exists, check whether the encrypted passwords match (which will result in a successful login).

Protecting your form from spam

The registration form will have a username field, a password field with a confirmation field, and a special field named a `reCAPTCHA` field. A `CAPTCHA` is a special field on a web form that checks whether the person who is entering data into the form is actually a person, or an automated program that is spamming your site. The `reCAPTCHA` field is simply one implementation of a `CAPTCHA` field. The `reCAPTCHA` method has been integrated into WTForms, as it is the most popular implementation on the web.

To use `reCAPTCHA`, you will need a `reCAPTCHA` login from `https://www.google.com/recaptcha/intro/index.html`. As `reCAPTCHA` is a Google product, you can log in with your Google account.

Once you log in, it will ask you to add a site. In this case, any name will do, but the domain field must have `localhost` as an entry. Once you deploy your site, your domain must also be added to this list.

Now that you have added a site, dropdowns with instructions on server and client integration will appear. The given `script` tag will need to be added to the templates of our login and registration views when we create them. What WTForms needs from this page are the keys, as shown in the following screenshot:

Remember to never show these keys to the public. As these keys are only registered to `localhost`, they can be shown here without any problem.

Add these keys to the `config` object in the `config.py` file so that WTForms can access them as follows:

```
class Config(object):
    SECRET_KEY =
'736670cb10a600b695a55839ca3a5aa54a7d7356cdef815d2ad6e19a2031182b'
    RECAPTCHA_PUBLIC_KEY = "6LdKkQQTAAAAAEH0GFj7NLg5tGicaoOus7G9Q5Uw"
    RECAPTCHA_PRIVATE_KEY = '6LdKkQQTAAAAAMYroksPTJ7pWhobYb88fTAcxcYn'
```

The following code is our registration form in `auth/forms.py`:

```
class RegisterForm(Form):
    username = StringField('Username', [
      DataRequired(),
      Length(max=255)
    ])
    password = PasswordField('Password', [
      DataRequired(),
      Length(min=8)
    ])
    confirm = PasswordField('Confirm Password', [
      DataRequired(),
      EqualTo('password')
    ])
    recaptcha = RecaptchaField()
    def validate(self):
      check_validate = super(RegisterForm, self).validate()
      # if our validators do not pass
      if not check_validate:
        return False
      user = User.query.filter_by(
        username=self.username.data
      ).first()
      # Is the username already being used
      if user:
        self.username.errors.append(
          "User with that name already exists"
        )
        return False
      return True
```

Note how we are preventing a user from registering itself twice by overriding the `validate` method. This is the right way to add extra form validation logic, as we previously explained.

The post creation form will just contain a text input for the title and a text area input for the post content. So the `blog/forms.py` will contain the following:

```
class PostForm(Form):
  title = StringField('Title', [
    DataRequired(),
    Length(max=255)
  ])
  text = TextAreaField('Content', [DataRequired()])
```

Creating views

The login and registration views will create our form objects and pass them to the templates. After the `LoginForm` validates the user's credentials, we will use Flask-Login to actually log the user in.

In the `auth/controllers.py` controller, we will find the `login` view, as shown in the following code:

```
...
from flask_login import login_user, logout_user
...

@auth_blueprint.route('/login', methods=['GET', 'POST'])
@oid.loginhandler
def login():
    form = LoginForm()
    ...
    if form.validate_on_submit():
        user = User.query.filter_by(username=form.username.data).one()
        login_user(user, remember=form.remember.data)
        ...
        flash("You have been logged in.", category="success")
        return redirect(url_for('main.index'))

    ...
    return render_template('login.html', form=form,
openid_form=openid_form)
```

The `logout` view is very simple, and will redirect the user to the main index page, as follows:

```
@auth_blueprint.route('/logout', methods=['GET', 'POST'])
def logout():
  logout_user()
  flash("You have been logged out.", category="success")
  return redirect(url_for('main.index'))
```

The `register` view is used to register database users only, and will redirect users to the login page so that they can immediately log in, as follows:

```
@auth_blueprint.route('/register', methods=['GET', 'POST'])
def register():
  form = RegisterForm()
  if form.validate_on_submit():
    new_user = User()
    new_user.username = form.username.data
    new_user.set_password(form.username.data)
    db.session.add(new_user)
    db.session.commit()
    flash(
      "Your user has been created, please login.",
      category="success"
    )
    return redirect(url_for('.login'))
  return render_template('register.html', form=form)
```

Your login page should now resemble the following screenshot:

Your registration page should look like the following screenshot:

Now we need to create the post creation and editing page so that something can be secured. The two pages will need to transform the text area field into a **WYSIWYG** (short for **what you see is what you get**) editor to handle wrapping the post text in HTML. In the `blog/controllers.py` controller, you will find the following view to add new posts:

```
...
from flask_login import login_required, current_user
from .forms import CommentForm, PostForm
...
@blog_blueprint.route('/new', methods=['GET', 'POST'])
@login_required
def new_post():
  form = PostForm()
  if form.validate_on_submit():
    new_post = Post()
    new_post.user_id = current_user.id
    new_post.title = form.title.data
    new_post.text = form.text.data
```

```
        db.session.add(new_post)
        db.session.commit()
        flash("Post added", info)
        return redirect(url_for('blog.post', post_id=new_post.id)
    return render_template('new.html', form=form)
```

We are protecting our view using the Flask-Login decorator @login_required to ensure that only authenticated users can submit new posts. Next, using the proxy method current_user, we fetch the currently logged user ID so that the post is associated with the user.

The new.html template will need a JavaScript file for the WYSIWYG editor; **CKEditor** is very simple to install and use. Now, our new.html file can be created as follows. Name it templates/blog/new.html:

```
{% extends "base.html" %}
{% block title %}Post Creation{% endblock %}
{% block body %}
<div class="p-4 shadow-sm">
    <div class="row">
        <div class="col">
            <h1>Create a New Post</h1>
        </div>
    </div>
</div>

<div class="row">
    <form method="POST" action="{{ url_for('.new_post') }}">
        {{ form.hidden_tag() }}
        <div class="form-group">
            {{ form.title.label }}
            {% if form.title.errors %}
            {% for e in form.title.errors %}
            <p class="help-block">{{ e }}</p>
            {% endfor %}
            {% endif %}
            {{ form.title(class_='form-control') }}
        </div>
        <div class="form-group">
            {{ form.text.label }}
            {% if form.text.errors %}
            {% for e in form.text.errors %}
            <p class="help-block">{{ e }}</p>
            {% endfor %}
            {% endif %}
            {{ form.text(id="editor", class_='form-control') }}
        </div>
        <input class="btn btn-primary" type="submit" value="Submit">
```

```
        </form>
    </div>
    </div>
{% endblock %}

{% block js %}
<script src="//cdn.ckeditor.com/4.4.7/standard/ckeditor.js">
</script>
<script>
    CKEDITOR.replace('editor');
</script>
{% endblock %}
```

This is all that is needed to have the user's input stored as HTML in the database. Because we passed the `safe` filter in our post template, the HTML code appears correctly on our post pages. The `edit.html` template is similar to the `new.html` template. The only difference is the `form` opening tag, shown in the following code:

```
<form method="POST" action="{{ url_for('.edit_post', id=post.id)
    }}">
...
</form>
```

The `post.html` template will need a button for authors to link them to the edit page, as shown in the following code:

```
<div class="row">
  <div class="col-lg-6">
    <p>Written By <a href="{{ url_for('.user',
      username=post.user.username) }}">{{ post.user.username
      }}</a> on {{ post.publish_date }}</p>
  </div>
  ...
  {% if current_user == post.user_id %}
  <div class="row">
    <div class="col-lg-2">
    <a href="{{ url_for('.edit_post', id=post.id) }}" class="btn
      btn-primary">Edit</a>
  </div>
  {% endif %}
</div>
```

Once again, we are using the `current_user` proxy to fetch the currently logged-in user, this time on a Jinja2 template, so that we only show the **Edit** button to the user that previously create the blog post.

Finally, we should add an entry to create new posts in the main navigation bar. We should also take a look at how the login, logout, and register options are enabled and disabled. In `templates/navbar.html`, enter the following:

```
{% if current_user.is_authenticated %}
<li class="nav-item">
    <a class="nav-link" href="{{url_for('auth.logout')}}">
    <i class="fa fa-fw fa-sign-out"></i>Logout</a>
</li>
{% else %}
<li class="nav-item">
    <a class="nav-link" href="{{url_for('auth.login')}}">
    <i class="fa fa-fw fa-sign-in"></i>Login</a>
</li>
<li class="nav-item">
    <a class="nav-link" href="{{url_for('auth.register')}}">
    <i class="fa fa-fw fa-sign-in"></i>Register</a>
</li>
{% endif %}
```

OpenID

To integrate OpenID authentication with our application, we are going to use a new Flask extension named **Flask-OpenID,** implemented by the **Flask** creator itself. As always, the extension needs to be added to the `requirements.txt` file, as follows:

```
...
Flask-OpenID
...
```

Our app will also need a couple of things to implement OpenID:

- A new form object
- The form validation in the login and registration pages
- A callback after the form submission to log the user in or create a new user

In the `auth/__init__.py` file, the `OpenID` object can be initialized as follows:

```
...
from flask_openid import OpenID
...
oid = OpenID()
```

In the `create_module` function, the `oid` object is registered to the `app` object, as follows:

```
def create_module(app, **kwargs):
    ...
    oid.init_app(app)
    ...
```

The new `form` object will only need the URL of the `OpenID` provider. In `auth/forms.py`, enter the following:

```
from wtforms.validators import DataRequired, Length, EqualTo, URL
class OpenIDForm(Form):
    openid = StringField('OpenID URL', [DataRequired(), URL()])
```

In the login and registration views, `OpenIDForm()` will be initialized, and if the data is valid, a login request will be sent. In `auth/views.py`, enter the following:

```
    ...

@auth_blueprint.route('/login', methods=['GET', 'POST'])
@oid.loginhandler
def login():
    form = LoginForm()
    openid_form = OpenIDForm()
    if openid_form.validate_on_submit():
        return oid.try_login(
            openid_form.openid.data,
            ask_for=['nickname', 'email'],
            ask_for_optional=['fullname']
        )
    if form.validate_on_submit():
        flash("You have been logged in.", category="success")
        return redirect(url_for('blog.home'))
    openid_errors = oid.fetch_error()
    if openid_errors:
        flash(openid_errors, category="danger")
    return render_template(
        'login.html',
        form=form,
        openid_form=openid_form
    )

@main_blueprint.route('/register', methods=['GET', 'POST'])
@oid.loginhandler
def register():
    form = RegisterForm()
    openid_form = OpenIDForm()
    if openid_form.validate_on_submit():
```

```
    return oid.try_login(
      openid_form.openid.data,
      ask_for=['nickname', 'email'],
      ask_for_optional=['fullname']
    )
  if form.validate_on_submit():
    new_user = User(form.username.data)
    new_user.set_password(form.password.data)
    db.session.add(new_user)
    db.session.commit()
    flash(
      "Your user has been created, please login.",
      category="success"
    )
    return redirect(url_for('.login'))
  openid_errors = oid.fetch_error()
  if openid_errors:
    flash(openid_errors, category="danger")
  return render_template(
    'register.html',
    form=form,
    openid_form=openid_form
  )
```

Both the views have the new decorator `@oid.loginhandler`, which tells Flask-OpenID to listen for authentication information coming back from the provider. With OpenID, logging in and registering are the same. It is possible to create a user from the login form and to log in from the registration form. The same field appears on both pages to avoid confusing the user.

To handle the user creation and login, a new function in the `auth/__init__.py` file is needed, as shown in the following code:

```
@oid.after_login
def create_or_login(resp):
    from models import db, User
    username = resp.fullname or resp.nickname or resp.email
    if not username:
        flash('Invalid login. Please try again.', 'danger')
        return redirect(url_for('main.login'))
    user = User.query.filter_by(username=username).first()
    # if the user does not exist create it
    if user is None:
        user = User(username)
        db.session.add(user)
```

```
    db.session.commit()
login_user(user)
return redirect(url_for('main.index'))
```

This function is called after every successful response from the provider. If the login is successful and a user object does not exist for the identity, then this function creates a new User object. If one already exists, the upcoming authentication methods will log the user in. OpenID does not require all possible information to be returned, so it is possible that not a full name, but only an email address will be returned. This is why the username can be the nickname, full name, or email address. The db and User object are imported inside the function to avoid cyclical imports from the models.py file that is importing the bcrypt object.

OAuth

To log in with Facebook and Twitter, the **OAuth** protocol is used as previously described. Our app will not use OAuth directly; instead, another Flask extension will be used, named **Flask Dance**. In the requirements.txt, enter the following:

```
...
flask-dance
...
```

As previously described, the OAuth protocol needs a previously created application in each provider's developer page. After our application is created, we will have a key and secret token for each provider. For now, we are going to keep these credentials on the configuration file as is. Later, we will be using environment variables to handle them. So, in the configuration file config.py, add the following:

```
...
class Config(object):
    ...
    TWITTER_API_KEY = "XXX"
    TWITTER_API_SECRET = "XXXX"
    FACEBOOK_CLIENT_ID = "YYYY"
    FACEBOOK_CLIENT_SECRET = "YYYY"
```

Now we are ready to initialize and configure our OAuth extension. **Flask-Dance** will help us create a new Flask blueprint for each provider we want to add. Once again, `auth/__init__.py` is the place where we configure all our authentication extensions, as follows:

```
...
from flask_dance.contrib.twitter import make_twitter_blueprint, twitter
from flask_dance.contrib.facebook import make_facebook_blueprint, facebook
...
def create_module(app, **kwargs):
...
    twitter_blueprint = make_twitter_blueprint(
        api_key=app.config.get("TWITTER_API_KEY"),
        api_secret=app.config.get("TWITTER_API_SECRET"),
    )
    app.register_blueprint(twitter_blueprint, url_prefix="/auth/login")

    facebook_blueprint = make_facebook_blueprint(
        client_id=app.config.get("FACEBOOK_CLIENT_ID"),
        client_secret=app.config.get("FACEBOOK_CLIENT_SECRET"),
    )
    app.register_blueprint(facebook_blueprint, url_prefix="auth/login"
...
```

Flask-Dance will create the following routes for us:

- `/auth/login/twitter/authorized`: Here, the user is redirected after authorization is successful on Twitter
- `/auth/login/twitter`: This is the initial login view for Twitter OAuth
- `/auth/login/facebook/authorized`
- `/auth/login/facebook`

After a successful login/authorization is accomplished, we need to log the user in on Flask-Login; if the user does not exist on the database, add them. To do this, we register for the authorized signal event. Enter the following in `auth/__init__.py`:

```
...
from flask_dance.consumer import oauth_authorized
...
@oauth_authorized.connect
def logged_in(blueprint, token):
    from .models import db, User
    if blueprint.name == 'twitter':
        username = session.get('screen_name')
    elif blueprint.name == 'facebook':
        resp = facebook.get("/me")
```

```
    username = resp.json()['name']
user = User.query.filter_by(username=username).first()
if not user:
    user = User()
    user.username = username
    db.session.add(user)
    db.session.commit()

login_user(user)
flash("You have been logged in.", category="success")
```

The `@oauth_authorized` is the decorator from Flask-Dance that we use to register our function to handle the after-authorized signal. This is a generic signal handler for all our providers, so we need to know what provider are we currently handling. We need to know this because we need to fetch our username, and each provider is going to expose different user information in a different way. On Twitter, we will use the `screen_name` key that has already been returned by the provider and has already been pushed to our Flask session object by Flask-Dance. But on Facebook, we need to make a further request to Facebook's API to fetch the username.

 During development, you will probably not use HTTPS. This will trigger an error when using `OAuth2`. To get around this, you have to tell `oauthlib` to accept insecure connections. In the command line, enter `$ export OAUTHLIB_INSECURE_TRANSPORT=1`.

Finally, in the register and login templates, we have the following links to start the login process:

```
<h2 class="text-center">Register/Login With Facebook</h2>
<a href="{{ url_for('facebook.login') }}">Login</a>

<h2 class="text-center">Register/Login With Twitter</h2>
<a href="{{ url_for('twitter.login') }}">Login</a>
```

Role-based access control (RBAC)

To implement a simple role-based access control system, we need to create a new database entity `Role` model that will need a many-to-many relationship for our `User` model so that a user can have multiple roles.

With our code from Chapter 2, *Creating Models with SQLAlchemy*, adding a many-to-many relationship to the User object is easy, as shown in the following code:

```
roles = db.Table(
    'role_users',
    db.Column('user_id', db.Integer, db.ForeignKey('user.id')),
    db.Column('role_id', db.Integer, db.ForeignKey('role.id'))
)


class User(db.Model):
    ...
    roles = db.relationship(
        'Role',
        secondary=roles,
        backref=db.backref('users', lazy='dynamic')
    )

    def __init__(self, username=""):
        default = Role.query.filter_by(name="default").one()
        self.roles.append(default)
        self.username = username

    ...
    def has_role(self, name):
        for role in self.roles:
            if role.name == name:
                return True
        return False
    ...
class Role(db.Model):
    id = db.Column(db.Integer(), primary_key=True)
    name = db.Column(db.String(80), unique=True)
    description = db.Column(db.String(255))

    def __init__(self, name):
        self.name = name

    def __repr__(self):
        return '<Role {}>'.format(self.name)
```

Also, when a user is created, a default role is always inserted into it. Note the has_role method that will help us easily check whether a user has a certain role; this will be useful for templates.

Our test data Python script has already populated the `Role` model with admin, poster, and default.

Next, we will need a decorator function to enable RBAC in our views. Python's decorator functions are very useful, and security is certainly a context where they can be welcome. Without them, we would have to write the same code over and over again (violating the DRY principal). We need a decorator function that receives an argument—on our case, the role name—and then checks whether the user has the required role. It returns `HTTP 403` if they do not. This is enabled using the following code:

```
import functools
...
def has_role(name):
    def real_decorator(f):
        def wraps(*args, **kwargs):
            if current_user.has_role(name):
                return f(*args, **kwargs)
            else:
                abort(403)
        return functools.update_wrapper(wraps, f)
    return real_decorator
```

The `functools.update_wrapper` is needed so that the decorated function returns the function definition instead of the wrapper definition; without it, we would lose the routing definition from Flask.

Now, we are ready to protect our **new post** view and **edit** view. Since only a user with the **poster** role can access them, this is now very simple using the `has_access` decorator.

Look at the `auth/__init__.py` file:

```
...
from ..auth import has_role
...
@blog_blueprint.route('/new, methods=['GET', 'POST'])
@login_required
@has_role('poster')
def new_post(id):
    ...
```

We can also add a user check to the view, to ensure that only a user that has created a post can actually edit it. We have already disabled the edit option, but a user can always access the view by typing the URL directly in the browser.

Go to the file named `blog/controllers.py`:

```
@blog_blueprint.route('/edit/<int:id>', methods=['GET', 'POST'])
@login_required
@has_role('poster')
def edit_post(id):
    post = Post.query.get_or_404(id)
    # We want admins to be able to edit any post
    if current_user.id == post.user.id:
        form = PostForm()
        if form.validate_on_submit():
            post.title = form.title.data
            post.text = form.text.data
            post.publish_date = datetime.datetime.now()
            db.session.add(post)
            db.session.commit()
            return redirect(url_for('.post', post_id=post.id))
        form.title.data = post.title
        form.text.data = post.text
        return render_template('edit.html', form=form, post=post)
    abort(403)
```

Also, in the navigation bar, we want to show the **New Post** option only to the users that have the poster role.

Summary

Our users now have secure logins, multiple login and registration options, and explicit access permissions. Our app has everything that is needed to be a fully fledged blog app. In the next chapter, we will stop following this example application in order to introduce a technology named **NoSQL**.

Using NoSQL with Flask

7

A **NoSQL** (short for **Not Only SQL**) database is any non-relational data store. It usually focuses on speed and scalability. NoSQL has been taking the web development world by storm for the past seven years. Huge companies, such as Netflix and Google, have announced that they are moving many of their services to NoSQL databases, and many smaller companies have followed their example.

This chapter will deviate from the rest of the book in that it will not mostly focus on Flask. The focus on the database design might seem odd in a book about Flask, but choosing the correct database for your application is arguably the most important decision that you can make while designing your technology stack. In the vast majority of web applications, the database is the bottleneck, so the database you pick will determine the overall speed of your app. A study conducted by Amazon showed that even a 100 ms delay caused a one percent reduction in sales, so speed should always be one of the main concerns of a web developer. There is also an abundance of horror stories in the programmer community of web developers involving developers choosing a popular NoSQL database and then not really understanding what the database requires in terms of administration. This leads to large amounts of data loss and crashes, which in turn means the loss of customers. All in all, it's no exaggeration to say that your choice of database for your application can be the difference between your app succeeding and failing.

In this chapter, we will illustrate the strengths and weaknesses of NoSQL databases by examining each type of NoSQL database and the differences between NoSQL and traditional databases.

Types of NoSQL database

NoSQL is a blanket term used to describe nontraditional methods of storing data in a database. The vast majority of NoSQL databases are not relational—unlike RDBMS—which means that they normally cannot perform operations such as JOIN. There are a number of other features that distinguish an SQL database from a NoSQL database. With a NoSQL database, we have the ability to not impose a fixed schema—for example, a collection on MongoDB can hold different fields, and so they can accept any kind of document. With NoSQL you can (and should) take advantage of denormalization, making a tradeoff between storage and speed.

Modern NoSQL databases include key-value stores, document stores, column family stores, and graph databases.

Key-value stores

A **key-value** NoSQL database acts much like a dictionary in Python. A single value is associated with one key and is accessed via that key. Also, like a Python dictionary, most key-value databases have the same read speed regardless of how many entries there are. Advanced programmers would know this as **O(1) reads**. In some key-value stores, only one key can be retrieved at a time, rather than multiple rows in traditional SQL databases. In most key-value stores, the content of the value is not queryable, but the keys are. Values are just binary blobs: they can be literally anything, from a string to a movie file. However, some key-value stores give default types, such as strings, lists, sets, and dictionaries, while still giving the option of adding binary data.

Because of their simplicity, key-value stores are typically very fast. However, their simplicity makes them unsuitable as the main database for most applications. As such, most key-value store use cases involve storing simple objects that need to expire after a certain amount of time. Two common examples of this pattern are storing users' session data and shopping cart data. Also, key-value stores are commonly used as caches for the application or for other databases. For example, results from a commonly run, or CPU-intensive, query or function are stored with the query or function name as a key. The application will check the cache in the key-value store before running the query on the database, thereby decreasing page load times and stress on the database. An example of this functionality will be shown in Chapter 10, *Useful Flask Extensions*.

The most popular key–value stores are **Redis**, **Riak**, and **Amazon DynamoDB**.

Document stores

Document store is one of the most popular NoSQL database types, and is typically used to replace RDBMSes. Databases store data in collections of key-value pairs called documents. These documents are schemaless, meaning that no document follows the structure of any other document. Also, extra keys may be appended to each document after its creation. Document stores can store data in **JSON**, BSON, and XML. For example, the following are two different post objects stored in JSON:

```
{
  "title": "First Post",
  "text": "Lorem ipsum...",
  "date": "2015-01-20",
  "user_id": 45
},
{
  "title": "Second Post",
  "text": "Lorem ipsum...",
  "date": "2015-01-20",
  "user_id": 45,
  "comments": [
    {
      "name": "Anonymous",
      "text": "I love this post."
    }
  ]
}
```

Note that the first document has no comments array. As stated before, documents are schemaless, so this format is perfectly valid. The lack of a schema also means that there are no type checks at the database level. There is nothing in the database to stop an integer from being entered into the title field of a post. Schemaless data is the most powerful feature of document stores and attracts many developers to adopt it for their apps. However, it can also be considered very dangerous, as there is one less check to stop faulty or malformed data from getting into your database.

Some document stores collect similar objects into collections of documents to make querying objects easier. However, in some document stores, all objects are queried at once. Document stores store the metadata of each object, which allows all of the values in each document to be queried and return matching documents.

The most popular document stores are **MongoDB**, **CouchDB**, and **Couchbase**.

Column family stores

Column family stores, also known as **wide column stores**, have many things in common with both key-value stores and document stores. Column family stores are the fastest type of NoSQL database because they are designed for large applications. Their main advantage is their ability to handle terabytes of data and still have very fast read and write speeds by distributing the data across several servers in an intelligent way.

Column family stores are also the hardest to understand, due in part to the vernacular of column family stores, as they use many of the same terms as RDBMSes, but with wildly different meanings. In order to clearly understand what a column family store is, let's jump straight into an example. Let's create a simple *user-to-posts* association in a typical column family store.

First, we need a user table. In column family stores, data is stored and accessed via a unique key, such as a key-value store, but the content consists of unstructured columns, such as a document store. Consider the following user table:

Key	Jack				John	
Column	Full Name	Bio		Location	Full Name	Bio
Value	Jack Stouffer	This is my about me		Michigan, USA	John Doe	This is my about me

Note that each key holds columns, which are key-value pairs as well. Also, it is not necessary for each key to have the same number or type of columns. Each key can store hundreds of unique columns, or they can all have the same number of columns to make application development easier. This is in contrast to key-value stores, which can hold any type of data with each key. This is also slightly different than document stores, which can store types, such as arrays and dictionaries, in each document. Now let's create our posts table:

Key	Post/1			Post/2		
Column	Title	Date	Text	Title	Date	Text
Value	Hello World	2015-01-01	Post text...	Still Here	2015-02-01	Post text...

There are several things to understand about column family stores before we continue. Firstly, in column family stores, data can only be selected via a single key or key range; there is no way to query the contents of the columns. To get around this, many programmers use an external search tool with their database—such as **Elasticsearch**—that stores the contents of columns in a searchable format (Lucene's inverted indexes) and returns matching keys to be queried on the database. This limitation is why proper *schema* design is so crucial in column family stores, and must be carefully thought through before storing any data.

Secondly, data cannot be ordered by the content of the columns. Data can only be ordered by key, which is why the keys to the posts are integers. This allows the posts to be returned in the order in which they were entered. This is not a requirement for the user table because there is no need to sequentially order users.

Thirdly, there are no `JOIN` operators, and we cannot query for a column that would hold a user key. With our current schema, there is no way to associate a post with a user. To create this functionality, we need a third table that holds the user to post associations, as follows:

Key	Jack		
Column	Posts	Posts/1	Post/1
Value		Posts/2	Post/2

This is slightly different from the other tables we have seen so far. The `Posts` column is named a **super column**, which is a column that holds other columns. In this table, a super column is associated with our user key, which is holding an association of the position of a post to one post. Clever readers might ask why we wouldn't just store this association in our `user` table, much like how the problem would be solved in document stores. This is because regular columns and super columns cannot be held in the same table. You must choose one at the creation of each table.

To get a list of all the posts by a user, we would first have to query the post association table with our user key, use the returned list of associations to get all of the keys in the posts' table, and query the post table with the keys.

If that query seems like a roundabout process to you, that's because it is, and it is made that way by design. The limiting nature of a column family store is what allows it to be so fast and handle so much data. Removing features such as searching by value and column name gives column family stores the ability to handle hundreds of terabytes of data. It's not an exaggeration to say that SQLite is a more complex database for the programmer than a typical column family store.

For this reason, most Flask developers should steer clear of column family stores as they add complexity to applications that isn't necessary. Unless your application is going to handle millions of reads and writes a second, using a column family store is like pounding in a nail with an atomic bomb.

The most popular column family stores are **BigTable**, **Cassandra**, and **HBase**.

Graph databases

Designed to describe and then query relationships, **graph databases** are like document stores, but have mechanisms to create and describe links between two nodes.

A **node** is like an instance of an object, usually a collection of key-value pairs or a JSON document. Nodes can be given labels to mark them as part of a category—for example, a user or a group. After your nodes have been defined, an arbitrary number of one-way relationships between the nodes, named **links**, can be created with their own attributes. For example, if our data had two user nodes and each of the two users knew each other, we would define two knows links between them to describe that relationship, as shown in the following diagram. This would allow you to query all the people that know one user or all the people that a user knows:

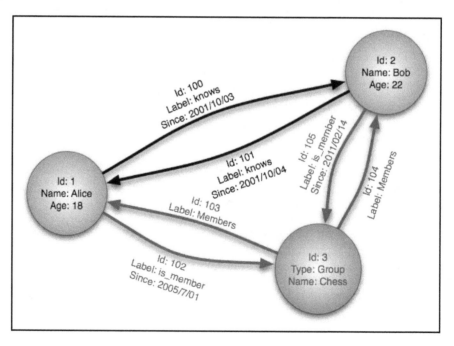

Graph stores also allow you to query by the link's attributes. This allows you to easily create otherwise complex queries, such as a search for all of the users that one user marked as known in October 2001. Graph stores can follow links from node to node to create even more complex queries. If this example dataset had more groups, we can query for groups that people we know have joined but that we haven't joined. Otherwise, we can query for people who are in the same groups as a user, but who the user doesn't know. Queries in a graph store can also follow a large number of links to answer complex questions, such as "which restaurants in New York that serve burgers and have a three-star rating or higher have my friends liked?"

The most common use case for a graph database is to build a recommendation engine. For example, say that we had a graph store that is filled with our friend data from a social networking site. Using this data, we could build a mutual friend finder by querying for users that have been marked as friends by more than two of our friends.

It is very rare for a graph database to be used as the primary data store of an application. Most uses of graph stores have each node acting as a representation of a piece of data in their main database by storing its unique identifier and a small amount of other identifying information.

The most popular graph stores are **Neo4j** and **InfoGrid**.

RDBMS versus NoSQL

NoSQL is a tool, and like any tool there are specific use cases where it excels and there are use cases where some other tool would be a better fit. No one would use a screwdriver to pound in a nail; it's possible, but using a hammer would make the job easier. One large problem with NoSQL databases is that people adopt them when an RDBMS would solve the problem just as well, or better.

To understand which tool should be used when, we must understand the strengths and weaknesses of both systems.

The strengths of RDBMS databases

One of the biggest strengths of RDBMSes is their maturity. The technology behind RDBMSes has existed for over 40 years and is based on the solid theory of relational algebra and relational calculus. Because of their maturity, they have a long, proven track record across many different industries of handling data in a safe and secure way.

Data integrity

Integrity is also one of the biggest selling points of RDBMSes. RDBMSes have several methods in place to ensure that the data entered into a database will not only be correct, but that data loss will be practically nonexistent. These methods combine to form what is known as **ACID** (short for **atomicity**, **consistency**, **isolation**, and **durability**). ACID is a set of rules for transactions that guarantee that the transaction is handled safely.

The principle of atomicity requires that each transaction is all or nothing. If one part of the transaction fails, the entire transaction fails. This is much like the following quote from *The Zen of Python*:

"Errors should never pass silently. Unless explicitly silenced."

If there is a problem with the data that has been changed or entered, the transaction should not keep operating because the proceeding operations most likely require that the previous operations were successful.

The principle of consistency requires that any data that the transaction modifies or adds follows the rules of each table. Such rules include type checks, user-defined constraints—such as *foreign keys*—cascade rules, and triggers. If any of the rules are broken, then according to the atomicity rule, the transaction will be thrown out.

The principle of isolation requires that if the database runs transactions concurrently to speed up writes, then the outcome of the transactions would be the same as if they were run serially. This is mostly a rule for database programmers, and is not something that web developers need to worry about.

Finally, the principle of durability requires that once a transaction is accepted, the data must never be lost, barring a hard drive failure after the transaction is accepted. If the database crashes or loses power, then the durability principle requires that any data written before the problem occurred should still be present when the server is backed up. This essentially means that all transactions must be written to the disk once they are accepted.

Speed and scale

A common misconception is that the ACID principle makes RDBMSes slow and unable to scale. This is only half true—it is completely possible for an RDBMS to scale. For example, an Oracle database configured by a professional database administrator can handle tens of thousands of complex queries a second. Huge companies, such as Facebook, Twitter, Tumblr, and Yahoo!, are using MySQL to great effect, and PostgreSQL is emerging as a favorite of many programmers because of its speed advantage over MySQL.

Tools

When evaluating a programming language, the strongest points for or against adopting it are the size and activity of its community. A larger and more active community means more help if you get stuck and more open source tools available for you to use in your projects.

It's no different with databases. RDBMSes, such as MySQL and PostgreSQL, have official libraries for almost every language that is used in commercial environments and unofficial libraries for everything else. Tools, such as Excel, can easily download the latest data from one of these databases and allow the user to treat it like it was any other dataset. Several free desktop GUIs exist for each database, and some are officially supported by the databases' corporate sponsor.

The strengths of NoSQL databases

The main reason that many people use NoSQL databases is its speed advantage over traditional databases. Out of the box, many NoSQL databases can outperform RDBMSes. However, a well-tuned and properly scaled SQL database with read slaves can outperform NoSQL databases. Many NoSQL databases, especially document stores, sacrifice consistency for availability. This means that they can handle many concurrent reads and writes, but those writes may be in conflict with one another. Yet, this is not straightforward, as you will soon see when we look at the CAP theorem.

The second feature that pulls people to NoSQL is its ability to handle unformatted data. Storing data in XML or JSON allows an arbitrary structure to each document. Applications that store user-designed data have benefited greatly from the adoption of NoSQL. For example, a video game that allows players to submit their custom levels to some central repository can now store the data in a queryable format rather than in a binary blob.

The third feature that draws people to NoSQL is the ease of creating a cluster of databases working in tandem. Not having JOIN operators or only accessing values via keys makes splitting the data across servers a rather trivial task when compared with RDBMSes. This is due to the fact that JOIN operators require a scan of the entire table, even if it is split across many different servers. The JOIN operators become even slower when documents or keys can be assigned to a server by an algorithm as simple as the starting character of its unique identifier—for example, everything that starts with the letters A–H is sent to server 1, I–P to server 2, and Q–Z to server 3. This makes looking up the location of data for a connected client very fast.

Next, we will briefly explain the CAP theorem, to give you some background on the underlying problems behind database-distributed systems.

CAP theorem

The **CAP** theorem stands for **consistency**, **availability**, and **partition** tolerance, and states that it's not possible for a distributed system to guarantee all three, so a trade-off must be made.

The following list shows exactly what each of these guarantees means on a distributed system:

- **Consistency:** Guarantees that each node on a cluster returns the most recent write and preserves linear consistency
- **Availability:** Every non failing node is able to respond to a request with a non error response
- **Partition tolerance**: The system continues to operate despite network outages/delays

The theorem states that in case of a network partition, a distributed system has to choose between consistency or availability, so in the case of a network partition, systems must fall into two main categories, CP and AP.

A simple visualization of such a distributed system would be two instances serving many clients concurrently on distinct data centers. One client sends: write the key-value **a:0** to **server1**. Then **server1** sends **a:0** to **server2**, **server2** sends an acknowledgement back to **server1** which then sends an acknowledgement back to the client. This is shown in the following diagram:

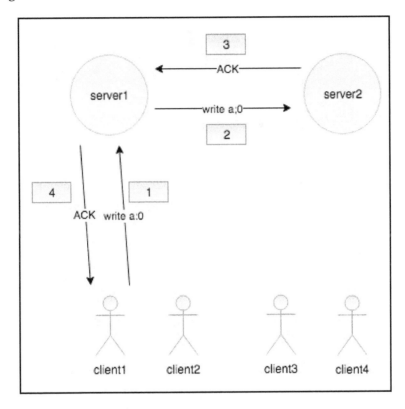

Imagine that a network partition occurs and this prevents **server1** from communicating with **server2**. Meanwhile, **client1** requests that **server1** changes **a:0** to **a:1**. If the system aims for consistency, then it would reject the transaction since it can't send the write to **server2** and **server2** would deny any transactions since it could serve dirty reads, and we are aiming for consistency. This relationship is shown in the following diagram:

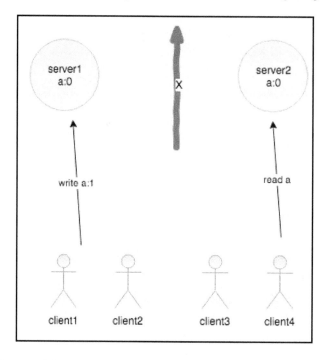

If we want to aim for availability, we must relax consistency. In today's database RDBMS or NoSQL, systems are not 100% CP or AP, but they can be configured to be more or less relaxed as to their consistency and availability to a certain degree.

Although not 100% correct, MongoDB aims for consistency and partition tolerance. MongoDB in a cluster architecture uses a single-master setup, which means that a single node can accept writes. It avoids a **single point of failure** (**SPOF**) by having the ability to switch if the majority of the other nodes lose contact with their current master. This increases availability by lowering consistency for the following reasons:

- If you use a single node, then reads and writes to the same system on MongoDB will make it a very consistent system, but if you use multiple instances for reads with asynchronous replication, then the entire system will eventually become consistent

- When the old master node recovers, it will rejoin the cluster as a slave node, and all the dirty writes it might have will be rolled back

What database to use and when

So, each database has different uses. It was stated at the beginning of the section that the main problem when programmers choose a NoSQL database for their technology stack is that they choose it when an RDBMS would work just as well. This is born out of some common misconceptions. Firstly, people try to use a relational mindset and data model and think that they will work just as well in a NoSQL database. People usually come to this misunderstanding because the marketing on the various websites of NoSQL databases is misleading, and encourages users to drop their current database without considering whether a non-relational model will work for their project.

Secondly, people believe that you must use only one data store for your application. Many applications can benefit from using more than one data store. Take a Facebook clone as an example. It could use MySQL for holding user data, Redis to store session data, a document store to hold the data for the quizzes and surveys that people share with each other, and a graph database to implement a feature for finding friends.

If an application feature needs very fast writes, and write safety is not a primary concern, then you should use a document store database. If you need to store and query schemaless data, then you should use a document store database.

If an application feature needs to store something that deletes itself after a specified time, or if the data does not need to be searched, then you should use a key-value store.

If an application feature involves finding or describing complex relationships between two or more sets of data, then you should use a graph store.

If an application feature needs guaranteed write safety, or if it needs each entry to fit into a specified schema, different sets of data in the database to be compared using JOIN operators, or constraints on the entered data, then you should use an RDBMS.

MongoDB in Flask

MongoDB is far and away the most popular NoSQL database. MongoDB is also the best-supported NoSQL database for Flask and Python in general. Therefore, our examples will focus on MongoDB.

MongoDB is a document storage NoSQL database. Documents are stored in collections, which allow the grouping of similar documents, but no similarities between documents are necessary to store a document in a collection. Documents are defined in a JSON superset named **BSON** (short for **Binary JSON**). BSON allows JSON to be stored in binary format rather than in string format, saving a lot of space. BSON also distinguishes between several different ways of storing numbers, such as 32-bit integers and doubles.

To understand the basics of MongoDB, we will use **Flask-MongoEngine** to cover the same functionality of Flask-SQLAlchemy in the previous chapters. Remember that these are just examples. There is no benefit of refactoring our current code to use MongoDB because MongoDB cannot offer any new functionality for our use case. New functionality with MongoDB will be shown in the next section.

Installing MongoDB

To install MongoDB, go to https://www.mongodb.org/downloads and select your OS from the tabs under the heading **Download MongoDB**. Every OS that has a supported version has installation instructions listed next to the download button of the installer.

To run MongoDB, go to Bash and run the following:

```
$ mongod
```

This will run a server for as long as the window is open.

Using Docker, you can easily launch a MongoDB server without needing to install anything else on your computer.

To start a MongoDB server on Docker, enter the following:

```
$docker run -d -p 27017:27017 mongo:3.2.20-jessie
$docker container list
CONTAINER ID IMAGE COMMAND CREATED STATUS PORTS NAMES
4c6706af399b mongo:3.2.20-jessie "docker-entrypoint.s..." About a minute ago
Up About a minute 0.0.0.0:27017->27017/tcp silly_ardinghelli
```

Setting up MongoEngine

If you're following the example code provided with this book (which you can find at https://github.com/PacktPublishing/Hands-On-Web-Development-with-Flask), then all you need to do is create a new Python virtual environment and install all the necessary dependencies. You will notice the provided init.sh and requirements.txt. Inside the init.sh, we have all the necessary commands to get us set up, as shown in the following code:

```
if [ ! -d "venv" ]; then
    virtualenv venv
fi
source venv/bin/activate
pip install -r requirements.txt
```

And, of course, our requirements.txt contains the following necessary packages:

```
Flask
Flask-MongoEngine
```

In the __init__.py file, a mongo object will be created that represents our database, as shown in the following code:

```
from flask_mongoengine import MongoEngine

mongo = MongoEngine

def create_app(object_name):
...
    mongo.init_app(app)
...
```

Before our app will run, our `DevConfig` object in `config.py` needs to set up the parameters of the `mongo` connection:

```
MONGODB_SETTINGS = {
  'db': 'local',
  'host': 'localhost',
  'port': 27017
}
```

These are the defaults for a brand new MongoDB installation.

Defining documents

MongoEngine is an ORM that is based around Python's object system, and is specifically designed for MongoDB. Unfortunately, there is no SQLAlchemy-style wrapper that supports all NoSQL drivers. In RDBMSes, the implementations of SQL are so similar that creating a universal interface is possible. However, the underlying implementations of each document store are different enough that the task of creating a similar interface would be more trouble than it is worth.

Each collection in your Mongo database is represented by a class that inherits from `mongo.Document`, as shown in the following code:

```
class Post(mongo.Document):
    title = mongo.StringField(required=True)
    text = mongo.StringField()
    publish_date = mongo.DateTimeField(default=datetime.datetime.now())
    def __repr__(self):
        return "<Post '{}'>".format(self.title)
```

Each class variable is a representation of a key belonging to a document, which is represented in this example of a `Post` class. The class variable name is used as the key in the document.

Unlike SQLAlchemy, there is no need to define a primary key. A unique ID will be generated for you under the `id` attribute. The preceding code would generate a BSON document that would resemble the following:

```
{
  "_id": "55366ede8b84eb00232da905",
  "title": "Post 0",
  "text": "<p>Lorem ipsum dolor...",
  "publish_date": {"$date": 1425255876037}
}
```

Field types

There are a large number of fields, and each represents a distinct category of data in Mongo. Unlike the underlying database, each field provides a type check before the document is allowed to be saved or altered. The most-used fields are as follows:

- BooleanField
- DateTimeField
- DictField
- DynamicField
- EmbeddedDocumentField
- FloatField
- IntField
- ListField
- ObjectIdField
- ReferenceField
- StringField

> For a full list of fields and detailed documentation, go to the MongoEngine website at http://docs.mongoengine.org.

The majority of these are named after the Python type they accept and work in the same way as the SQLAlchemy types. However, there are some new types that have no counterpart in SQLAlchemy. Let's take a look at them in detail:

- DynamicField is a field that can hold any type of value and performs no type checks on values.
- DictField can store any Python dictionary that can be serialized by json.dumps().
- ReferenceField simply stores the unique ID of a document, and when queried, MongoEngine will return the referenced document.
- EmbeddedDocumentField stores the passed document in the parent document, so there is no need for a second query.
- ListField represents a list of fields of a specific type. This is typically used to store a list of references to other documents or a list of embedded documents to create a one-to-many relationship. If a list of unknown types is needed, then DynamicField can be used.

Each field type takes some common arguments, as shown in the following code:

```
Field(
    primary_key=None
    db_field=None,
    required=False,
    default=None,
    unique=False,
    unique_with=None,
    choices=None
)
```

- The `primary_key` argument specifies that you do not want MongoEngine to autogenerate a unique key, but the value of the field should be used as the ID. The value of this field will now be accessible from both the `id` attribute and the name of the field.
- `db_field` defines what the key will be named in each document. If it is not set, it will default to the name of the class variable.
- If `required` is defined as `True`, then that key must be present in the document. Otherwise, the key does not have to exist for documents of that type. When a class is defined, the nonexistent key is queried, and it will return `None`.
- `default` specifies the value that this field will be given if no value is defined.
- If `unique` is set to `True`, then MongoEngine checks to make sure that no other documents in the collection will have the same value for this field:
  - When passed a list of field names, `unique_with` will make sure that—when taken in combination—the values of all the fields will be unique for each document. This is much like multicolumn `UNIQUE` indexes in RDBMSes.

- Finally, when given a list, the `choices` option limits the allowable values for that field to the elements in the list.

Types of documents

MongoEngine's method to define documents allows either flexibility or rigidity on a collection-by-collection basis. Inheriting from `mongo.Document` means that only the keys defined in the class can be saved to the database. Those keys defined in the class can be empty, but everything else will be ignored. On the other hand, if your class inherits `mongo.DynamicDocument`, then any extra fields that are set will be treated as `DynamicField` and will be saved with the document, as follows:

```
class Post(mongo.DynamicDocument):
    title = mongo.StringField(required=True, unique=True)
    text = mongo.StringField()
    ...
```

To show the extreme case (which is not recommended), the following class is perfectly valid; it has no required fields and allows any fields to be set:

```
class Post(mongo.DynamicDocument):
    pass
```

The last type of document is `EmbeddedDocument`. A `EmbeddedDocument` is simply a document that is passed to `EmbeddedDocumentField` and is stored as is in the document, as follows:

```
class Comment(mongo.EmbeddedDocument):
    name = mongo.StringField(required=True)
    text = mongo.StringField(required=True)
    date = mongo.DateTimeField(default=datetime.datetime.now())
```

Why use `EmbeddedDocumentField` over `DictField` when they seem to perform the same function? The end result of using each is the same. However, an embedded document defines a structure for the data, while `DictField` can be anything. To understand this better, think of it this way: `Document` is to `DynamicDocument` what `EmbeddedDocument` is to `DictField`.

The meta attribute

Using the `meta` class variable, many attributes of a document can be manually set. If you are working with an existing set of data and want to connect your classes to the collections, then set the collection key of the `meta` dictionary, as follows:

```
class Post(mongo.Document):
    ...
    meta = {'collection': 'user_posts'}
```

You can also manually set the maximum number of documents in the collection and the maximum size of each document. In the following example, there can be only 10,000 documents, and each document can't be larger than 2 MB:

```python
class Post(mongo.Document):
    ...
    meta = {
        'collection': 'user_posts',
        'max_documents': 10000,
        'max_size': 2000000
    }
```

Indexes can also be set through MongoEngine. Indexes can be made single field by using a string or multifield by using a tuple, as follows:

```python
class Post(mongo.Document):
    ...
    meta = {
        'collection': 'user_posts',
        'max_documents': 10000,
        'max_size': 2000000,
        'indexes': [
            'title',
            ('title', 'user')
        ]
    }
```

The default ordering of a collection can be set through the `meta` variable using the **ordering key**, as shown in the following code. When – is prepended, it tells MongoEngine to order results in descending order of that field. If + is prepended, it tells MongoEngine to order results in ascending order of that field. This default behavior is overridden if the `order_by` function is specified in a query, which will be shown in the *CRUD* section:

```python
class Post(mongo.Document):
    ...
    meta = {
        'collection': 'user_posts',
        'max_documents': 10000,
        'max_size': 2000000,
        'indexes': [
            'title',
            ('title', 'user')
        ],
        'ordering': ['-publish_date']
    }
```

The `meta` variable can also enable inheritance from user-defined documents, which is disabled by default. The subclass of the original document will be treated as a member of the parent class and will be stored in the same collection, as follows:

```
class Post(mongo.Document):
    ...
    meta = {'allow_inheritance': True}

class Announcement(Post):
    ...
```

CRUD

As stated in `Chapter 2`, *Creating Models with SQLAlchemy*, there are four main forms of data manipulation that any data store must implement. They are the creation of new data, the reading of existing data, the updating of existing data, and the deletion of data.

Create

To create a new document, just create a new instance of the class and call the `save` method, as follows:

```
>>> post = Post()
>>> post.title = "Post From The Console"
>>> post.text = "Lorem Ipsum..."
>>> post.save()
```

Otherwise, the values can be passed as keywords in the object creation, as follows:

```
>>> post = Post(title="Post From Console", text="Lorem Ipsum...")
```

Unlike SQLAlchemy, MongoEngine does not automatically save related objects that are stored in `ReferenceFields`. To save any changes to referenced documents along with the changes to the current document, pass `cascade` as `True`, as shown in the following code:

```
>>> post.save(cascade=True)
```

If you wish to insert a document and skip its checks against the defined parameters in the class definition, then pass `validate` as `False`, as shown in the following code:

```
>>> post.save(validate=False)
```

Remember that these checks exist for a reason. Turn them off only for a very good reason.

Write safety

By default, MongoDB does not wait for the data to be written to disk before acknowledging that the write occurred. This means that it is possible for writes that were acknowledged to have failed, either by hardware failure or some error when the write occurred. To ensure that the data is written to disk before Mongo confirms the write, use the `write_concern` keyword. The `write_concern` parameter tells Mongo when it should return with an acknowledgement of the write, as shown in the following code:

```
# will not wait for write and not notify client if there was an error
>>> post.save(write_concern={"w": 0})
# default behavior, will not wait for write
>>> post.save(write_concern={"w": 1})
# will wait for write
>>> post.save(write_concern={"w": 1, "j": True})
```

As stated in the *RDBMS versus NoSQL* section, it's very important that you understand how the NoSQL database that you are using treats writes. To learn more about MongoDB's write concern, go to
`http://docs.mongodb.org/manual/reference/write-concern/`.

Read

The `objects` attribute is used to access the documents from the database. To read all of the documents in a collection, use the `all` method, as follows:

```
>>> Post.objects.all()
[<Post: "Post From The Console">]
```

To limit the number of items returned, use the `limit` method as follows:

```
# only return five items
>>> Post.objects.limit(5).all()
```

This `limit` command is slightly different than the SQL version. In SQL, the `limit` command can also be used to skip the first results. To replicate this functionality, use the `skip` method as follows:

```
# skip the first 5 items and return items 6-10
>>> Post.objects.skip(5).limit(5).all()
```

By default, MongoDB returns the results in the order of the time of their creation. To control this, there is the `order_by` function, which is used as follows:

```
# ascending
>>> Post.objects.order_by("+publish_date").all()
# descending
>>> Post.objects.order_by("-publish_date").all()
```

If you want only the first result from a query, use the `first` method. If your query returns nothing, and you expected it to, then use `first_or_404` to automatically abort with a `404` error. This acts in exactly the same way as its Flask-SQLAlchemy counterpart, and is provided by Flask-MongoEngine, as follows:

```
>>> Post.objects.first()
<Post: "Post From The Console">
>>> Post.objects.first_or_404()
<Post: "Post From The Console">
```

The same behavior is available for the `get` method, which expects that the query will only return one result and will raise an exception otherwise, as follows:

```
# The id value will be different your document
>>> Post.objects(id="5534451d8b84ebf422c2e4c8").get()
<Post: "Post From The Console">
>>> Post.objects(id="5534451d8b84ebf422c2e4c8").get_or_404()
<Post: "Post From The Console">
```

The `paginate` method is also present and has the exact same API as its Flask-SQLAlchemy counterpart, as follows:

```
>>> page = Post.objects.paginate(1, 10)
>>> page.items()
[<Post: "Post From The Console">]
```

Also, if your document has a `ListField` method, then the `paginate_field` method on the document object can be used to paginate through the items of the list.

Filtering

If you know the exact value of the field you wish to filter by, then you can pass its value as a keyword to the `objects` method, as follows:

```
>>> Post.objects(title="Post From The Console").first()
<Post: "Post From The Console">
```

Unlike SQLAlchemy, we cannot pass truth tests to filter our results. Instead, special keyword arguments are used to test values. For example, to find all posts published after January 1 2015, enter the following:

```
>>> Post.objects(
        publish_date__gt=datetime.datetime(2015, 1, 1)
).all()
[<Post: "Post From The Console">]
```

The `__gt` appended to the end of the keyword is called an operator. MongoEngine supports the following operators:

- `ne`: Not equal to
- `lt`: Less than
- `lte`: Less than or equal to
- `gt`: Greater than
- `gte`: Greater than or equal to
- `not`: Negate an operator—for example, `publish_date__not__gt`
- `in`: Value is in the list
- `nin`: Value is not in the list
- `mod`: Value % a == b—a and b are passed as (a, b)
- `all`: Every item in the provided list of values is in the field
- `size`: The size of the list
- `exists`: Value for the field exists

MongoEngine also provides the following operators to test string values:

- `exact`: String equals the value
- `iexact`: String equals the value (case-insensitive)
- `contains`: String contains the value
- `icontains`: String contains the value (case-insensitive)

- `startswith`: String starts with the value
- `istartswith`: String starts with the value (case-insensitive)
- `endswith`: String ends with the value
- `iendswith`: String ends with the value (case insensitive) Update

These operators can be combined to create the same powerful queries that were created in the previous sections. For example, to find all of the posts that were created after January 1 2015 don't use the word `post` in the title. Instead, the body text should start with the word `Lorem` and should be ordered by the publish date, starting with the latest one. You can do this using the following code:

```
>>> Post.objects(
        title__not__icontains="post",
        text__istartswith="Lorem",
        publish_date__gt=datetime.datetime(2015, 1, 1),
).order_by("-publish_date").all()
```

However, if there is a complex query that cannot be represented by these tools, then a raw Mongo query can be passed as well, as follows:

```
>>> Post.objects(__raw__={"title": "Post From The Console"})
```

Update

To update objects, the `update` method is called on the results of a query, as follows:

```
>>> Post.objects(
        id="5534451d8b84ebf422c2e4c8"
).update(text="Ipsum lorem")
```

If your query should only return one value, then use `update_one` to only modify the first result, as follows:

```
>>> Post.objects(
        id="5534451d8b84ebf422c2e4c8"
).update_one(text="Ipsum lorem")
```

Unlike traditional SQL, there are many different ways to change a value in MongoDB. Operators are used to change the values of a field in the following different ways:

- `set`: Sets a value (same as given earlier)
- `unset`: Deletes a value and removes the key
- `inc`: Increments a value

- dec: Decrements a value
- push: Appends a value to a list
- push_all: Appends several values to a list
- pop: Removes the first or last element of a list
- pull: Removes a value from a list
- pull_all: Removes several values from a list
- add_to_set: Adds a value to a list only if it's not in the list already

For example, if a `Python` value needs to be added to a `ListField` named tags for all `Post` documents that have the `MongoEngine` tag, as follows:

```
>>> Post.objects(
        tags__in="MongoEngine",
        tags__not__in="Python"
).update(push__tags="Python")
```

The same write concern parameters to save exist for updates, as shown in the following code:

```
>>> Post.objects(
        tags__in="MongoEngine"
    ).update(push__tags="Python", write_concern={"w": 1, "j": True})
```

Delete

To delete a document instance, call its `delete` method as follows:

```
>>> post = Post.objects(
        id="5534451d8b84ebf422c2e4c8"
).first()
>>> post.delete()
```

Relationships in NoSQL

Just as we created relationships in SQLAlchemy, we can create relationships between objects in MongoEngine. Only with MongoEngine, we will be doing so without `JOIN` operators.

One-to-many relationships

There are two ways to create a one-to-many relationship in MongoEngine. The first method is to create a relationship between two documents by using `ReferenceField` to point to the ID of another object, as follows:

```
class Post(mongo.Document):
    ...
    user = mongo.ReferenceField(User)
```

Accessing the property of `ReferenceField` gives us direct access to the referenced object, as follows:

```
>>> user = User.objects.first()
>>> post = Post.objects.first()
>>> post.user = user
>>> post.save()
>>> post.user
<User Jack>
```

Unlike SQLAlchemy, MongoEngine has no way to access objects that have relationships to other objects. With SQLAlchemy, a `db.relationship` variable could be declared, which allowed a user object to access all of the posts with a matching `user_id` column. No such variable exists in MongoEngine.

A solution is to get the user ID for the posts you wish to search for and filter with the `user` field. This is the same thing that SQLAlchemy did behind the scenes, but we are doing it manually, as follows:

```
>>> user = User.objects.first()
>>> Post.objects(user__id=user.id)
```

The second way to create a one-to-many relationship is to use `EmbeddedDocumentField` with `EmbeddedDocument`, as follows:

```
class Post(mongo.Document):
    title = mongo.StringField(required=True)
    text = mongo.StringField()
    publish_date = mongo.DateTimeField(default=datetime.datetime.now())
    user = mongo.ReferenceField(User)
    comments = mongo.ListField(mongo.EmbeddedDocumentField(Comment))
```

Accessing the `comments` property gives a list of all the embedded documents. To add a new comment to the post, treat it like a list and append `comment` documents to it, as follows:

```
>>> comment = Comment()
>>> comment.name = "Jack"
>>> comment.text = "I really like this post!"
>>> post.comments.append(comment)
>>> post.save()
>>> post.comments
[<Comment 'I really like this post!'>]
```

Note that there was no call to a `save` method on the `comment` variable. This is because the comment document is not a real document; it is only an abstraction of `DictField`. Also, keep in mind that documents can only be up to 16 MB in size, so be careful how many `EmbeddedDocumentFields` are on each document and how many `EmbeddedDocuments` each one is holding.

Many-to-many relationships

The concept of a many-to-many relationship does not exist in document store databases. This is because with `ListFields`, they become completely irrelevant. To idiomatically create the tag feature for the `Post` object, add a list of strings as follows:

```
class Post(mongo.Document):
    title = mongo.StringField(required=True)
    text = mongo.StringField()
    publish_date = mongo.DateTimeField(default=datetime.datetime.now())
    user = mongo.ReferenceField(User)
    comments = mongo.ListField(mongo.EmbeddedDocumentField(Comment))
    tags = mongo.ListField(mongo.StringField())
```

Now, when we wish to query for all of the `Post` objects that have a specific tag or many tags, all we need is a simple query, as shown in the following code:

```
>>> Post.objects(tags__in="Python").all()
>>> Post.objects(tags__all=["Python", "MongoEngine"]).all()
```

For the list of roles on each user object, we use a list of references using the `ListField` of `ReferenceField(Role)`, as shown in the highlighted text in the following code:

```
...
class Role(mongo.Document):
    name = mongo.StringField(max_length=64, required=True, unique=True)
    description = mongo.StringField()
```

```
. . .

class User(mongo.Document):
    username = mongo.StringField(required=True)
    password = mongo.StringField()
    roles = mongo.ListField(mongo.ReferenceField(Role))

. . .
```

Leveraging the power of NoSQL

To show the unique power of NoSQL, let's add a feature that would be possible with SQLAlchemy, but which would be much more difficult: different post types, each with their own custom bodies. This will be much like the functionality of the popular blog platform Tumblr.

To begin, allow your post type to act as a parent class and remove the text field from the Post class, as not all posts will have text on them. This is shown in the following code:

```
class Post(mongo.Document):
    title = mongo.StringField(required=True)
    publish_date = mongo.DateTimeField(default=datetime.datetime.now())
    user = mongo.ReferenceField(Userm)
    comments = mongo.ListField(
    mongo.EmbeddedDocumentField(Commentm)
)
    tags = mongo.ListField(mongo.StringField())
    meta = {
        'allow_inheritance': True
    }
```

Each post type will inherit from the Post class. Doing so will allow the code to treat any Post subclass as if it were a post. Our blogging app will have four types of post: a normal blog post, an image post, a video post, and a quote post. These are shown in the following code:

```
class BlogPost(Post):
    text = db.StringField(required=True)
    @property
    def type(self):
        return "blog"

class VideoPost(Post):
    url = db.StringField(required=True)
    @property
    def type(self):
```

```
          return "video"

class ImagePost(Post):
    image_url = db.StringField(required=True)
    @property
    def type(self):
      return "image"

class QuotePost(Post):
    quote = db.StringField(required=True)
    author = db.StringField(required=True)
    @property
    def type(self):
      return "quote"
```

Our post-creation page needs to be able to create each of these post types. The `PostForm` object in `forms.py`, which handles post creation, will need to be modified to handle the new fields first. We will add a selection field that determines the type of post, an `author` field for the quote type, an `image` field to hold a URL, and a `video` field that will hold the embedded HTML iframe. The `quote` and `blog` post content will both share the `text` field, as follows:

```
class PostForm(Form):
    title = StringField('Title', [
      DataRequired(),
      Length(max=255)
    ])
    type = SelectField('Post Type', choices=[
      ('blog', 'Blog Post'),
      ('image', 'Image'),
      ('video', 'Video'),
      ('quote', 'Quote')
    ])
    text = TextAreaField('Content')
    image = StringField('Image URL', [URL(), Length(max=255)])
    video = StringField('Video Code', [Length(max=255)])
    author = StringField('Author', [Length(max=255)])
```

The `new_post` view function in the `blog/controllers.py` controller will also need to be updated to handle the new post types, as follows:

```
@blog_blueprint.route('/new', methods=['GET', 'POST'])
@login_required
@poster_permission.require(http_exception=403)
def new_post():
  form = PostForm()
  if form.validate_on_submit():
```

```
  if form.type.data == "blog":
    new_post = BlogPost()
    new_post.text = form.text.data
  elif form.type.data == "image":
    new_post = ImagePost()
    new_post.image_url = form.image.data
  elif form.type.data == "video":
    new_post = VideoPost()
    new_post.video_object = form.video.data
  elif form.type.data == "quote":
    new_post = QuotePost()
    new_post.text = form.text.data
    new_post.author = form.author.data
  new_post.title = form.title.data
  new_post.user = User.objects(
    username=current_user.username
  ).one()
  new_post.save()
return render_template('new.html', form=form)
```

The new.html file that renders our form object will need to display the new fields that are added to the form, as follows:

```
<form method="POST" action="{{ url_for('.new_post') }}">
...
<div class="form-group">
  {{ form.type.label }}
  {% if form.type.errors %}
    {% for e in form.type.errors %}
      <p class="help-block">{{ e }}</p>
    {% endfor %}
  {% endif %}
  {{ form.type(class_='form-control') }}
</div>
...
<div id="image_group" class="form-group">
  {{ form.image.label }}
  {% if form.image.errors %}
    {% for e in form.image.errors %}
      <p class="help-block">{{ e }}</p>
    {% endfor %}
  {% endif %}
  {{ form.image(class_='form-control') }}
</div>
<div id="video_group" class="form-group">
  {{ form.video.label }}
  {% if form.video.errors %}
    {% for e in form.video.errors %}
```

```
      <p class="help-block">{{ e }}</p>
    {% endfor %}
  {% endif %}
  {{ form.video(class_='form-control') }}
</div>
<div id="author_group" class="form-group">
  {{ form.author.label }}
    {% if form.author.errors %}
      {% for e in form.author.errors %}
        <p class="help-block">{{ e }}</p>
      {% endfor %}
    {% endif %}
    {{ form.author(class_='form-control') }}
</div>
<input class="btn btn-primary" type="submit" value="Submit">
</form>
```

Now that we have our new inputs, we can add some JavaScript to show and hide the fields based on the type of post, as follows:

```
{% block js %}
<script src="//cdn.ckeditor.com/4.4.7/standard/ckeditor.js"></script>
<script>
  CKEDITOR.replace('editor');

  $(function () {
    $("#image_group").hide();
    $("#video_group").hide();
    $("#author_group").hide();

    $("#type").on("change", function () {
      switch ($(this).val()) {
        case "blog":
          $("#text_group").show();
          $("#image_group").hide();
          $("#video_group").hide();
          $("#author_group").hide();
          break;
        case "image":
          $("#text_group").hide();
          $("#image_group").show();
          $("#video_group").hide();
          $("#author_group").hide();
          break;
        case "video":
          $("#text_group").hide();
          $("#image_group").hide();
          $("#video_group").show();
```

```
                    $("#author_group").hide();
                    break;
                 case "quote":
                    $("#text_group").show();
                    $("#image_group").hide();
                    $("#video_group").hide();
                    $("#author_group").show();
                    break;
              }
           });
        })
     </script>
     {% endblock %}
```

Finally, the `post.html` file needs to be able to display our post types correctly. We have the following code:

```
<div class="col-lg-12">
{{ post.text | safe }}
</div>
```

All that is needed is to replace this with the following:

```
<div class="col-lg-12">
   {% if post.type == "blog" %}
     {{ post.text | safe }}
   {% elif post.type == "image" %}
     <img src="{{ post.image_url }}" alt="{{ post.title }}">
   {% elif post.type == "video" %}
     {{ post.video_object | safe }}
   {% elif post.type == "quote" %}
     <blockquote>
        {{ post.text | safe }}
     </blockquote>
     <p>{{ post.author }}</p>
   {% endif %}
</div>
```

Summary

In this chapter, the fundamental differences between NoSQL and traditional SQL systems were laid out. We explored the main types of NoSQL systems and why an application might need, or not need, to be designed with a NoSQL database. We addressed the CAP theorem and its implications regarding modern database systems.

Using our app's models as a base, the power of MongoDB and MongoEngine was shown by demonstrating how simple it was to set up complex relationships and inheritance.

In the next chapter, our blogging application will be extended with a feature designed for other programmers who wish to use our site to build their own service—that is, RESTful endpoints.

8
Building RESTful APIs

Representational State Transfer (**REST**) is an architectural style that is used to implement web services. It was defined by Roy Fielding in his PhD dissertation in 2000. REST aims to implement a standard for uniform and predefined operations between systems. These systems can be client browsers, mobile applications, servers running parallel worker processes—you name it. By using HTTP methods, REST is platform- and programming-language-agnostic, and decouples the client and the server for easier development. This is typically used in web **single-page applications** (**SPAs**) that need to pull or update user information on the server. REST is also used to provide outside developers with a common interface to access user data. For example, Facebook and Twitter use REST in their application program interface, or API.

 You can take a look at Roy Fielding's original dissertation on REST at `https://www.ics.uci.edu/~fielding/pubs/dissertation/rest_arch_style.htm`.

In this chapter, you will learn about the following topics:

- The HTTP protocol: requests, responses, methods, headers, and the URI format
- How to build a REST service
- How to secure a REST service using JWT

What is REST?

Before getting into the details of REST, and since it is a style for communication between systems, let's first have a quick dive into the actual protocol that it uses, on which this whole book is based.

HTTP

The **Hypertext Transfer Protocol** (**HTTP**) is a request–response protocol that belongs to layer 7 (the application layer). This layer interacts with the application itself. Some other protocols that belong to layer 7 are the **Simple Mail Transfer protocol** (**SMTP**), **Network File System** (**NFS**), and the **File Transfer Protocol** (**FTP**), to name a few.

HTTP was designed to be used by clients (user agents) to request resources from a server. These resources can be HTML files or any other content, such as JSON, XML, or media files. These requests for resources are identified by the network using **unified resource locators** (**URLs**).

A URL is a specific type of URI, composed of the following elements:

```
<scheme>://<authority>/<path>/<query><fragment>
```

The preceding `<authority>` part:

```
<userinfo>@<host>:<port>
```

The following is an example URL using our application:

```
http://someserver.com:5000/blog/user/user1?title=sometitle#1
```

Let's separate out the elements of this:

Scheme	HTTP
authority.host	someserver.com
authority.port	5000
path	blog/user/user1
query	title=sometitle
fragment	1

Next, we will quickly look at an HTTP request message from a user agent to a server. This is a GET request from a Mozilla browser, as shown in the highlighted text in the following code:

```
GET /blog/user/user1 HTTP/1.1
Host: someserver.com
Accept: image/gif, image/jpeg, */*
Accept-Language: en-us
Accept-Encoding: gzip, deflate
User-Agent: Mozilla/4.0 (compatible; MSIE 6.0; Windows NT 5.1)
Cookie: cookie1=somevalue; cookie2=othervalue;
session:dsofksdfok439349i3sdkfoskfoskfosdkfo
(blank line)
```

So an HTTP request is composed of the following:

- **Request line**: Further composed of `<Request method> <Request URI> <HTTP version>`
- **Request header**: Contains information about what the client accepts, the user agent, cookies, and even basic authentication credentials
- **A blank line**: Separates the header from the body section
- **Request body**: Optional

Accepted HTTP request methods are `GET`, `HEAD`, `POST`, `PUT`, `DELETE`, `CONNECT`, `OPTIONS`, `TRACE`, and `PATCH`. The REST specification will use them to identify application type operations.

An HTTP response to a request looks like the following:

```
HTTP/1.0 200 OK
Content-Type: application/json
Content-Length: 1330
Server: Werkzeug/0.14.1 Python/2.7.10
Date: Thu, 19 Jul 2018 11:14:16 GMT
{ "author": "user1" ... }
```

It's composed of the following elements:

- **Status line**: The status of the response
- **Response headers**: Contains information about the content type, length, the server type (in our example, it's Flask's development server itself), date, and whether it can send set-cookie operations
- A blank line
- **Response body**: In our example, this is a JSON response, probably a REST service response

Status response codes are also very significant to REST. These fall into the following categories:

- **Informational**: 1XX
- **Successful**: 2XX
- **Redirection**: 3XX
- **Client error**: 4XX
- **Server error**: 5XX

For further details on status response codes, take a look at RFC2616 at `https://www.w3.org/Protocols/rfc2616/rfc2616-sec10.html`.

REST definition and best practices

Before getting into the details of REST, let's look at an example. With a client—in this case, a web browser—and a server, the client sends a request to the server over HTTP for some models, as follows:

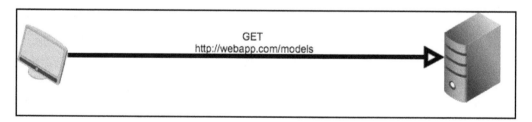

The server will then respond with a document containing all the models, as follows:

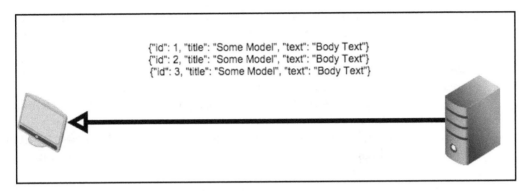

The client can then modify the data on the server through a PUT HTTP request, as follows:

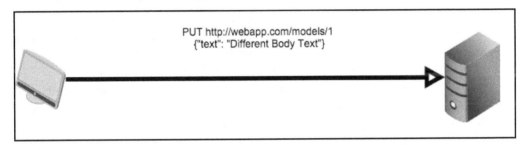

Then, the server will respond that it has modified the data. This is a very simplified example, but it will serve as a backdrop to how REST is defined.

Rather than a strict standard, REST lays out a set of constraints on communications to define a methodology that can be implemented in many ways. These constraints are born out of years of trial and error with other communication protocols, such as the **Remote Procedure Call** (**RPC**) or **Simple Object Access Protocol** (**SOAP**). These protocols fell by the wayside because of their strictness, verbosity, and the fact that it is difficult to use them to create APIs. The issues with these systems were identified, and REST's constraints were created to keep these issues from happening again.

REST provides the following guiding constraints:

- **Separation of concerns between the client and server**: The client and server should be able to evolve or change independently as long as the API does not change.
- **Stateless**: Any information that is necessary to handle requests is stored in the request itself or by the client. An example of the server being stateless is the `session` object in Flask. The `session` object does not store its information on the server, but stores it on the client in a cookie. The cookie is sent along with every request for the server to parse and determine whether the necessary data for the requested resource is stored inside it, rather than the server storing session information for every user.
- **Uniform interface**: There are many different parts to this constraint, which are as follows:
    - The interface is based around resources, which in our case are models.
    - Data sent by the server is not the actual data in the server, but a representation. For example, a JSON abstraction of the data is sent with each request, rather than the actual database.
    - The data sent by the server is enough to allow the client to modify the data on the server. In the preceding example, the IDs that are passed to the client fill this role.
    - Every resource provided by the API must be represented and accessed in the same manner. For example, one resource cannot be represented in XML and while another is represented in JSON.
- **Layered system:** Load balancers, proxies, caches, and other servers and services can act between the client and the server, as long as the final result is the same as if they were not there. This improves performance, scalability, and availability.
- **Cacheability:** Clients can cache responses, so a server must define whether a response is cacheable or not. This improves performance.

When a system adheres to all these constraints, it is considered to be a RESTful system. The most common forms of RESTful systems are built of HTTP and JSON. Each resource is located on its own URL path and is modified with different HTTP request methods. Generally, this takes the following form:

HTTP method	URL	Action
GET	http://host/resource	Get all the resource representations
GET	http://host/resource/1	Get the resource with an ID of 1

POST	http://host/resource	Create a new resource from the form data in the POST
PUT	http://host/resource/1	Modify the existing data of the resource with the ID of 1
DELETE	http://host/resource/1	Delete the resource with the ID of 1

As an example, a response to the second GET request would look like the following:

```
HTTP/1.0 200 OK
Content-Type: application/json
Content-Length: 1330
Server: Werkzeug/0.14.1 Python/2.7.10
Date: Thu, 19 Jul 2018 11:14:16 GMT

{ "id": 100, "title": "Some blog post title" }
```

In RESTful APIs, it is also very important that we return the correct HTTP status code with the response data to notify the clients of what actually happened on the server without the clients resorting to parsing the returned message. Here is a list of the main HTTP codes that are used in RESTful APIs, along with their meaning:

HTTP code	Name	Meaning
200	OK	The default code of HTTP. The request was successful, and the data was returned.
201	Created	The request was successful, and a new resource was created on the server.
204	No content	The request was successful, but the response returned no content.
400	Bad request	The request was denied because of some perceived client error—either it was a malformed request or it was missing the required data.
401	Unauthorized	The request was denied because the client was not authenticated, and it should be authenticated before requesting this resource again.
403	Forbidden	The request was denied because the client does not have permission to access this resource. This is in contrast to the 401 code, which assumes that the user is not authenticated. The 403 code says the resource is not accessible regardless of authentication.
404	Not found	The requested resource does not exist.

405	Method not allowed	The request was denied because the HTTP method is not available for the URL.
500	Internal server error	The web server responds with this status code when it has encountered an unexpected condition that prevented it from fulfilling the request from the client.
501	Not implemented	This error is shown when it does not support the functionality required to process the request. This is the appropriate response when the server does not recognize the request method.
502	Bad gateway	When the server is acting as a gateway or proxy and receives an invalid response from the upstream server.
503	Service unavailable	Currently unable to handle the request because of temporary overloading or maintenance of the server.
504	Gateway timeout	Did not receive a timely response from the upstream server.

Setting up a RESTful Flask API

In our app, we will create a RESTful interface to the blog post data in our database. The representations of the data will be sent as JSON. The data will be retrieved and modified using the general form in the preceding table, but the URI will be `/api/posts`.

If you haven't already downloaded and accessed the example code given for this chapter and taken a look at the Flask URL maps for the API, then a simple way of doing this can be seen in the root directory of the application, as shown in the following code:

```
$ # Initialise the virtual environment and database with test data
$ ./init.sh
$ # Activate the python virtual environment
$ source venv/bin/activate
$ export FLASK_APP=main.py
$ echo app.url_map | flask shell | grep api
..
  <Rule '/auth/api' (POST, OPTIONS) -> auth.api>,
  <Rule '/api/post' (HEAD, GET, PUT, POST, OPTIONS, DELETE) -> postapi>,
  <Rule '/api/post/<post_id>' (HEAD, GET, PUT, POST, OPTIONS, DELETE)
  -> postapi>,
```

We are going to implement an authentication endpoint for the API and the necessary endpoints to create a CRUD API for the blog posts.

We could just use the standard Flask views to create the API, but the Flask extension **Flask Restful** makes the task much easier and will help us adhere to a full REST compliance (RESTful).

To include this new dependency in our application, you can find the following in the `requirements.txt` file:

```
...
Flask-Restful
...
```

We are going to create a new module for the API. The application structure looks like the following code:

```
./
  main.py
  config.py
  ...
  webapp/
    blog/
    main/
    auth/
    api/
       __init__.py
       blog/
           controlers.py
           fields.py
           parsers.py
    templates/
    static/
```

Once again, the idea is to structure our application so that it can grow easily. This time, for each application module we add—such as a blog, shared photos, you name it—we create a new module inside the `api/` module itself where all the API logic is defined. A different approach could be to include the REST API inside each module.

Just like with all the other modules, there is a `create_module` function on the `api/__init__.py` that handles its own initialization for the main factory function, `create_app`. The `PostApi` class will also have its route defined with the `add_resource()` method of the `Api` object.

This can be seen in the provided code file, `api/__init__.py`, as follows:

```
from flask_restful import Api
from .blog.controllers import PostApi
```

```
rest_api = Api()


def create_module(app, **kwargs):
    rest_api.add_resource(
        PostApi,
        '/api/post',
        '/api/post/<int:post_id>',
    )
    rest_api.init_app(app)
```

It can also be seen in the `create_app` function in `__init__.py` file, as follows:

```
...
def create_app(object_name):
...
    from api import create_module as api_create_module
    ...
    api_create_module(app)

    return app
```

The control logic and views for our `Post` API are stored in a new folder named `api/blog` in the `controllers.py` file. Inside the `controllers.py`, we are going to create the API itself, as follows:

```
from flask_restful import Resource

class PostApi(Resource):
    ...
```

In Flask Restful, every REST resource is defined as a class that inherits from the `Resource` object. Much like the `MethodView` object shown in `Chapter 4`, *Creating Controllers with Blueprints*, any class that inherits from the `Resource` object defines its logic with methods named after the HTTP methods. For example, when the GET HTTP method hits the `PostApi` class, the `get` method will be executed.

JWT authentication

To solve our authentication problems, `Flask-Login` could be used and the cookie data from the login could be checked. However, this would require developers who wish to use our API to have their program login through the web interface. We could also have developers send their login data with every request, but it's a good design practice to only send sensitive information when absolutely necessary. Instead, our API will provide an `auth/api` endpoint that allows them to send login credentials and get an access token back.

For the authentication mechanism, we are going to use **JSON Web Token** (**JWT**) to create access tokens for the consumers of our API upon login. A JWT token asserts which user is logged in, thereby saving the server another call to the database for authentication. This token has an expiration date encoded inside it that will not allow the token to be used after it expires. This means that even if the token is stolen by a malicious user, it will only be useful for a limited amount of time before the client has to reauthenticate. As always, be sure to use HTTPS to encrypt all your client–server connections.

To leverage this feature, we are going to use another Flask extension—Flask-JWT-extended. You will find its dependency declared in the `requirements.txt` file, as follows:

```
...
flask-jwt-extended
...
```

The initialization of the extension is going to be made on the `auth` module.

Look at the following `auth/__init__.py` file:

```
from flask_jwt_extended import JWTManager
...
jwt = JWTManager()
...
def create_module(app, **kwargs):
    ...
    jwt.init_app(app)
    ...
```

Next, we use the following helper function to authenticate users that are defined on the same file:

```
def authenticate(username, password):
    from .models import User
    user = User.query.filter_by(username=username).first()
    if not user:
        return None
    # Do the passwords match
    if not user.check_password(password):
        return None
    return user
```

The definition of the login endpoint itself can be found at `auth/controllers.py`, as shown in the following code:

```
@auth_blueprint.route('/api', methods=['POST'])
def api():
    if not request.is_json:
        return jsonify({"msg": "Missing JSON in request"}), 400

    username = request.json.get('username', None)
    password = request.json.get('password', None)
    if not username:
        return jsonify({"msg": "Missing username parameter"}), 400
    if not password:
        return jsonify({"msg": "Missing password parameter"}), 400
    user = authenticate(username, password)
    if not user:
        return jsonify({"msg": "Bad username or password"}), 401
    # Identity can be any data that is json serializable
    access_token = create_access_token(identity=user.id)
    return jsonify(access_token=access_token), 200
```

First, we verify whether the request includes a JSON body. For this, we use a `request.is_json` function from Flask. Next, we extract the username and password from the JSON body using `request.json.get`. Then we check the user's credentials using the previous help function, `authenticate`. Finally, we return the JWT access token using the username as our identity.

Users of our API will have to pass the token that is received from this resource to any method that requires user credentials. In order to test this code, a tool named **curl** will be used. Curl is a command-line tool included in Bash that allows for the creation and manipulation of HTTP requests. To test it, use the `curl` utility to first log in, as shown in the following code:

```
$ curl -H "Content-Type: application/json" -d
'{"username":"user1","password":"password"}' http://localhost:5000/auth/api
{
  "access_token":
"eyJhbGciOiJIUzI1NiIsInR5cCI6IkpXVCJ9.eyJqdGkiOiIyOGZjMDNkOC0xY2MyLTQwZDQtO
DJlMS0xMGQ0Mjc2YTk1ZjciLCJleHAiOjE1MzIwMTg4NDMsImZyZXNoIjpmYWxzZSwiaWF0Ijox
NTMyMDE3OTQzLCJ0eXBlIjoiYWNjZXNzIiwibmJmIjoxNTMyMDE3OTQzLCJpZGVudGl0eSI6InV
zZXIxIn0.Cs-ANWq0I2M2XMrZpQof-_cX0gsKE7U4UG1t1rB0UoY"
}
```

We then use the `-H` flag to send the request header stating that the content body is JSON and the `-d` flag to send the request body data. Next, we can use the token to access API-protected resources, as follows:

```
$ export
ACCESS="eyJhbGciOiJIUzI1NiIsInR5cCI6IkpXVCJ9.eyJqdGkiOiIyOGZjMDNkOC0xY2MyLT
QwZDQtODJlMS0xMGQ0Mjc2YTk1ZjciLCJleHAiOjE1MzIwMTg4NDMsImZyZXNoIjpmYWxzZSwia
WF0IjoxNTMyMDE3OTQzLCJ0eXBlIjoiYWNjZXNzIiwibmJmIjoxNTMyMDE3OTQzLCJpZGVudGl0
eSI6InVzZXIxIn0.Cs-ANWq0I2M2XMrZpQof-_cX0gsKE7U4UG1t1rB0UoY"
$ curl -H "Authorization: Bearer $ACCESS" http://localhost:5000/api/post
```

Note how the access token is sent on the request header user `Authorization: Bearer <TOKEN>` convention. If we try to access the same resource without any token, we get the following:

```
$ curl -v http://localhost:5000/api/post
...
< HTTP/1.0 401 UNAUTHORIZED
...
{
  "msg": "Missing Authorization Header"
}
```

As expected, we get an HTTP `401` status code. To protect API endpoints, we just have to use the `flask-jwt-extended` decorator `@jwt_required`, and to fetch the username, we use the `get_jwt_identity()` function.

The `flask-jwt-extended` decorator provides some extra functionalities, such as token expiration, the ability to refresh token endpoints, and many configuration options. You can read more about it at `http://flask-jwt-extended.readthedocs.io/en/latest/`.

Get requests

For some of our GET, PUT, and DELETE requests, our API will need the ID of the post that is to be modified.

The data to be sent to the client must be a representation of the Post objects in JSON, so how will our Post objects be translated? Flask Restful provides a way of translating any object into JSON through the `fields` object and the `marshal_with` function decorator.

Output formatting

The output format is defined by creating a dictionary of `field` objects that represent basic types. The key of the field defines what attribute the field will try to translate. By passing the dictionary to the `marshal_with` decorator, any object that the `get` method attempts to return will be first translated using the dictionary. This also works for lists of objects. Let's look at a simple way of implementing this API endpoint. The following example code takes pagination into account, but we will show you how this works later.

Look at the following `api/blog/controllers.py` file:

```
import datetime

from flask import abort
from flask_restful import Resource, fields, marshal_with
from flask_jwt_extended import jwt_required, get_jwt_identity
from webapp.blog.models import db, Post, Tag
from webapp.auth.models import User
...

post_fields = {
    'id': fields.Integer(),
    'author': fields.String(attribute=lambda x: x.user.username),
    'title': fields.String(),
    'text': HTMLField(),
    'tags': fields.List(fields.Nested(nested_tag_fields)),
    'publish_date': fields.DateTime(dt_format='iso8601')
}
```

```
class PostApi(Resource):
    @marshal_with(post_fields)
    @jwt_required
    def get(self, post_id=None):
        if post_id:
            post = Post.query.get(post_id)
            if not post:
                abort(404)
            return post
        else:
            posts = Post.query.all()
            return posts
```

While reloading the API in the browser, every `Post` object will be shown in JSON format. Note the `HTMLField` on the fields declaration. The problem is that the API should not return HTML from the WYSIWYG editor in the post creation form. As stated earlier, the server should not be concerned with the UI, and the HTML is purely for output specification. To solve this, we will need a custom field object that strips HTML from the strings. In a new file in the `api/blog/` folder named `fields.py`, we have the following:

```
try:
    # Try python3
    from html.parser import HTMLParser
except Exception as e:
    # Nop python2
    from HTMLParser import HTMLParser

from flask_restful import fields


class HTMLStripper(HTMLParser):
    fed = list()

    def __init__(self):
        self.reset()
        self.fed = []

    def handle_data(self, d):
        self.fed.append(d)

    def get_data(self):
        return ''.join(self.fed)


def strip_tags(html):
    s = HTMLStripper()
    s.feed(html)
```

```
        return s.get_data()


    class HTMLField(fields.Raw):
        def format(self, value):
            return strip_tags(str(value))
```

The exception block is to take into account Python2 and Python3 compatibility, since the standard library has changed for the `HTMLParser` module in Python3. We now have a `strip_tags` function that will return any string that has been cleaned of HTML tags. A new field type, called `HTMLfield`, is defined by inheriting from the `fields.Raw` class and sending values through the `strip_tags` function. If the page is reloaded, all HTML is gone and only the text will remain.

Flask Restful provides many default fields, as shown in the following list:

- `fields.String`: This converts the value using `str()`.
- `fields.FormattedString`: This passes the formatted string in Python with the variable name in brackets.
- `fields.Url`: This provides the same functionality as the Flask `url_for` function.
- `fields.DateTime`: This converts a Python `date` or `datetime` object to a string. The `format` keyword argument specifies whether the string should be an `ISO8601` date or an `RFC822` date.
- `fields.Float`: This converts the value to a string representation of a float.
- `fields.Integer`: This converts the value to a string representation of an integer.
- `fields.Nested`: This allows nested objects to be represented by another dictionary of field objects.
- `fields.List`: Much like the MongoEngine API, this field takes another field type as an argument and tries to convert a list of values into a JSON list of the field types.
- `fields.Boolean`: This converts the value to a string representation of a `boolean` argument.

There are two more fields that are added to the returned data: the author and the tags. The comments will be left out because they should be contained under their own resource.

The author field uses the attribute keyword argument of the field class. This allows any attribute of the object to be represented rather than just base-level properties. Because the many-to-many relationship of the tags returns a list of objects, the same solution cannot be used with the tags. A list of tag dictionaries can now be returned using the NestedField type inside a ListField and another dictionary of fields. This has the added benefit of giving the end users of the API a tag ID so that they can query as easily as if there were a tag API.

Request arguments

While sending a GET request to the base of the resource, our API currently sends all the Post objects in the database. This is acceptable if the number of objects is low or the number of people using the API is low. However, if either increases, the API will put a large amount of stress on the database. Much like the web interface, the API should be paginated as well.

In order to achieve this, our API will need to accept a GET query string parameter called page that specifies which page is to be loaded. Flask Restful provides a method to grab request data and parse it. If the required arguments aren't there, or the types don't match, Flask Restful will autocreate a JSON error message. In a new file in the api/blog/ folder named parsers.py, you will find the following code:

```
...
from flask_restful import reqparse
...
post_get_parser = reqparse.RequestParser()
post_get_parser.add_argument(
    'page',
    type=int,
    location=['args', 'headers'],
    required=False,
)
```

The following code is what we should have on the PostApi class when the request has no post ID key:

```
from .parsers import post_get_parser
...
class PostApi(Resource):
    @marshal_with(post_fields)
    @jwt_required
    def get(self, post_id=None):
        if post_id:
```

```
  ..
  return post
else:
  args = post_get_parser.parse_args()
  page = args['page'] or 1
  ...
  posts = Post.query.order_by(
    Post.publish_date.desc()
  ).paginate(page, current_app.config.get('POSTS_PER_PAGE', 10))
  ...
  return posts.items
```

In the preceding example, RequestParser looks for the page variable in either the query string or the request header and returns the page of Post objects from that page. Again, we are making the page size configurable with the same value as for the web view page version. We use the current_app Flask proxy to fetch any value from our configuration.

After a parser object is created with RequestParser, arguments can be added using the add_argument method. The first argument of add_argument is the key of the argument that is to be parsed, but add_argument also takes a lot of keyword arguments, as shown in the following list:

- action: This is what the parser does with the value after it has been successfully parsed. The two available options are store and append. The store option adds the parsed value to the returned dictionary. The append options adds the parsed value to the end of a list in the dictionary.
- case_sensitive: This is a boolean argument to allow or disallow the keys to be case insensitive.
- choices: This is like MongoEngine, a list of the allowed values for the argument.
- default: This is the value that is produced if the argument is absent from the request.
- dest: This is the key to add the parsed value to in the returned data.
- help: This is a message to return to the user if validation fails.
- ignore: This is a boolean argument to allow or disallow failures of the type conversion.
- location: This indicates where to look for the data. The locations available are as follows:
  - args to look in the GET query string
  - headers to look in the HTTP request headers
  - form to look in the HTTP POST data

- `cookies` to look in the HTTP cookies
- `json` to look in any sent JSON
- `files` to look in the `POST` file data

- `required`: This is a boolean argument to determine whether the argument is optional.
- `store_missing`: This is a boolean argument to determine whether the default value should be stored if the argument is not in the request.
- `type`: This is the Python type to convert the passed value.

Using the Flask Restful parser, it is very easy to add new parameters to the API. For example, let's add a user argument that allows us to search for all posts that have been made by a user. First, in the `api/blog/parsers.py` file, we have the following:

```
post_get_parser = reqparse.RequestParser()
post_get_parser.add_argument('page', type=int, location=['args',
'headers'])
post_get_parser.add_argument('user', type=str, location=['args',
'headers'])
```

Then, in the `api/blog/controllers.py` file, we have the following:

```
class PostApi(Resource):
    @marshal_with(post_fields)
    @jwt_required
    def get(self, post_id=None):
        if post_id:
            ...
            return post
        else:
            args = post_get_parser.parse_args()
            page = args['page'] or 1

            if args['user']:
                user = User.query.filter_by(username=args['user']).first()
                if not user:
                    abort(404)

                posts = user.posts.order_by(
                    Post.publish_date.desc()
            ).paginate(page, current_app.config.get('POSTS_PER_PAGE', 10))
            else:
                posts = Post.query.order_by(
                    Post.publish_date.desc()
            ).paginate(page, current_app.config.get('POSTS_PER_PAGE', 10))
            return posts.items
```

When Flask's `abort` function is called from `Resource`, Flask Restful will automatically create an error message to be returned with the status code.

To test the API, we use `curl` for the sake of simplicity, but feel free to use any other tool available to interact with HTTP APIs. After requesting an access token from our authentication endpoint, request `post` with `id=1`, as follows:

```
$ curl -H "Authorization: Bearer $ACCESS"
"http://localhost:5000/api/post/1"
```

Or you can request all posts as follows:

```
$ curl -H "Authorization: Bearer $ACCESS" "http://localhost:5000/api/post"
```

Note that the response only fetches the first page, as intended. Now let's request page two, as follows:

```
$ curl -H "Authorization: Bearer $ACCESS"
"http://localhost:5000/api/post?page=2"
```

Finally, you can request for posts from a certain user as follows:

```
$ curl -H "Authorization: Bearer $ACCESS"
"http://localhost:5000/api/post?user=user1"
```

Post requests

The `POST` methods on REST are used for resource creation, not that this isn't considered an idempotent method. Using our new knowledge of the Flask Restful parser, we can cover the `POST` endpoint. First, we will need a parser that will take a title, the body text, and a list of tags. In the `parser.py` file, find the following:

```
post_post_parser = reqparse.RequestParser()
post_post_parser.add_argument(
    'title',
    type=str,
    required=True,
    help="Title is required",
    location=('json', 'values')
)
post_post_parser.add_argument(
    'text',
    type=str,
    required=True,
    help="Body text is required",
```

```
        location=('json', 'values')
    )
    post_post_parser.add_argument(
        'tags',
        type=str,
        action='append',
        location=('json', 'values')
    )
```

Next, we have created a helper function, called `add_tags_to_post`, to add tags to a post. If the tags don't exist, it will add them to the database. We will use it on POST and PUT requests. Nothing new here—just a simple SQLAlchemy helper function to help us keep our code concise.

Next, the `PostApi` class will need a `post` method to handle incoming requests. The `post` method will use the given values for the title and body text. Also, if the `tags` key exists, then add the tags to the post, which creates new tags if the passed ones do not exist, as shown in the following code:

```
import datetime
from .parsers import (
    post_get_parser,
    post_post_parser
)
from webapp.models import db, User, Post, Tag
class PostApi(Resource):
    ...
    @jwt_required
    def post(self, post_id=None):
        args = post_post_parser.parse_args(strict=True)
        new_post = Post(args['title'])
        new_post.user_id = get_jwt_identity()
        new_post.text = args['text']
        if args['tags']:
            add_tags_to_post(post, args['tags'])
        db.session.add(new_post)
        db.session.commit()
        return {'id': new_post.id}, 201
```

At the `return` statement, if a tuple is returned, the second argument is treated as the status code. There is also a third value that acts as extra header values by passing a dictionary. Also, note the `get_jwt_identity` that we use to fetch the user ID from the JWT token. This was set up at the login phase where we used the user ID to set the JWT identity.

To pass POST variables, the d flag is used, as follows:

```
$ curl -X POST -H "Authorization: Bearer $ACCESS" -H "Content-Type:
application/json" -d '{"title":"Text Title", "text":"Some text"}'
"http://localhost:5000/api/post"
{
    "id": 310
}
```

The ID of the newly created post should be returned. If you go to the browser, you should see our newly created post, which was made by the user that you used to generate the authentication token.

Put requests

As listed in the table at the beginning of this chapter, PUT requests are used to change the values of an existing resource. Like the post method, the first thing that we should do is create a new parser in parsers.py, as follows:

```
post_put_parser = reqparse.RequestParser()
post_put_parser.add_argument(
    'title',
    type=str,
    location=('json', 'values')
)
post_put_parser.add_argument(
    'text',
    type=str,
    location=('json', 'values')
)
post_put_parser.add_argument(
    'tags',
    type=str,
    action='append',
    location=('json', 'values')
)
```

The logic for the put method is very similar to the post method. The main difference is that each change is optional and any request that does not provide post_id is denied, as shown in the following code:

```
...
def add_tags_to_post(post, tags_list):
    for item in tags_list:
        tag = Tag.query.filter_by(title=item).first()
```

```
    # Add the tag if it exists. If not, make a new tag
    if tag:
        post.tags.append(tag)
    else:
        new_tag = Tag(item)
        post.tags.append(new_tag)
...

    @jwt_required
    def put(self, post_id=None):
        if not post_id:
            abort(400)
        post = Post.query.get(post_id)
        if not post:
            abort(404)
        args = post_put_parser.parse_args(strict=True)
        if get_jwt_identity() != post.user_id:
            abort(403)
        if args['title']:
            post.title = args['title']
        if args['text']:
            post.text = args['text']
        if args['tags']:
            print("Tags %s" % args['tags'])
            add_tags_to_post(post, args['tags'])

        db.session.merge(post)
        db.session.commit()
        return {'id': post.id}, 201
```

Also note that, just as we did with the controller for web views, we are denying any request to change a blog post that was not made by the creator of the blog post him or herself.

To test this method, `curl` can also create PUT requests with the −X flag, as follows:

```
$ curl −X PUT −H "Authorization: Bearer $ACCESS" −H "Content−Type:
application/json" \
    −d '{"title": "Modified From REST", "text": "this is from REST",
"tags": ["tag1","tag2"]}' \
http://localhost:5000/api/post/5
```

Delete requests

Finally, in the following code we have the DELETE request, which is the simplest of the four supported methods. The main difference with the delete method is that it returns no content, which is the accepted standard with DELETE requests:

```
@jwt_required
def delete(self, post_id=None):
    if post_id:
        abort(400)
    post = Post.query.get(post_id)
    if not post:
        abort(404)
    if get_jwt_identity() != post.user_id:
        abort(401)
    db.session.delete(post)
    db.session.commit()
    return "", 204
```

Again, we can test using the following:

```
$ curl -X DELETE -H "Authorization: Bearer $ACCESS"
http://localhost:5000/api/post/102
```

If everything is successfully deleted, you should receive a 204 status code and nothing should show up.

Before we move on from REST completely, there is one final challenge for you to test your understanding of Flask Restful. Try to create a comments API that is not only modifiable from http://localhost:5000/api/comments, but that also allows developers to modify only those comments on a specific post by using the URL format http://localhost:5000/api/post/<int:post_id>/comments.

Summary

Our Post API is now a complete feature. If a developer wants, then they can create a desktop or mobile application using this API, all without using HTML scraping, which is a very long and tedious process. Giving the developers who wish to use your website as a platform the ability to do so will increase your site's popularity, as they will essentially give you free advertising with their app or website.

In the next chapter, we will use the popular program Celery to run programs and tasks asynchronously with our application.

Creating Asynchronous Tasks with Celery

9

While creating web apps, it is vital to keep the time taken to process a request below or around 50 ms. On web applications or web services that have a medium to high rate of requests per second, response time becomes even more paramount. Think of requests such as a flow of liquid that needs to be handled at least as quickly as its flow rate, or else it will overflow. Any extra processing on the server that can be avoided, should be avoided. However, it is quite common to have requirements to operations in a web app that take longer than a couple of seconds, especially when complex database operations or image processing are involved.

In building an application that is able to scale horizontally, it should be possible to decouple all the heavy processing procedures from the web server's layer, and couple them to a worker's layer that can independently scale itself.

To protect our user experience and site reliability, a task queue named Celery will be used to move these operations out of the Flask process.

In this chapter, we will cover the following topics:

- Using Docker to run RabbitMQ and Redis
- Celery and Flask integration
- Learning to identify processes that should run outside the web server
- Creating and calling several types of tasks from simple asynchronous to complex workflows
- Using Celery as a scheduler with beats

What is Celery?

Celery is an asynchronous task queue written in Python. Celery runs multiple tasks, which are user-defined functions, concurrently, through the Python multiprocessing library. Celery receives messages that tell it to start a task from a **broker**, which is usually called a message queue, as shown in the following diagram:

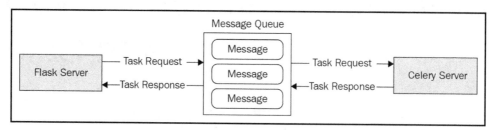

A **message queue** is a system specifically designed to send data between producer processes and consumer processes. **Producer processes** are any programs that create messages to be sent to the queue, and **consumer processes** are any programs that take the messages out of the queue. Messages sent from a producer are stored in a **First In, First Out** (**FIFO**) queue, where the oldest items are retrieved first. Messages are stored until a consumer receives the message, after which the message is deleted. Message queues provide real-time messaging without relying on polling, which means continuously checking the status of a process. As messages are sent from producers, consumers are listening on their connection to the message queue for new messages; the consumer is not constantly contacting the queue. This difference is like the difference between **AJAX** and **WebSockets**, in that AJAX requires constant contact with the server, while WebSockets are just a continuous bidirectional communication stream.

It is possible to replace the message queue with a traditional database. Celery even comes with built-in support for SQLAlchemy to allow this. However, using a database as a broker for Celery is highly discouraged. Using a database in place of a message queue requires the consumer to constantly poll the database for updates. Also, because Celery uses multiprocessing for concurrency, the number of connections making lots of reads goes up quickly. Under medium loads, using a database requires the producer to make lots of writes to the database at the same time as the consumer is reading.

It is also possible to use a message queue as a broker and a database to store the results of the tasks. In the preceding diagram, the message queue was used for sending task requests and task results. However, using a database to store the end result of the task allows the final product to be stored indefinitely, whereas the message queue will throw out the data as soon as the producer receives the data, as shown in the following diagram:

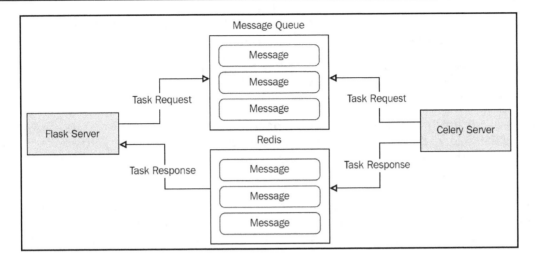

This database is often a key/value NoSQL store to help handle the load. This is useful if you plan on doing analytics on previously run tasks, but otherwise it's safer to just stick with the message queue.

There is even an option to drop the results of tasks entirely, and not have the results returned at all. This has the downside that the producer has no way of knowing if a task was successful or not, but often, this is permissible in smaller projects.

For our stack, we will use RabbitMQ as the message broker. RabbitMQ runs on all major operating systems and is very simple to be set up and run. Celery also supports RabbitMQ without any extra libraries, and is the recommended message queue in the Celery documentation.

At the time of writing, there is no way to use RabbitMQ with Celery in Python 3. You can use Redis, however, instead of RabbitMQ. The only difference will be the connection strings. For more information, see `http://docs.celeryproject.org/en/latest/getting-started/brokers/redis.html`.

Setting up Celery and RabbitMQ

To install Celery on our `virtualenv`, we need to add it to our `requirements.txt` file:

```
...
Celery
...
```

As always, use the provided `init.sh` script, or use the procedure explained here to create and install all dependencies on a Python virtual environment.

We will also need a Flask extension to help handle the initialization of Celery:

```
$ pip install Flask-Celery-Helper
```

The Flask documentation states that Flask extensions for Celery are unnecessary. However, getting the Celery server to work with Flask's application context, when your app is organized with an application factory, is significant. So, we will use `Flask-Celery-Helper` to do the heavy lifting.

Next, RabbitMQ needs to be up and running. To do this easily, we will use a Docker container. Make sure you have Docker installed and properly set up; if not, then check out `Chapter 1`, *Getting Started*, for instructions. First, we will need a very simple Dockerfile:

```
FROM rabbitmq:3-management

ENV RABBITMQ_ERLANG_COOKIE "SWQOKODSQALRPCLNMEQG"
ENV RABBITMQ_DEFAULT_USER "rabbitmq"
ENV RABBITMQ_DEFAULT_PASS "rabbitmq"
ENV RABBITMQ_DEFAULT_VHOST "/"
```

This is all it takes to build and run a RabbitMQ Docker image with the management interface. We are using a Docker Hub image that is available for download at `https://hub.docker.com/_/rabbitmq/`. Visit the Hub page for further configuration details.

Next, let's build our image issue the following command:

```
$ docker build -t blog-rmq .
```

The `-t` flag is used to tag our image with a friendly name; in this case, `blog-rmq`. Then run the newly created image in the background using the following command:

```
$ docker run -d -p 15672:15672 -p 5672:5672 blog-rmq
```

The `-d` flag is to run the container in the background (daemon). The `-p` flag is for port mapping between the container and our host/desktop.

Let's check if it's properly running:

```
$ docker ps
CONTAINER ID IMAGE COMMAND CREATED STATUS PORTS NAMES
6eb2ab1da516 blog-rmq "docker-entrypoint.s..." 13 minutes ago Up 14 minutes
4369/tcp, 5671/tcp, 0.0.0.0:5672->5672/tcp, 15671/tcp, 25672/tcp,
0.0.0.0:15672->15672/tcp xenodochial_kepler
```

Let's check out the RabbitMQ management interface. In your browser, navigate to `http://localhost:15672` and log in using the configured credentials set up on the Dockerfile. In this case, our username is `rabbitmq`, and our password is also `rabbitmq`.

If you need more information, RabbitMQ maintains a detailed list of installation and configuration instructions for each operating system at `https://www.rabbitmq.com/download.html`.

After RabbitMQ is installed, go to a Terminal window and run the following command:

```
$ rabbitmq-server
```

Creating tasks in Celery

As stated before, Celery tasks are just user-defined functions that perform some operations. But before any tasks can be written, our Celery object needs to be created. This is the object that the Celery server will import to handle running and scheduling all of the tasks.

At a bare minimum, Celery needs one configuration variable to run, and that is the connection to the message broker. The connection is defined the same as the SQLAlchemy connection; that is, as a URL. The backend, which stores our tasks' results, is also defined as a URL, as shown in the following code:

```
class DevConfig(Config):
    DEBUG = True
    SQLALCHEMY_DATABASE_URI = 'sqlite:///../database.db'
    CELERY_BROKER_URL = "amqp://rabbitmq:rabbitmq@localhost//"
    CELERY_RESULT_BACKEND = "amqp://rabbitmq:rabitmq@localhost//"
```

In the `__init__.py` file, the `Celery` class from `Flask-Celery-Helper` will be initialized:

```
from flask_celery import Celery
...
celery = Celery()
...
def create_app(object_name):
...
    celery.init_app(app)
...
```

So, in order for our Celery process to work with the database and any other Flask extensions, it needs to work within our application context. In order to do so, Celery will need to create a new instance of our application for each process. Like most Celery apps, we need a Celery factory to create an application instance and register our Celery instance on it. In a new file, named `celery_runner.py`, in the top-level directory—the same location where `manage.py` resides—we have the following:

```python
import os
from webapp import create_app
from celery import Celery


def make_celery(app):
    celery = Celery(
        app.import_name,
        broker=app.config['CELERY_BROKER_URL'],
        backend=app.config['CELERY_RESULT_BACKEND']
    )
    celery.conf.update(app.config)
    TaskBase = celery.Task

    class ContextTask(TaskBase):
        abstract = True

        def __call__(self, *args, **kwargs):
            with app.app_context():
                return TaskBase.__call__(self, *args, **kwargs)

    celery.Task = ContextTask
    return celery

env = os.environ.get('WEBAPP_ENV', 'dev')
flask_app = create_app('config.%sConfig' % env.capitalize())

celery = make_celery(flask_app)
```

The `make_celery` function wraps every call to each Celery task in a Python `with` block. This makes sure that every call to any Flask extension will work as it is working with our app. Also, make sure not to name the Flask app instance `app`, as Celery tries to import any object named `app` or `celery` as the Celery application instance. So naming your Flask object `app` will cause Celery to try to use it as a Celery object.

Now we can write our first task. It will be a simple task to start with; one that just returns any string passed to it. We have a new file in the blog module directory, named `tasks.py`. In this file, find the following:

```
from .. import celery

@celery.task()
def log(msg):
    return msg
```

Now, the final piece of the puzzle is to run the Celery process, which is called a **worker**, in a new Terminal window. Again, this is the process that will be listening to our message broker for commands to start new tasks:

```
$ celery worker -A celery_runner --loglevel=info
```

The `loglevel` flag is there, so you will see the confirmation that a task was received, and its output was available, in the Terminal window.

Now, we can send commands to our Celery worker. Open a Flask shell session, as follows:

```
$ export FLASK_APP=main.py
$ flask shell
>>> from webapp.blog.tasks import log
>>> log("Message")
Message
>>> result = log.delay("Message")
```

The function can be called as if it were any other function, and doing so will execute the function in the current process. However, calling the `delay` method on the task will send a message to the worker process to execute the function with the given arguments.

In the Terminal window that is running the Celery worker, you should see something like the following:

```
Task webapp.blog.tasks.log succeeded in 0.0005873600021s: 'Message'
```

As with any asynchronous task, the `ready` method can be used to tell if the task has successfully been completed. If `True`, the `get` method can be used to retrieve the result of the tasks as follows:

```
>>> result.ready()
True
>>> result.get()
"Message"
```

The get method causes the current process to wait until the ready function returns True to retrieve the result. So, calling get immediately after calling the task essentially makes the task synchronous. Because of this, it's rather rare for tasks to actually return a value to the producer. The vast majority of tasks perform some operation and then exit.

When a task is run on the Celery worker, the state of the task can be accessed via the state attribute. This allows for a more fine-grained understanding of what the task is currently doing in the worker process. The available states are as follows:

- FAILURE: The task failed, and all of the retries failed as well.
- PENDING: The task has not yet been received by the worker.
- RECEIVED: The task has been received by the worker, but is not yet processing.
- RETRY: The task failed and is waiting to be retried.
- REVOKED: The task was stopped.
- STARTED: The worker has started processing the task.
- SUCCESS: The task was completed successfully.

In Celery, if a task fails, then the task can recall itself with the retry method, as follows:

```
@celery.task(bind=True)
def task(self, param):
  try:
    some_code
  except Exception, e:
    self.retry(exc=e)
```

The bind parameter in the decorator function tells Celery to pass a reference to the task object as the first parameter in the function. Using the self parameter, the retry method can be called, which will rerun the task with the same parameters. There are several other parameters that can be passed to the function decorator to change the behavior of the task:

- max_retries: This is the maximum number of times the task can be retried before it is declared as failed.
- default_retry_delay: This is the time in seconds to wait before running the task again. It's a good idea to keep this at around a minute or so if you expect that the conditions that led to the task failing are transitory; for example, network errors.

- `rate_limit`: This specifies the total number of unique calls to this task that are allowed to run in a given interval. If the value is an integer, then it represents the total number of calls that this task that is allowed to run per second. The value can also be a string in the form of *x/m*, for *x* number of tasks per minute, or *x/h*, for *x* number of tasks per hour. For example, passing in *5/m* will only allow this task to be called five times a minute.
- `time_limit`: If this is specified, then the task will be killed if it runs longer than the specified number of seconds.
- `ignore_result`: If the task's return value isn't used, then don't send it back.

It's a good idea to specify all of these for each task to avoid any chance that a task will not be run.

Running Celery tasks

The `delay` method is a shorthand version of the `apply_async` method, which is called in this format:

```
task.apply_async(
    args=[1, 2],
    kwargs={'kwarg1': '1', 'kwarg2': '2'}
)
```

However, the `args` keyword can be implicit, as shown here:

```
apply_async([1, 2], kwargs={'kwarg1': '1', 'kwarg2': '2'})
```

Calling `apply_async` allows you to define some extra functionality in the task call that you cannot specify in the `delay` method. First, the `countdown` option specifies the amount of time in seconds that the worker, upon receiving the task, should wait before running it:

```
>>> from webapp.blog.tasks import log
>>> log.apply_async(["Message"], countdown=600)
```

The `countdown` is not a guarantee that the task will be run after 600 seconds. The `countdown` option only says that the task is up for processing after *x* number of seconds. If all of the worker processes are busy with the other tasks, then it will not be run immediately.

Another keyword argument that `apply_async` gives is the `eta` argument. `eta` is passed through a Python `datetime` object that specifies exactly when the task should be run. Again, `eta` is not reliable:

```
>>> import datetime
>>> from webapp.blog.tasks import log
# Run the task one hour from now
>>> eta = datetime.datetime.now() + datetime.timedelta(hours=1)
>>> log.apply_async(["Message"], eta=eta)
```

Celery workflows

Celery provides many ways to group multiple, dependent tasks together, or to execute many tasks in parallel. These methods take a large amount of influence from language features found in functional programming languages. However, to understand how this works, we first need to understand signatures. Consider the following task:

```
@celery.task()
def multiply(x, y):
    return x * y
```

Let's see a **signature** in action to understand it. Open up a Flask shell and enter the following:

```
# Export FLASK_APP if you haven't already
$ export FLASK_APP=main.py
$ flask shell
>>> from celery import signature
>>> from webapp.blog.tasks import multiply
# Takes the same keyword args as apply_async
>>> signature('webapp.tasks.multiply', args=(4, 4), countdown=10)
webapp.tasks.multiply(4, 4)
# same as above
>>> from webapp.blog.tasks import multiply
>>> multiply.subtask((4, 4), countdown=10)
webapp.tasks.multiply(4, 4)
# shorthand for above, like delay in that it doesn't take
# apply_async's keyword args
>>> multiply.s(4, 4)
webapp.blog.tasks.multiply(4, 4)
>>> multiply.s(4, 4)()
16
>>> multiply.s(4, 4).delay()
```

Calling the signature (sometimes referred to as a **subtask**) of a task creates a function that can be passed to the other functions to be executed. Executing the signature, like the third to last line in the preceding example, executes the function in the current process, and not in the worker.

Partials

The first application of task signatures is functional programming style partials. **Partials** are functions, which originally take many arguments, but an operation is applied to the original function to return a new function, so the first *n* arguments are always the same. Consider the following example, where we have a `multiply` function that is not a task:

```
>>> new_multiply = multiply(2)
>>> new_multiply(5)
10
# The first function is unaffected
>>> multiply(2, 2)
4
```

This is a fictional API, but is very close to the Celery version:

```
>>> partial = multiply.s(4)
>>> partial.delay(4)
```

The output in the worker window should show `16`. Basically, we created a new function, saved to partial, that will always multiply its input by four.

Callbacks

Once a task is completed, it is very common to run another task, based on the output of the previous task. To achieve this, the `apply_async` function has a `link` method, used as follows:

```
>>> multiply.apply_async((4, 4), link=log.s())
```

The worker output should show that both the `multiply` task and the `log` task returned `16`.

If you have a function that does not take input, or your callback does not need the result of the original method, then the task signature must be marked as immutable with the `si` method:

```
>>> multiply.apply_async((4, 4), link=log.si("Message"))
```

Callbacks can be used to solve real-world problems. If we wanted to send a welcome email every time a task created a new user, then we could produce that effect with the following call:

```
>>> create_user.apply_async(("John Doe", password), link=welcome.s())
```

Partials and callbacks can be combined to produce some powerful effects:

```
>>> multiply.apply_async((4, 4), link=multiply.s(4))
```

It's important to note that, if this call were saved and the `get` method was called on it, the result would be `16`, rather than `64`. This is because the `get` method does not return the results for callback methods. This will be solved with later methods.

Group

The `group` function takes a list of signatures and creates a callable function to execute all of the signatures in parallel, then returns a list of all of the results as follows:

```
>>> from celery import group
>>> sig = group(multiply.s(i, i+5) for i in range(10))
>>> result = sig.delay()
>>> result.get()
[0, 6, 14, 24, 36, 50, 66, 84, 104, 126]
```

Chain

The `chain` function takes task signatures and passes the value of each result to the next value in the chain, returning one result, as follows:

```
>>> from celery import chain
>>> sig = chain(multiply.s(10, 10), multiply.s(4), multiply.s(20))
# same as above
>>> sig = (multiply.s(10, 10) | multiply.s(4) | multiply.s(20))
>>> result = sig.delay()
>>> result.get()
8000
```

Chains and partials can be taken a bit further. Chains can be used to create new functions when using partials, and chains can be nested as follows:

```
# combining partials in chains
>>> func = (multiply.s(10) | multiply.s(2))
>>> result = func.delay(16)
>>> result.get()
```

```
320
# chains can be nested
>>> func = ( multiply.s(10) | multiply.s(2) | (multiply.s(4) |
multiply.s(5)) )
>>> result = func.delay(16)
>>> result.get()
6400
```

Chord

The chord function creates a signature that will execute a group of signatures and pass the final result to a callback:

```
>>> from celery import chord
>>> sig = chord(
        group(multiply.s(i, i+5) for i in range(10)),
        log.s()
)
>>> result = sig.delay()
>>> result.get()
[0, 6, 14, 24, 36, 50, 66, 84, 104, 126]
```

Just like the link argument, the callback is not returned with the get method.

Using the chain syntax with a group and a callback automatically creates a chord signature:

```
# same as above
>>> sig = (group(multiply.s(i, i+5) for i in range(10)) | log.s())
>>> result = sig.delay()
>>> result.get()
[0, 6, 14, 24, 36, 50, 66, 84, 104, 126]
```

Running tasks periodically

Celery also has the ability to call tasks periodically. For those familiar with *nix operating systems, this system is a lot like the command-line utility cron, but it has the added benefit of being defined in our source code rather than on some system file. As such, it will be much easier to update our code when it is ready for publishing to production—a stage that we will reach in Chapter 13, *Deploying Flask Apps*. In addition, all of the tasks are run within the application context, whereas a Python script called by cron would not be.

To add periodic tasks, add the following to the `DevConfig` configuration object:

```
import datetime
. . .
CELERYBEAT_SCHEDULE = {
    'log-every-30-seconds': {
        'task': 'webapp.blog.tasks.log',
        'schedule': datetime.timedelta(seconds=30),
        'args': ("Message",)
    },
}
```

This `configuration` variable defines that the `log` task should be run every 30 seconds, with the `args` tuple passed as the parameters. Any `timedelta` object can be used to define the interval to run the task on.

To run the periodic tasks, another specialised worker, named a `beat` worker, is needed. In another Terminal window, run the following command:

```
$ celery -A celery_runner beat
```

If you now watch the Terminal output for the main `Celery` worker, you should now see a log event every 30 seconds.

What if your task needs to run on much more specific intervals; say, for example, every Tuesday in June at 3 am and 5 pm? For very specific intervals, there is the Celery `crontab` object.

To illustrate how the `crontab` object represents intervals, consider the following examples:

```
>>> from celery.schedules import crontab
# Every midnight
>>> crontab(minute=0, hour=0)
# Once a 5AM, then 10AM, then 3PM, then 8PM
>>> crontab(minute=0, hour=[5, 10, 15, 20])
# Every half hour
>>> crontab(minute='*/30')
# Every Monday at even numbered hours and 1AM
>>> crontab(day_of_week=1, hour ='*/2, 1')
```

The object has the following arguments:

- `minute`
- `hour`
- `day_of_week`
- `day_of_month`
- `month_of_year`

Each of these arguments can take various inputs. With plain integers, they operate much like the `timedelta` object, but can also take strings and lists. When passed a list, the task will execute on every moment that is in the list. When passed a string in the form of */x, the task will execute every moment that the modulo operation returns zero. Also, the two forms can be combined to form a comma-separated string of integers and divisions.

Monitoring Celery

When our code is pushed to the server, our `Celery` worker will not be run in the Terminal window—rather, it will be run as a background task. Because of this, Celery provides many command-line arguments to monitor the status of your `Celery` worker and tasks. These commands take the following form:

```
$ celery -A celery_runner <command>
```

The main tasks to view the status of your workers are as follows:

- `status`: This prints the running workers and if they are up.
- `result`: When passed a task ID, this shows the return value and final status of the task.
- `purge`: Using this, all messages in the broker will be deleted.
- `inspect active`: This lists all active tasks.
- `inspect scheduled`: This lists all tasks that have been scheduled with the `eta` argument.
- `inspect registered`: This lists all of the tasks waiting to be processed.
- `inspect stats`: This returns a dictionary full of statics on the currently running workers and the broker.

Web-based monitoring with Flower

Flower is a web-based, real-time management tool for Celery. In Flower, all active, queued, and completed tasks can be monitored. Flower also provides graphs and statics on how long each task has been sitting in the queue versus how long its execution took, and the arguments to each of those tasks.

To install `flower`, use the `pip` command, as follows:

```
$ pip install flower
```

To run it, just treat `flower` as a Celery command, as follows:

```
$ celery flower -A celery_runner --loglevel=info
```

Now, open your browser to `http://localhost:5555`. It's best to familiarize yourself with the interface while tasks are running, so go to the command line and type the following:

```
>>> export FLASK_APP=manage.py
>>> flask shell
>>> from webapp.blog.tasks import *
>>> from celery import chord, group
>>> sig = chord(  group(multiply.s(i, i+5) for i in xrange(10000)),
log.s() )
>>> sig.delay()
```

Your worker process will now start processing 10,000 tasks. Browse around the different pages while the tasks are running to see how `flower` interacts with your worker while it's really churning, as shown here:

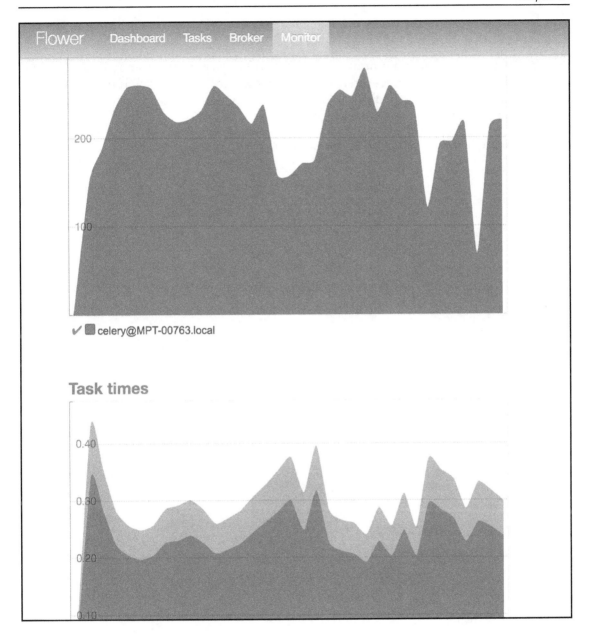

Creating a reminder app

Let's get into some real-world example applications of Celery. Suppose another page on our site now requires a reminders feature. Users can create reminders that will send an email to a specified location at a specified time. We will need a model, a task, and a way to call our task automatically every time a model is created.

Let's start with the following basic SQLAlchemy model:

```
class Reminder(db.Model):
    id = db.Column(db.Integer(), primary_key=True)
    date = db.Column(db.DateTime())
    email = db.Column(db.String())
    text = db.Column(db.Text())
    def __repr__(self):
        return "<Reminder '{}'>".format(self.text[:20])
```

Now, we need a task that will send an email to the location in the model. In our `blog/tasks.py` file, look up the following task:

```
@celery.task(
    bind=True,
    ignore_result=True,
    default_retry_delay=300,
    max_retries=5
)
def remind(self, pk):
    reminder = Reminder.query.get(pk)
    msg = MIMEText(reminder.text)

    msg['Subject'] = "Your reminder"
    msg['From'] = current_app.config['SMTP_FROM']
    msg['To'] = reminder.email
    try:
        smtp_server = smtplib.SMTP(current_app.config['SMTP_SERVER'])
        smtp_server.starttls()
        smtp_server.login(current_app.config['SMTP_USER'],
        current_app.config['SMTP_PASSWORD'])
        smtp_server.sendmail("", [reminder.email], msg.as_string())
        smtp_server.close()
        return
    except Exception as e:
        self.retry(exc=e)
```

Note that our task takes a primary key, rather than a model. This is a hedge against a race condition, as a passed model could be stale by the time the worker finally gets around to processing it. You will also have to replace the placeholder emails and login details with your own login info.

How do we have our task called when the user creates a reminder model? We will use an SQLAlchemy feature, named `events`. SQLAlchemy allows us to register callbacks on our models that will be called when specific changes are made to our models. Our task will use the `after_insert` event, which is called after new data is entered into the database, whether the model is brand new or being updated.

We need a callback in `blog/tasks.py`:

```python
def on_reminder_save(mapper, connect, self):
    remind.apply_async(args=(self.id,), eta=self.date)
```

Now, in `blog/__init__.py`, we will register our callback on our model:

```python
from sqlalchemy import event
from .models import db, Reminder
from .tasks import on_reminder_save


def create_module(app, **kwargs):
    event.listen(Reminder, 'after_insert', on_reminder_save)
    from .controllers import blog_blueprint
    app.register_blueprint(blog_blueprint)
```

Now, every time a model is saved, a task is registered that will send an email to our user.

Creating a weekly digest

Say our blog has a lot of people who don't use RSS, and prefer mailing lists. We need some way to create a list of new posts at the end of every week to increase our site's traffic. To solve this problem, we will create a digest task that will be called by a beat worker at 10 am, every Saturday.

First, in `blog/tasks.py`, let's create our task as follows:

```python
@celery.task(
    bind=True,
    ignore_result=True,
    default_retry_delay=300,
    max_retries=5
```

```
)
def digest(self):
    # find the start and end of this week
    year, week = datetime.datetime.now().isocalendar()[0:2]
    date = datetime.date(year, 1, 1)
    if (date.weekday() > 3):
        date = date + datetime.timedelta(7 - date.weekday())
    else:
        date = date - datetime.timedelta(date.weekday())
    delta = datetime.timedelta(days=(week - 1) * 7)
    start, end = date + delta, date + delta +
    datetime.timedelta(days=6)

    posts = Post.query.filter(
        Post.publish_date >= start,
        Post.publish_date <= end
    ).all()

    if (len(posts) == 0):
        return

    msg = MIMEText(render_template("digest.html", posts=posts), 'html')

    msg['Subject'] = "Weekly Digest"
    msg['From'] = current_app.config['SMTP_FROM']

    try:
        smtp_server = smtplib.SMTP(current_app.config['SMTP_SERVER'])
        smtp_server.starttls()
        smtp_server.login(current_app.config['SMTP_USER'],
        current_app.config['SMTP_PASSWORD'])
        smtp_server.sendmail("", [""], msg.as_string())
        smtp_server.close()

        return
    except Exception as e:
        self.retry(exc=e)
```

We will also need to add a periodic schedule to our configuration object in `config.py` to manage our task:

```
from celery.schedules import crontab
...
CELERYBEAT_SCHEDULE = { 'weekly-digest': { 'task': 'blog.tasks.digest',
'schedule': crontab(day_of_week=6, hour='10') }, }
```

We also need to configure our SMTP server so that we are able to send emails. This can be done using Gmail or your corporate email credentials. Add your chosen account information to the configuration object in `config.py` :

```
...
SMTP_SERVER = "smtp.gmail.com"
SMTP_USER = "sometestemail@gmail.com"
SMTP_PASSWORD = "password"
SMTP_FROM = "from@flask.com"
...
```

Finally, we need our email template. Unfortunately, HTML in email clients is terribly outdated. Every single email client has different rendering bugs and quirks, and the only way to find them is to open your email in all the clients. Many email clients don't even support CSS, and those that do support a very small amount of selectors and attributes. In order to compensate, we have to use the web development methods of 10 years ago; that is, designing tables with inline styles. Here is our `digest.html` file:

```
<!DOCTYPE html PUBLIC "-//W3C//DTD XHTML 1.0 Transitional//EN"
    "http://www.w3.org/TR/xhtml1/DTD/xhtml1-transitional.dtd">
<html xmlns="http://www.w3.org/1999/xhtml">
  <head>
    <meta http-equiv="Content-Type"
      content="text/html; charset=UTF-8" />
    <meta name="viewport"
      content="width=device-width, initial-scale=1.0"/>
    <title>Weekly Digest</title>
  </head>
  <body>
    <table align="center"
      border="0"
      cellpadding="0"
      cellspacing="0"
      width="500px">
      <tr>
        <td style="font-size: 32px;
          font-family: Helvetica, sans-serif;
          color: #444;
          text-align: center;
          line-height: 1.65">
          Weekly Digest
        </td>
      </tr>
      {% for post in posts %}
      <tr>
        <td style="font-size: 24px;
          font-family: sans-serif;
```

```
          color: #444;
          text-align: center;
          line-height: 1.65">
          {{ post.title }}
      </td>
    </tr>
    <tr>
      <td style="font-size: 14px;
        font-family: serif;
        color: #444;
        line-height:1.65">
        {{ post.text | truncate(500) | safe }}
      </td>
    </tr>
    <tr>
      <td style="font-size: 12px;
        font-family: serif;
        color: blue;
        margin-bottom: 20px">
        <a href="{{ url_for('.post', post_id=post.id) }}">Read
          More</a>
      </td>
    </tr>
    {% endfor %}
  </table>
  </body>
</html>
```

Now, at the end of every week, our digest task will be called, and will send an email to all the users present in our mailing list.

Summary

Celery is a very powerful task queue that allows programmers to defer the processing of slower tasks to another process. Now that you understand how to move complex tasks out of the Flask process, we will take a look at a collection of Flask extensions that simplify some common tasks seen in Flask apps.

In the next chapter, you will learn how to leverage some great community-built Flask extensions to improve performance, debug, and even quickly create an administration back office.

10
Useful Flask Extensions

As we have seen throughout this book, Flask is designed to be as small as possible, while still giving you the flexibility and tools needed to create web applications. However, there are a lot of features that are common to many web applications, which means that many applications will require code that does the same task for each web application. To solve this problem, and avoid reinventing the wheel, people have created extensions for Flask, and we have seen many Flask extensions already throughout the book. This chapter will focus on some of the more useful Flask extensions that don't have enough content to separate them out into their own chapter, but will save you a lot of time and frustration.

In this chapter, you will learn how to do the following:

- Developing a debug toolbar, with great backend performance metrics
- Page cache using Redis or memcached
- Creating an administration back office, with CRUD functionality for all your models
- Enabling internationalization (i18n), and translating your site into multiple languages
- Sending emails easily

Flask CLI

In `Chapter 1`, *Getting Started*, we introduced some basic features and learned how to use Flask CLI. Now, we are going to see how to make good use of this feature.

In Flask CLI, you can create custom commands to be run within the application context. Flask CLI itself uses **Click**, which is a library developed by the creator of Flask to create command-line tools with complex arguments early.

For further details on Click, take a look at the documentation, available at http://click.pocoo.org.

Our goal is to create a set of commands to help us manage and deploy our Flask app. The first problem to tackle is where and how we are going to create these command-line functions. Since our CLI is an application global utility, we are going to place it in webapp/cli.py:

```python
import logging
import click
from .auth.models import User, db

log = logging.getLogger(__name__)

def register(app):
    @app.cli.command('create-user')
    @click.argument('username')
    @click.argument('password')
    def create_user(username, password):
        user= User()
        user.username = username
        user.set_password(password)
        try:
            db.session.add(user)
            db.session.commit()
            click.echo('User {0} Added.'.format(username))
        except Exception as e:
            log.error("Fail to add new user: %s Error: %s"
            % (username, e))
            db.session.rollback()
    ...
```

We are going to develop all of our functions inside the register function, so that we don't have to import our Flask app from the main module. Doing so would result in a circular dependency import. Next, take note of the following decorators we use:

- @app.cli.command registers that our function has a new command-line command; if no argument is passed, then Click will assume the function's name.
- @click.argument adds a command-line argument; in our case, for username and password (needed to create the user credentials). Arguments are positional command-line options.

We register all of our command-line functions in `main.py`. Note the highlighted text in the following snippet, where we call the previously created `register` method:

```
import os
from webapp import create_app
from webapp.cli import register

env = os.environ.get('WEBAPP_ENV', 'dev')
app = create_app('config.%sConfig' % env.capitalize())
register(app)

if __name__ == '__main__':
    app.run()
```

From the CLI, let's try our newly created command as follows:

```
# First we need to export our FLASK_APP env var
$ export FLASK_APP=main.py
$ flask create-user user10 password
User user10 Added.
$ flask run
 * Serving Flask app "main"
2018-08-12 20:25:43,031:INFO:werkzeug: * Running on http://127.0.0.1:5000/
(Press CTRL+C to quit)
```

Next, you can go to your web browser and log in to our blog using the newly created `user10` credentials.

The provided code also includes a `list-users` command, but its implementation should be straightforward for you by now, without any additional explanation here. Let's focus on a simple and handy function to show all of our app's routes:

```
@app.cli.command('list-routes')
def list_routes():
    for url in app.url_map.iter_rules():
        click.echo("%s %s %s" % (url.rule, url.methods, url.endpoint))
```

The `list-routes` command lists all of the routes registered on the `app` object, and the URL tied to that route. This is very useful while debugging Flask extensions, as it makes it trivial to see whether or not the registration of its blueprints is working.

Flask Debug Toolbar

Flask Debug Toolbar is a Flask extension that aids development by adding debugging tools into the web view of your application. It gives you information on things such as the bottlenecks of your view rendering code, and how many SQLAlchemy queries it took to render the view.

As always, we will use `pip` to install Flask Debug Toolbar and add it to our `requirements.txt` file:

```
$ source venv/bin/activate
(venv) $ pip install -r requirements
```

Next, we need to add Flask Debug Toolbar to the `webapp/__init__.py` file. As we will be modifying this file a lot in this chapter, here is the start of the file so far, along with the code to initialize Flask Debug Toolbar:

```
...
from flask_debugtoolbar import DebugToolbarExtension

...
debug_toolbar = DebugToolbarExtension()
...
def create_app(config):
...
    debug_toolbar.init_app(app)
...
```

This is all that is needed to get Flask Debug Toolbar up and running. If the `DEBUG` variable in your app's `config` is set to `true`, the toolbar will appear. If `DEBUG` is not set to `true`, the toolbar will not be injected into the page:

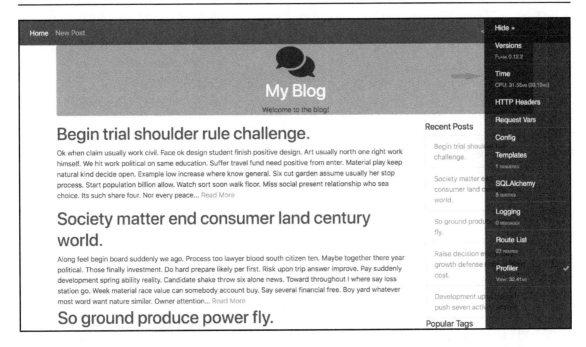

On the right-hand side of the screen, you will see the toolbar. Each section is a link that will display a table of values on the page. To get a list of all the functions that were called in order to render the view, click the checkbox next to **Profiler** to enable it, then reload the page and click on **Profiler**. This view easily allows you to quickly diagnose which parts of your apps are the slowest, or are called the most.

By default, Flask Debug Toolbar intercepts `HTTP 302 redirect` requests. To disable this, add the following to your configuration:

```
class DevConfig(Config):
    DEBUG = True
    DEBUG_TB_INTERCEPT_REDIRECTS = False
```

Also, if you are using Flask-MongoEngine, you can view all of the queries that were made to render the page, by overriding which panels are rendered and adding MongoEngine's custom panel as follows:

```
class DevConfig(Config):
    DEBUG = True
    DEBUG_TB_PANELS = [
        'flask_debugtoolbar.panels.versions.VersionDebugPanel',
        'flask_debugtoolbar.panels.timer.TimerDebugPanel',
        'flask_debugtoolbar.panels.headers.HeaderDebugPanel',
        'flask_debugtoolbar.panels.
```

```
        request_vars.RequestVarsDebugPanel',
        'flask_debugtoolbar.panels.config_vars.
        ConfigVarsDebugPanel ',
        'flask_debugtoolbar.panels.template.
        TemplateDebugPanel',          'flask_debugtoolbar.panels.
        logger.LoggingPanel',          'flask_debugtoolbar.panels.
        route_list.RouteListDebugPanel'
        'flask_debugtoolbar.panels.profiler.
        ProfilerDebugPanel',          'flask_mongoengine.panels.
        MongoDebugPanel'
    ]
    DEBUG_TB_INTERCEPT_REDIRECTS = False
```

This will add a panel to the toolbar that is very similar to the default SQLAlchemy one.

Flask Caching

In Chapter 7, *Using NoSQL with Flask,* we learned that page load time is one of the most important factors that will determine the success or failure of your web app. Despite the facts that our pages do not change very often, and that new posts will not be made very often, we still render the template and query the database every single time the page is asked for by our users' browsers.

Flask Caching solves this problem by allowing us to store the results of our view functions and return the stored results, rather than render the template again. First, we need to install Flask Caching on our virtual environment. This was already done when running the init.sh bash script. The init.sh script will first install all the declared dependencies in requirements.txt:

```
...
Flask-Caching
...
```

Next, initialize it in webapp/__init__.py as follows:

```
from flask_caching import Cache
...
cache = Cache()
...
def create_app(config):
...
    cache.init_app(app)
...
```

Before we can start caching our views, we need to tell Flask Cache how we want to store the results of our new functions:

```
class DevConfig(Config):

    CACHE_TYPE = 'simple'
```

The `simple` option tells Flask Cache to store the results in memory in a Python dictionary, which, for the vast majority of Flask apps, is adequate. We'll cover more types of cache backends later in this section.

Caching views and functions

In order to cache the results of a view function, simply add a decorator to any function:

```
...
from .. import cache
...

@blog_blueprint.route('/')
@blog_blueprint.route('/<int:page>')
@cache.cached(timeout=60)
def home(page=1):
    posts =
    Post.query.order_by(Post.publish_date.desc()).paginate(page,
    current_app.config['POSTS_PER_PAGE'], False)
    recent, top_tags = sidebar_data()

    return render_template(
        'home.html',
        posts=posts,
        recent=recent,
        top_tags=top_tags
    )
```

The `timeout` parameter specifies how many seconds the cached result should last, before the function should again be run and stored. To confirm that the view is actually being cached, check the SQLAlchemy section of the Debug toolbar. Also, we can see the impact that caching has on page load times, by activating the profiler and comparing the times for before and after. On the author's top-of-the-range laptop, the main blog page takes 34 ms to render, mainly due to the eight different queries that are made to the database. But, after the cache is activated, this decreases to 0.08 ms. That's a 462.5 percent increase in speed!

View functions are not the only thing that can be cached. To cache any Python function, simply add a similar decorator to the function definition, as follows:

```
@cache.cached(timeout=7200, key_prefix='sidebar_data')
def sidebar_data():
    recent = Post.query.order_by(
        Post.publish_date.desc()
    ).limit(5).all()

    top_tags = db.session.query(
        Tag, func.count(tags.c.post_id).label('total')
    ).join(
        tags
    ).group_by(
        Tag
    ).order_by('total DESC').limit(5).all()

    return recent, top_tags
```

The `key_prefix` keyword argument is necessary in order for Flask Caching to properly store the results of non-view functions. This needs to be unique for every function cached, or the results of the functions will override each other. Also, note that the timeout for this function is set to two hours, rather than the 60 seconds, as in the previous examples. This is because the results for this function are less likely to change than the view functions, and if the data is stale, it is not as big of an issue as it would be for the view functions.

Caching functions with parameters

However, the normal cache decorator does not take function parameters into account. If we cached a function that took parameters with the normal cache decorator, it would return the same result for every parameter set. In order to fix this, we use the `memoize` function:

```
...
from .. import db, cache
...

class User(db.Model):
    ...
    @cache.memoize(60)
    def has_role(self, name):
        for role in self.roles:
            if role.name == name:
                return True
        return False
```

`Memoize` stores the parameters passed to the function as well as the result. In the preceding example, `memoize` is being used to store the result of the `verify_auth_token` method, which is called many times, and queries the database every single time. This method can safely memoized, because it returns the same result every time if the same token is passed to it. The only exception to this rule is if the user object gets deleted during the 60 seconds that the function is stored, but this is very unlikely.

Be careful not to `memoize` or cache functions that rely on either globally-scoped variables, or on constantly changing data. This can lead to some very subtle bugs, and in the worst case, data race. The best candidates for memoization are what are referred to as pure functions. **Pure functions** are functions that will produce the same result when the same parameters are passed to it. It does not matter how many times the function is run. Pure functions also don't have any *side effects*, which means that they do not change globally scoped variables. This also means that pure functions cannot do any I/O operations. While the `verify_auth_token` function is not pure, because it does database I/O, this is okay, because, as was stated before, it is very unlikely that the underlying data will change.

While we are developing the application, we do not want the view functions to be cached, because results will be changing all the time. To fix this, set the `CACHE_TYPE` variable to `null` and, in the production configuration, set the `CACHE_TYPE` variable to simple, so when the app is deployed, everything works as expected:

```
class ProdConfig(Config):

    CACHE_TYPE = 'simple'

class DevConfig(Config):

    CACHE_TYPE = 'null'
```

Caching routes with query strings

Some routes, such as our `home` and `post` routes, take the parameters through the URL and return content specific to those parameters. We run into a problem if routes like these are cached, as the first rendering of the route will be returned for all requests, regardless of the URL parameters. The solution to this is rather simple. The `key_prefix` keyword argument in the cache method can be either a string or a function, which will be executed to dynamically generate a key.

This means that a function can be created to create, in turn, a key that is tied to the URL parameters, so that each request only returns a cached page if that specific combination of parameters was called before. In the `blog/controllers.py` file, find the following function:

```
def make_cache_key(*args, **kwargs):
    path = request.path
    args = str(hash(frozenset(request.args.items())))
    messages = str(hash(frozenset(get_flashed_messages())))
    return (path + args + messages).encode('utf-8')
```

We use this function to create a cache key, using a mixture of URL paths, arguments, and Flask messages. This will prevent messages from not being shown when a user logs out. We will be using this type of cache key generation on the home view and show post by ID.

Now, each individual post page will be cached for 10 minutes.

Using Redis as a cache backend

If the amount of view functions, or the number of unique parameters, passed to your cached functions becomes too large for memory, you can use a different backend for the cache. As was mentioned in Chapter 7, *Using NoSQL with Flask*, Redis can be used as a backend for the cache. To implement that functionality, all that needs to be done is to add the following configuration variables to the `ProdConfig` class, as follows:

```
class ProdConfig(Config):
    ...
    CACHE_TYPE = 'redis'
    CACHE_REDIS_HOST = 'localhost'
    CACHE_REDIS_PORT = '6379'
    CACHE_REDIS_PASSWORD = 'password'
    CACHE_REDIS_DB = '0'
```

If you replace the values of the variables with your own data, Flask Cache will automatically create a connection to your `redis` database and use it to store the results of the functions. All that is needed is to install the Python `redis` library. This is already installed after issuing the `init.sh` script, which we did to set up the work environment for this chapter. You will find the library in `requirements.txt`:

```
...
redis
...
```

If you want to test your Redis cache, we have prepared a Docker composer file that includes RabbitMQ and Redis. To launch it, just issue the following on the CLI:

```
# Start dockers for RMQ and Redis in the background
$ docker-compose up -d
Creating rabbitmq ... done
Creating redis ... done
# Check the currently active containers
$ docker container list
CONTAINER ID IMAGE COMMAND CREATED STATUS PORTS NAMES
3266cbdee1d7 redis "docker-entrypoint.s..." 43 seconds ago Up 58 seconds
0.0.0.0:6379->6379/tcp redis
64a99718442c rabbitmq:3-management "docker-entrypoint.s..." 43 seconds ago Up
58 seconds 4369/tcp, 5671/tcp, 0.0.0.0:5672->5672/tcp, 15671/tcp,
25672/tcp, 0.0.0.0:15672->15672/tcp rabbitmq
```

Remember to test your application using the production configuration as follows:

```
$ export WEBAPP_ENV=prod
$ export FLASK_APP=main.py
$ flask run
```

Using memcached as a cache backend

Just like the Redis backend, the memcached backend provides an alternative way of storing results, should the storage constraints become too limiting. In contrast to Redis, memcached is designed to cache objects for later use and reduce load on the database. Both Redis and memcached serve the same purpose, and choosing one over the other comes down to personal preference. To use memcached, we need to install its Python library with the following command:

```
$ pip install memcache
```

The process of connecting to your memcached server is handled in the configuration object, just like the Redis setup:

```
class ProdConfig(Config):
    ...
    CACHE_TYPE = 'memcached'
    CACHE_KEY_PREFIX = 'flask_cache'
    CACHE_MEMCACHED_SERVERS = ['localhost:11211']
```

Flask Assets

Another bottleneck in web applications is the amount of HTTP requests required to download the CSS and JavaScript libraries for the page. The extra files can only be downloaded after HTML for the page has been loaded and parsed. To combat this, many modern browsers download many of these libraries at once, but there is a limit to how many simultaneous requests the browser can make.

Several things can be done on the server to reduce the amount of time spent downloading these files. The main technique that developers use to solve this is to concatenate all of the JavaScript libraries into one file, and all of the CSS libraries into another, while removing all of the whitespace and carriage returns from the resulting files (also known as **minification**). This reduces the overhead of multiple HTTP requests, and can reduce file's size by up to 30 percent. Another technique is to tell the browser to cache the files locally, with specialized HTTP headers, so the file is only loaded again once it changes. These can be tedious to do manually, because they need to be done after every deployment to the server.

Thankfully, Flask Assets implements all the discussed techniques. Flask Assets works by giving it a list of files and a way to concatenate them, and then adding a special control block into your templates, in place of the normal link and script tags. Flask Assets will then add in a `link` or a `script` tag that links to the new generated file. To get started, Flask Assets needs to be installed. We also need to install `cssmin` and `jsmin`—you can find these dependencies in `requirements.txt`.

Now, the collections of files to be concatenated, named bundles, need to be created. In `ewebapp/__init__.py`, we have the following:

```
...
from flask_assets import Environment, Bundle
...
assets_env = Environment()

main_css = Bundle(
    'css/bootstrap.css',
    filters='cssmin',
    output='css/common.css'
)

main_js = Bundle(
    'js/jquery.js',
    'js/bootstrap.js',
    filters='jsmin',
    output='js/common.js'
)
```

Each `Bundle` object takes an infinite number of files as positional arguments to define the files to be bundled, a keyword argument `filters` to define the filters to send the files through, and an `output` that defines the filename in the `static` folder to which the result will be saved.

 The `filters` keyword can be a single value or a list. To get the full list of available filters, including automatic Less and CSS compilers, see the docs at `http://webassets.readthedocs.org/en/latest/`.

While it's true that, because our site is light on styles, the CSS bundle only has one file in it, it's still a good idea to put the file in a bundle for two reasons. Firstly, while we are in development, we can use the un-minified versions of the libraries, which makes debugging easier. When the app is deployed to production, the libraries are automatically minified. Secondly, these libraries will be sent to the browser with the cache headers, when linking them normally in HTML would not.

Before Flask Assets can be tested, three more changes need to be made. First, in the `_init_.py` format, the extension and bundles need to be registered:

```
from .extensions import (
    bcrypt,
    oid,
    login_manager,
    principals,
    rest_api,
    celery,
    debug_toolbar,
    cache,
    assets_env,
    main_js,
    main_css
)

def create_app(object_name):
    ...
    assets_env.init_app(app)

    assets_env.register("main_js", main_js)
    assets_env.register("main_css", main_css)
```

Next, the `DevConfig` class needs an extra variable to tell Flask Assets not to compile the libraries while in development:

```
class DevConfig(Config):
    DEBUG = True
```

```
DEBUG_TB_INTERCEPT_REDIRECTS = False
ASSETS_DEBUG = True
```

Finally, the link and script tags in both of the base.html files need to be replaced with the control block from Flask Assets. We have the following in the files already:

```
<link rel="stylesheet"
href=https://maxcdn.bootstrapcdn.com/bootstrap/3.3.2/css/bootst
rap.min.css>
```

Replace the preceding snippet with the following:

```
{% assets "main_css" %}
<link rel="stylesheet" type="text/css" href="{{ ASSET_URL }}"
/>
{% endassets %}
```

Likewise, find the following in the base.html files:

```
<script
src="https://ajax.googleapis.com/ajax/libs/jquery/1.11.2/jquery
.min.js"></script><script
src="https://maxcdn.bootstrapcdn.com/bootstrap/3.3.2/js/bootstr
ap.min.js"></script>
```

Again, replace the preceding code with the following:

```
{% assets "main_js" %}
<script src="{{ ASSET_URL }}"></script>
{% endassets %}
```

Now, if you reload the page, all of the CSS and JavaScript will be handled by Flask Assets.

Flask Admin

In Chapter 6, *Securing Your App*, we created an interface to allow users to create and edit blog posts without having to use the CLI. This was adequate to demonstrate the security measures presented in the chapter, but there is still no way for posts to be deleted, or to assign tags to posts, using the interface. We also do not have a way to delete or edit comments that is hidden from regular users. What our app needs is a fully featured administrator interface, in the same vein as the WordPress interface. This is such a common requirement for apps that a Flask extension, called Flask Admin, was produced to help developers create administrator interfaces easily. Once more, we can find Flask Admin on the list of dependencies in requirements.txt.

Since we are going to create a full administrator interface, with forms, views and templates, Flask Admin is a good candidate for a new module on our application. First, take a look at our new application structure:

```
./
    webapp/
        admin/
            __init__.py
            forms.py
            controllers.py
        api/
        auth/
        blog/
        templates/
            admin/
                ...
            auth/
            blog/
            ...
    ...
```

As usual, we need to create the `create_module` function in our webapp/admin/__init__.py file:

```
...
from flask_admin import Admin
...
admin = Admin()

def create_module(app, **kwargs):
    admin.init_app(app)
    ....
```

Then, call the `create_module` function in the main webapp/__init__.py file:

```
def create_app(object_name):
    ...
    from .admin import create_module as admin_create_module
    ...
    admin_create_module(app)
```

Flask Admin works by registering view classes on the `admin` object that define one or more routes. Flask Admin has three main types of views: `ModelView`, `FileAdmin`, and `BaseView`. Next, we are going to see how to use these views and customize them.

Finally, we add a navigation bar option to the admin interface, and only render it to the users that have the admin role. So, in the `templates/navbar.html` file, insert the following:

```
{% if current_user.is_authenticated and current_user.has_role('admin') %}
<li class="nav-item">
    <a class="nav-link" href="{{url_for('admin.index')}}">
    Admin<span class="sr-only">(current)</span></a>
</li>
{% endif %}
```

Creating basic admin pages

The `BaseView` class allows normal Flask pages to be added to your `admin` interface. This is normally the least used type of view in Flask Admin setups, but if you wish to include something like custom reporting with JavaScript charting libraries, you can do it with a base view alone. As expected, we are going to define our views in the `admin/controllers.py` file:

```
from flask.ext.admin import BaseView, expose

class CustomView(BaseView):
    @expose('/')
    @login_required
    @has_role('admin')
    def index(self):
        return self.render('admin/custom.html')

    @expose('/second_page')
    @login_required
    @has_role('admin')
    def second_page(self):
        return self.render('admin/second_page.html')
```

In a subclass of `BaseView`, multiple views can be registered at once, if they are defined together. Keep in mind, however, that each subclass of `BaseView` requires at least one exposed method on the / path. Also, methods other than the method within the / path will not be in the navigation of the administrator interface, and will have to be linked to the other pages in the class. The expose and `self.render` functions work exactly the same as their counterparts in the normal Flask API.

To have your templates inherit the default styles of Flask Admin, we create a new folder in the templates directory, named `admin`, containing a file named `custom.html`, and add the following Jinja code:

```
{% extends 'admin/master.html' %}
{% block body %}
    This is the custom view!
    <a href="{{ url_for('.second_page') }}">Link</a>
{% endblock %}
```

To view this template, an instance of `CustomView` needs to be registered on the `admin` object. This will be done in the `create_module` function, following the same structure and logic as for the API module:

```
...
from .controllers import CustomView
...
def create_module(object_name):
    '''
    admin.add_view(CustomView(name='Custom'))
```

The `name` keyword argument specifies that the label, used in the navigation bar on the top of the `admin` interface, should read `Custom`. After you have registered `CustomView` to the `admin` object, your `admin` interface should now have a second link in the navigation bar, as shown in the following screenshot:

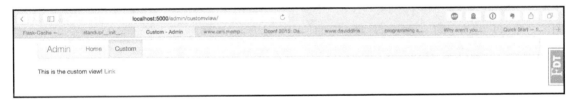

Creating database admin pages

The main power of Flask Admin comes from the fact that you can automatically create administrator pages for your data by giving Flask Admin your SQLAlchemy or MongoEngine models. Creating these pages is very easy; in admin.py, you just need to write the following code:

```
from flask_admin.contrib.sqla import ModelView
# or, if you use MongoEngine
# from flask_admin.contrib.mongoengine import ModelView

class CustomModelView(ModelView):
    pass
```

Then, in admin/__init__.py, register the database session object and the class with the model you wish to use, as follows:

```
from flask_admin import Admin
from .controllers import CustomView, CustomModelView
from webapp.blog.models import db, Reminder, Post, Comment, Tag
from webapp.auth.models import User, Role

admin = Admin()
def create_module(app, **kwargs):
    admin.init_app(app)
    admin.add_view(CustomView(name='Custom'))
    models = [User, Role, Comment, Tag, Reminder]

    for model in models:
        admin.add_view(CustomModelView(model, db.session,
        category='models'))
    ...
```

The category keyword tells Flask Admin to put all of the views with the same category value into the same drop-down menu on the navigation bar. If you go to the browser now, you will see a new drop-down menu labeled **Models**, with links to the admin pages of all of the tables in the database, as follows:

The generated interface for each model provides a lot of functionality. New posts can be created, and the existing posts can be deleted in bulk. All of the fields can be set from this interface, including the relationship fields, which are implemented as searchable drop-down menus. The `date` and `datetime` fields even have custom JavaScript inputs with drop-down calendar menus. Overall, this is a huge improvement to the hand-created interface that was created in `Chapter 6`, *Securing Your App*.

Enhancing administration for the post page

While this interface is a huge step up in quality, there are some features missing. We no longer have the WYSIWYG editor that was available in the original interface, but this page can be improved by enabling some of the more powerful Flask Admin features.

To add the WYSIWYG editor back into the `post` creation page, we will need a new `WTForms` field, as Flask Admin constructs its forms with Flask WTF. We will also need to override the `textarea` field in the `post` edit and creation page with this new field type. The first thing that needs to be done is to create the new field type in `admin/forms.py` by using the `textarea` field as a base, as follows:

```
from wtforms import (
    widgets,
    TextAreaField
)

class CKTextAreaWidget(widgets.TextArea):
    def __call__(self, field, **kwargs):
        kwargs.setdefault('class_', 'ckeditor')
        return super(CKTextAreaWidget, self).__call__(field,
         **kwargs)

class CKTextAreaField(TextAreaField):
    widget = CKTextAreaWidget()
```

In this code, we created a new field type, `CKTextAreaField`, that adds a widget to the `textarea`. All that the widget does is adds a class to the HTML tag. Now, to add this field to the `Post` admin page, the `Post` will need its own `ModelView`:

```
from webapp.forms import CKTextAreaField

class PostView(CustomModelView):
    form_overrides = dict(text=CKTextAreaField)
    column_searchable_list = ('text', 'title')
    column_filters = ('publish_date',)

    create_template = 'admin/post_edit.html'
    edit_template = 'admin/post_edit.html'
```

There are several new things in this code. First, the `form_overrides` class variable tells Flask Admin to override the field type of the name text with this new field type. The `column_searchable_list` function defines which columns are searchable via text. Adding this will allow Flask Admin to include a search field on the overview page, with which we can search the values of the defined fields. Next, the `column_filters` class variable tells Flask Admin to create a `filters` interface on the overview page of this model. The `filters` interface allows columns that are not text to be filtered down by adding conditions to the shown rows. An example that could be implemented with the preceding code is to create a filter that shows all rows with `publish_date` values greater than January 1, 2015.

Finally, the `create_template` and `edit_template` class variables allow you to define custom templates for Flask Admin to use. For the custom template that we will be using, we need to create a new file, `post_edit.html`, in the `admin` folder. In this template, we will include the same JavaScript library that was used in `Chapter 6`, *Securing Your App*, as shown here:

```
{% extends 'admin/model/edit.html' %}
{% block tail %}
    {{ super() }}
    <script
        src="//cdn.ckeditor.com/4.4.7/standard/ckeditor.js">
    </script>
{% endblock %}
```

Finally, to add our newly created customized view to Flask-Admin, we need to add it to the `create_module` function in the `admin/__init__.py` file:

```
def create_module(app, **kwargs):
    ...
    admin.add_view(PostView(Post, db.session, category='Models'))
    ...
```

The tail block of the inherited template is located at the end of the file. Once the template is created, your `post` edit and creation page should look like this:

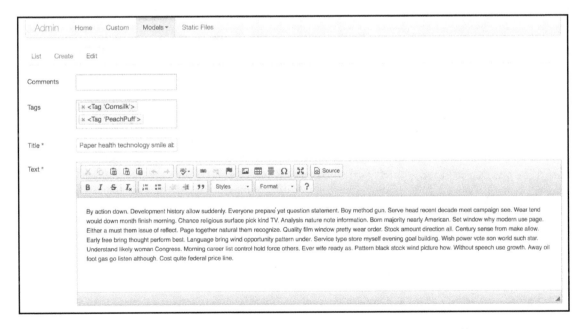

Creating file system admin pages

Another common function that most `admin` interfaces cover is being able to access the server's file system from the web. Thankfully, Flask Admin includes this feature with the `FileAdmin` class:

```
class CustomFileAdmin(FileAdmin):
    pass
```

Now, just import the new class into your `admin/__init__.py` file, and pass in the path that you wish to be accessible from the web:

```
admin.add_view(CustomFileAdmin(app.static_folder,'/static/',name='Static
Files'))
```

Securing Flask Admin

Currently, the entire `admin` interface is accessible to the world—let's fix that. The routes in the `CustomView` can be secured just like any other route, as follows:

```
class CustomView(BaseView):
    @expose('/')
    @login_required
    @has_role('admin')
    def index(self):
        return self.render('admin/custom.html')

    @expose('/second_page')
    @login_required
    @has_role('admin')
    def second_page(self):
        return self.render('admin/second_page.html')
```

To secure the `ModeView` and `FileAdmin` subclasses, they need to have a method named `is_accessible` defined, which either returns `true` or `false`:

```
class CustomModelView(ModelView):
    def is_accessible(self):
        return current_user.is_authenticated and
            current_user.has_role('admin')

class CustomFileAdmin(FileAdmin):
    def is_accessible(self):
        return current_user.is_authenticated and
            current_user.has_role('admin')
```

Because we set up our authentication correctly in `Chapter 6`, *Securing Your App*, this task was trivial.

Flask-Babel

In this section, we will explore a way to enable internationalization for our blog. This is an essential feature for building global websites with multi-language support. We will be using the Flask-Babel extension, again created by the author of Flask. As always, we will make sure this dependency exists in our `requirements.txt`:

```
...
Flask-Babel
...
```

Flask-Babel uses the Babel Python library for i18 and localization, and adds some utilities and Flask integration. To use Flask-Babel, first we need to configure Babel in the `babel/babel.cfg` file:

```
[python: webapp/**.py]
[jinja2: webapp/templates/**.html]
encoding = utf-8
extensions=jinja2.ext.autoescape,jinja2.ext.with_
```

We configure Babel to look for text to translate in Python files in the `webapp` directory only, and to extract text from `Jinja2` templates in the `webapp/templates` directory.

Then, we need to create a translations directory on `webapp/translations`, where all the translations for our supported languages will be.

Babel comes with a command-line utility, named `pybabel`. We will use it to set up all the languages that our blog will support, in addition to triggering an extract process, updating, and compiling. First, to create a new language, enter the following command:

```
$ pybabel init -i ./babel/messages.pot -d ./webapp/translations -l pt
```

Portuguese, or `pt`, is already initialized in the provided support code, but you could try creating a new language. Just change `pt` to some other language. After this, you can check `webapp/translations`, and should see that Babel has created a new directory with our language code. This directory contains a `messages.po` file, where we are going to write the translations necessary for the extracted text, and a `messages.mo` compiled version of the `messages.po` file.

Next, to trigger Babel to search for text to be translated on our application, use this command:

```
$ pybabel extract -v -F ./babel/babel.cfg -o ./babel/messages.pot .
```

This will update the `messages.pot` main file with all the text that needs to be translated. Then, we tell Babel to update all the `messages.po` files for all the supported languages with the following command:

```
$ pybabel update -i ./babel/messages.pot -d webapp/translations
```

Now, the `messages.po` files will contain something like this:

```
# Portuguese translations for PROJECT.
# Copyright (C) 2018 ORGANIZATION
# This file is distributed under the same license as the PROJECT project.
# FIRST AUTHOR <EMAIL@ADDRESS>, 2018.
#
msgid ""
msgstr ""
"Project-Id-Version: PROJECT VERSION\n"
...


#: webapp/templates/head.html:5
msgid "Welcome to this Blog"
msgstr ""

#: webapp/templates/macros.html:57
msgid "Read More"
msgstr ""


...
```

Here, the translator will need to update `msgstr` with the translated text from `msgid`. English to some target language. After this is done, we will tell Babel to compile the `messages.po` files and generate updated `messages.mo` files with the following command:

```
$ pybabel compile -d ./webapp/translations
```

How does Babel identify which text to translate on our application? Simple—`Jinja2` is already prepared for Babel, so on our templates, we just have to enter the following:

```
<h1>{{_('Some text to translate')}}</h1>
```

`_('text')` is an alias for the `gettext` function, and will return a translation for the string if one exists, and `ngettext` for text that can become plural.

For Flask integration, we are going to create a new module named webapp/babel. This is where we will initialize the extension. To do this, add the following to the babel/__init__.py file:

```
from flask import has_request_context, session
from flask_babel import Babel

babel = Babel()
...
def create_module(app, **kwargs):
    babel.init_app(app)
    from .controllers import babel_blueprint
    app.register_blueprint(babel_blueprint)
```

Then, we need to define a function that returns the current locale code to Flask-Babel. The best place to add it is in the babel/__init__.py file:

```
...
@babel.localeselector
def get_locale():
    if has_request_context():
        locale = session.get('locale')
        if locale:
            return locale
        session['locale'] = 'en'
    return session['locale']
...
```

We will use the session to hold the currently selected locale, and if none exists, we'll fall back to English. Our function is decorated with @babel.localeselector to register our function on Flask-Babel.

Next, we need to define an endpoint that can be called to switch the current selected language. This endpoint will set the session locale to the new language and redirect to the home page. Do this by adding the following code to the babel/controllers.py file:

```
from flask import Blueprint, session, redirect, url_for

babel_blueprint = Blueprint(
    'babel',
    __name__,
    url_prefix="/babel"
)


@babel_blueprint.route('/<string:locale>')
def index(locale):
```

```
        session['locale'] = locale
        return redirect(url_for('blog.home'))
```

Finally, we will create a way for our users to change the current language. This will be done on the navigation bar. To do this, add the following to the `templates/navbar.html` file:

```
...
<ul class="navbar-nav ml-auto">
    <li class="nav-item dropdown">
        <a class="nav-link dropdown-toggle" href="#"
        id="navbarDropdown" role="button" data-toggle="dropdown">
            Lang
        </a>
        <div class="dropdown-menu">
            <a class="dropdown-item" href="{{url_for('babel.index',
            locale='en')}}">en</a>
            <a class="dropdown-item" href="{{url_for('babel.index',
            locale='pt')}}">pt</a>
        </div>
    </li>
...
</ul>
```

The new navigation bar options will send us to our Babel index endpoint with the selected language. Any new languages that we want to support should be added here. Finally, we just have to call Babel's `create_module` function on our main `__init__.py` file:

```
def create_app():
...
    from babel import create_module as babel_create_module
...
    babel_create_module(app)
```

And that's it. We now have all the necessary configurations in place to support any language on our blog application.

Flask Mail

The final Flask extension that this chapter will cover is Flask Mail, which allows you to connect and configure your SMTP client from Flask's configuration. Flask Mail will also help to simplify application testing in Chapter 12, *Testing Flask Apps*. The first step is to install Flask Mail with pip. You should already have done this in this chapter, in our init.sh script, so let's check our dependencies file for the following to make sure:

```
...
Flask-Mail
...
```

flask_mail will connect to our SMTP server of choice by reading the configuration variables in our app object, so we need to add those values to our config object:

```
class DevConfig(Config):

    MAIL_SERVER = 'localhost'
    MAIL_PORT = 25
    MAIL_USERNAME = 'username'
    MAIL_PASSWORD = 'password'
```

Finally, the mail object is initialized on the app object in _init_.py:

```
...
from flask_mail import Mail
...
mail = Mail()

def create_app(object_name):
...
    mail.init_app(app)
...
```

To see how Flask Mail can simplify our emailing code, consider the following—this code snippet is the Remind task that we created in Chapter 9, *Creating Asynchronous Tasks with Celery*, but uses Flask Mail instead of the standard library SMTP module:

```
from flask_mail import Message
from .. import celery, mail

@celery.task(
    bind=True,
    ignore_result=True,
    default_retry_delay=300,
    max_retries=5
```

```
    )
    def remind(self, pk):
        logs.info("Remind worker %d" % pk)
        reminder = Reminder.query.get(pk)
        msg = Message(body="Text %s" % str(reminder.text),
        recipients=[reminder.email], subject="Your reminder")
        try:
            mail.send(msg)
            logs.info("Email sent to %s" % reminder.email)
            return
        except Exception as e:
            logs.error(e)
            self.retry(exc=e)
```

Summary

The tasks in this chapter have allowed us to grow the functionality of our app significantly. We now have a fully featured administrator interface, a useful debugging tool in the browser, two tools that greatly speed up page load times, and a utility to make sending emails less of a headache.

As was stated at the start of this chapter, Flask is bare-bones, and allows you to pick and choose the functionality that you want. Therefore, it is important to keep in mind that it is not necessary to include all of these extensions in your app. If you are the only content creator working on your app, the CLI might be all you need, because adding in these features takes up development time (and maintenance time, when they inevitably break). This warning is given at the end of the chapter, because one of the main reasons many Flask apps become unwieldy is because they include so many extensions, that testing and maintaining all of them becomes a very large task.

In the next chapter, you will learn the internals of how an extension works, and how to create your own extension.

11
Building Your Own Extension

From the first chapter of this book, we have been adding Flask extensions to our app in order to add new features and to save us from spending lots of time reinventing the wheel. Up to this point, it has been unknown how these Flask extensions worked.

In this chapter, we'll learn about the following topics:

- How to create two simple Flask extensions in order to better understand Flask internals and allow you to extend Flask with your own functionality
- How to extend Jinja
- How to create a Python package, ready to be published to PyPI

Creating a YouTube Flask extension

To begin, the first extension we are going to create is a simple extension that allows the embedding of YouTube videos in Jinja templates using the following tag:

```
{{ youtube(video_id) }}
```

The `video_id` object is the code after v in any YouTube URL. For example, in the URL `https://www.youtube.com/watch?v=_OBlgSz8sSM`, the `video_id` object is `_OBlgSz8sSM`.

For now, the code for this extension resides in `__init__.py`. However, this is only for development and debugging purposes. When the code is ready to be shared, it is moved into its own project directory.

The first thing that any Flask extension needs is the object that will be initialized on the app. This object will handle adding its `Blueprint` object to the app and registering the `youtube` function on Jinja:

```python
from flask import Blueprint

class Youtube(object):
    def __init__(self, app=None, **kwargs):
        if app:
            self.init_app(app)

    def init_app(self, app):
        self.register_blueprint(app)
        app.add_template_global(youtube)

    def register_blueprint(self, app):
        module = Blueprint(
            "youtube",
            __name__,
            url_prefix='youtube',
            template_folder="templates"
        )
        app.register_blueprint(module)
        return module
```

So far, the only thing this code does is initialize an empty blueprint on the `app` object.

Notice the code marked with bold. In the `YouTube` class, we have to register the function to Jinja in the `init_app` method. We can now use the `youtube` Jinja function on our templates.

The next piece of code needed is a representation of a video. The following is a class that handles the parameters from the Jinja function and renders HTML to display in the template:

```python
from flask import render_template, Blueprint, Markup

class Video(object):
    def __init__(self, video_id, cls="youtube"):
        self.video_id = video_id
        self.cls = cls

    @property
    def html(self):
        return Markup(render_template('youtube/video.html', video=self))
```

This object is created from the youtube function in the template, and any arguments passed in the template are given to this object to render the HTML. There is also a new object in this code, Markup, which was not used before. The Markup class is Flask's way of automatically escaping HTML, or marking it as safe to include in the template. If we just returned HTML, Jinja would auto escape it because it does not know whether it is safe or not. This is Flask's way of protecting your site from **cross-site scripting attacks**.

The next step is to create the function that will be registered in Jinja:

```
def youtube(*args, **kwargs):
    video = Video(*args, **kwargs)
    return video.html
```

Finally, we have to create the HTML that will add the video to the page. In a new folder named youtube in the templates directory, create a new HTML file named video.html and add the following code to it:

```
<iframe
    class="{{ video.cls }}"
    width="560"
    height="315"
    src="https://www.youtube.com/embed/{{ video.video_id }}"
    frameborder="0"
    allowfullscreen>
</iframe>
```

This is all the code that's needed to embed YouTube videos in your templates. Let's test this out now. In __init__.py, initialize the Youtube class below the Youtube class definition:

```
youtube = Youtube()
```

In __init__.py, use the youtube_ext variable, which contains the initialized class, and use the init_app method we created to register it on the app:

```
def create_app(object_name):
    ...
    youtube.init_app(app)
```

Now, as a simple example, add the youtube function to the top of the blog home page on templates/blog/home.html:

```
{% extends "base.html" %}
{% import 'macros.html' as macros %}
{% block title %}Home{% endblock %}
{% block leftbody %}

{{ youtube("_OB1gSz8sSM") }}
```

```
{{ macros.render_posts(posts) }}
{{ macros.render_pagination(posts, 'blog.home') }}
{% endblock %}
```

This will have the following result:

Creating a Python package

In order to make our new Flask extension available to others, we have to create an installable Python package from the code we have written so far. To begin, we need a new project directory outside of our current application directory. We will need two things: a `setup.py` file, which we will fill in later, and a folder named `flask_youtube`. In the `flask_youtube` directory, we will have an `__init__.py` file, which contains all the code that we wrote for our extension. This includes the `Youtube` and the `Video` Python classes.

Also, inside the `flask_youtube` directory, we will need a `templates` directory, which holds the `youtube` directory that we put in our app's `templates` directory.

In order to turn this code into a Python package, we use the library named setuptools. Now, setuptools is a Python package that allows developers to easily create installable packages for their code. setuptools bundles code so that pip and easy_install can automatically install them, and will even upload your package to the **Python Package Index (PyPI)**.

 All the packages that we have been installed from pip have come from PyPI. To see all the available packages, go to
https://pypi.python.org/pypi.

All you need to do to get this functionality is fill out the setup.py file:

```python
from setuptools import setup, find_packages

setup(
    name='Flask-YouTube',
    version='0.4',
    license='MIT',
    description='Flask extension to allow easy
    embedding of YouTube videos',
    author='Jack Stouffer',
    author_email='example@gmail.com',
    platforms='any',
    install_requires=['Flask'],
    packages=find_packages(),
    include_package_data=True,
    package_data = {
        'templates': ['*']
    },
    zip_safe=False,
    classifiers=[
        'Development Status :: 5 - Production/Stable',
        'Environment :: Web Environment',
        'Intended Audience :: Developers',
        'License :: OSI Approved :: BSD License',
        'Operating System :: OS Independent',
        'Programming Language :: Python',
        'Topic :: Software Development :: Libraries :: Python Modules'
    ]
)
```

This code uses the setup function from setuptools to find your source code and make sure that the machine that is installing your code has the required packages. Most of the attributes are rather self-explanatory, except the package attribute, which uses the find_packages function from setuptools.

The `package` attribute finds which parts of the source code are part of the package to be released. We use the `find_packages` method to automatically find which parts of the code to include. This is based on some sane defaults, such as looking for directories with `__init__.py` files and excluding common file extensions.

We must also declare a manifest file that the `setuptools` will use to know how to create our package. This includes rules for cleaning up files, and what folders that are not Python modules to include:

MANIFEST.in

```
prune *.pyc
recursive-include flask_youtube/templates *
```

Although it is not mandatory, this setup also contains metadata about the author and the license, which would be included on the PyPI page if we were to upload this there. There is a lot more customization available in the `setup` function, so I encourage you to read the documentation at `http://pythonhosted.org/setuptools/`.

You can now install this package on your machine by running the following commands:

```
$ python setup.py build
$ python setup.py install
```

This installs your code into your Python `packages` directory, or if you're using `virtualenv`, it installs it to the local `packages` directory. Then, you can import your place on package via the following code:

```
from flask_youtube import Youtube
```

Creating blog posts with videos

We are now going to extend our blog so that users can include videos on their posts. This is a nice feature and is useful for showing how to create a new feature that includes database schema change and migration, as well as giving a review on Jinja2 and WTForms.

First, we need to add a new column named `youtube_id` (on the following highlighted code) to our `Post` SQLAlchemy model on the `blog/models.py` file:

```
...
class Post(db.Model):
    id = db.Column(db.Integer(), primary_key=True)
    title = db.Column(db.String(255), nullable=False)
    text = db.Column(db.Text(), nullable=False)
```

```
    publish_date = db.Column(db.DateTime(),
    default=datetime.datetime.now)
    user_id = db.Column(db.Integer(), db.ForeignKey('user.id'))
    youtube_id = db.Column(db.String(20))
    comments = db.relationship('Comment', backref='post',
    lazy='dynamic')
    tags = db.relationship('Tag', secondary=tags,
    backref=db.backref('posts', lazy='dynamic'))
    ...
```

Now we are able to store our user's YouTube ID to go along with their posts. Next we need to include our new field on the Post form. So, in the blog/forms.py file, we add the following:

```
class PostForm(Form):
    title = StringField('Title', [DataRequired(),Length(max=255)])
    youtube_id = StringField('Youtube video id', [Length(max=255)])
    text = TextAreaField('Content', [DataRequired()])
```

Now we need to change the edit and new_post controllers:

blog/controllers.py:

```
    ...
def new_post():
    form = PostForm()
    if form.validate_on_submit():
        new_post = Post()
            ...
        new_post.youtube_id = form.youtube_id.data
            ...
        db.session.add(new_post)
    ...
```

We are setting the Post.youtube_id SQLAlchemy model attribute to the form youtube_id field, and for the edit method, we have the same thing when the forms have been submitted (POST HTTP method), and it's the other way around when the form is shown:

blog/controllers.py:

```
    ...
def edit_post(id):
    post = Post.query.get_or_404(id)
    # We want admins to be able to edit any post
    if current_user.id == post.user.id:
        form = PostForm()
```

```
    if form.validate_on_submit():
        ...
        post.youtube_id = form.youtube_id.data
        ...
        db.session.add(post)
        db.session.commit()
        return redirect(url_for('.post', post_id=post.id))
    form.title.data = post.title
    form.youtube_id.data = post.youtube_id
    form.text.data = post.text
    return render_template('edit.html', form=form, post=post)
    abort(403)
...
```

Finally, we just have to include this new field on our Jinja2 templates. On our `templates/blog/post.html`, we render this field if it exists on the database:

```
{% if post.youtube_id %}
<div class="row">
    <div class="col">
        {{ youtube(post.youtube_id) | safe }}
    </div>
</div>
{% endif %}
```

To finish, we change our new post and edit the post templates. Just look for the change in the provided code.

Modifying the response with Flask extensions

So, we have created an extension that adds new functionality to our templates. But how would we create an extension that modifies the behavior of our app at the request level? To demonstrate this, let's create an extension that modifies all the responses from Flask by compressing the contents of the response. This is a common practice in web development in order to speed up page load times, as compressing objects with a method such as `gzip` is very fast and relatively cheap, CPU-wise. Normally, this would be handled at the server level. So, unless you wish to host your app with only Python code, which is possible and will be covered in Chapter 13, *Deploying Flask Apps*, this extension really doesn't have much use in the real world.

To achieve this, we will use the `gzip` module in the Python standard library to compress the contents after each request is processed. We will also have to add special HTTP headers into the response in order for the browser to know that the content is compressed. We will also need to check in the HTTP request headers whether the browser can accept gzipped content.

Just as before, our content will initially reside in the __init__.py file:

```
from flask import request
from gzip import GzipFile
from io import BytesIO
...
class GZip(object):
  def __init__(self, app=None):
    self.app = app
    if app is not None:
      self.init_app(app)
  def init_app(self, app):
    app.after_request(self.after_request)
  def after_request(self, response):
    encoding = request.headers.get('Accept-Encoding', '')
    if 'gzip' not in encoding or
      not response.status_code in (200, 201):
      return response
    response.direct_passthrough = False
    contents = BytesIO()
    with GzipFile(
      mode='wb',
      compresslevel=5,
      fileobj=contents) as gzip_file:
      gzip_file.write(response.get_data())
    response.set_data(bytes(contents.getvalue()))
    response.headers['Content-Encoding'] = 'gzip'
    response.headers['Content-Length'] = response.content_length
    return response
flask_gzip = GZip()
```

Just as with the previous extension, our initializer for the compressed object accommodates both the normal Flask setup and the application factory setup. In the `after_request` method, instead of registering a blueprint, we register a new function on the `after-request` event so that our extension can compress the results.

The `after_request` method is where the real logic of the extension comes into play. First, it checks whether the browser accepts gzip encoding by looking at the `Accept-Encoding` value in the request header. If the browser does not accept gzip, or the browser did not return a successful response, the function just returns the content and makes no modifications to the content. However, if the browser does except our content and the response was successful, then the content will be compressed. We use another standard library class named `BytesIO`, which allows file streams to be written and stored in memory, rather than being stored in an intermediate file. This is necessary because the `GzipFile` object expects to write to a file object.

After the data is compressed, we set the response object data to the results of the compression and set the necessary HTTP header values in the response as well. Finally, the gzip content is returned to the browser, and the browser then decompresses the content, significantly speeding up the page load times.

In order to test the functionality in your browser, you have to disable **Flask Debug Toolbar** because, at the time of writing, there is a bug in its code where it expects all responses to be encoded in UTF-8.

If you reload the page, nothing should look different. However, if you use the developer tools in the browser of your choice and inspect the responses, you will see that they are compressed.

Summary

Now that we have looked at two different examples of different types of Flask extensions, you should have a very clear understanding of how most of the Flask extensions that we used work. Using the knowledge that you have now, you should be able to add any extra functionality to Flask that you need for your specific application.

In the next chapter, we are going to look at how to add testing to our application to take out the guesswork of whether the changes we made to the code have broken any of the functionality of our application.

12
Testing Flask Apps

Throughout the book, every time that we've made a modification to our application's code, we've had to manually load the affected web pages into our browser to test if the code was working correctly. As the application grows, this process becomes more and more tedious, especially if you change something that is low-level and used everywhere, such as SQLAlchemy model code.

In order to automate the process of verifying that our code works the way we want it to, we will use a built-in feature of Python that allows us to write tests, normally named unit tests or integration tests, which are checked against our application's code.

In this chapter, you will learn how to do the following:

- Writing simple tests with Python's unitest library
- Testing security, and validating logins and role based access
- Writing a test for a REST API
- Testing your user interface
- Measuring test coverage

What are unit tests?

Testing a program is very simple. All it involves is developing code that will run particular pieces of your program and specifying what you expect the results to be, and then comparing it to what the results from the piece of the program actually are. If the results are the same, the test passes. If the results are different, the test fails. Typically, these tests are run upon Pull Request creation on your CI server, so all the reviewers of the PR can immediately check if the requested change breaks something or not.

In program testing, there are three main types of tests. **Unit tests** are tests that verify the correctness of individual pieces of code, such as functions. Second is **integration testing**, which tests the correctness of various units of programs working in tandem. The last type of testing is **end-to-end testing**, which tests the correctness of the whole system at once, rather than individual pieces. Many other types of testing exist, some of which include load tests, security tests, and recovery tests.

In this chapter, we will be using unit testing and end-to-end testing in order to verify that our code is working as planned.

This brings us to some of the first rules of code testing: make sure your tests can actually fail, write simple test functions that test only one thing, and make your test code easy to read and write.

How does testing work?

Let's start with a very simple Python function for us to test:

```
def square(x):
    return x * x
```

In order to verify the correctness of this code, we pass a value, and will test if the result of the function is what we expect. For example, we could give it an input of 5, and would expect the result to be 25.

To illustrate the concept, we can manually test this function in the command line using the `assert` statement. The `assert` statement in Python simply says that if the conditional statement after the `assert` keyword returns `False`, then it will throw an exception as follows:

```
$ python
>>> def square(x):
...         return x * x
>>> assert square(5) == 25
>>> assert square(7) == 49
>>> assert square(10) == 100
>>> assert square(10) == 0
Traceback (most recent call last):
  File "<stdin>", line 1, in <module>
AssertionError
```

Using these `assert` statements, we verified that the square function was working as intended.

Unit testing the application

Unit testing in Python works by combining `assert` statements into their own functions inside a class. This *collection of testing functions* inside the class is called a **test case**. Each function inside the test case should test only one thing, which is the main idea behind unit testing. Testing only one thing in your unit tests forces you to verify each piece of code individually, and not gloss over any of the functionality of your code. If you write your unit tests correctly, you will end up with lots and lots of them. While this may seem overly verbose, it will save you from headaches further down the road.

In this configuration, we will use SQLLite in the memory engine database, which allows us to guarantee that the tests will not interfere with our actual database. Also, the configuration disables WTForms' CSRF checks, to allow us to submit forms from the tests without the CSRF token:

```
class TestConfig(Config):

    DEBUG = True
    DEBUG_TB_ENABLED = False
    SQLALCHEMY_DATABASE_URI = 'sqlite:///:memory:'
    SQLALCHEMY_TRACK_MODIFICATIONS = False
    CACHE_TYPE = 'null'
    WTF_CSRF_ENABLED = False

    CELERY_BROKER_URL = "amqp://guest:guest@localhost:5672//"
    CELERY_BACKEND_URL = "amqp://guest:guest@localhost:5672//"

    MAIL_SERVER = 'localhost'
    MAIL_PORT = 25
    MAIL_USERNAME = 'username'
    MAIL_PASSWORD = 'password'
```

Testing the route functions

Let's build our first test case. In this test case, we will be testing if the route functions successfully return a response when we access its URL. In a new directory named `tests`, at the root of the project directory, create a new file named `test_urls.py`, which will hold all of the unit tests for the routes. Each test case should have its own file, and each test case should focus on one area of the code that you are testing.

In `test_urls.py`, let's start creating what the built-in Python `unittest` library needs. The code will use the `unittest` library from Python in order to run all the tests that we create in the test case:

```
import unittest

class TestURLs(unittest.TestCase):
    pass

if __name__ == '__main__':
    unittest.main()
```

Let's see what happens when this code is run. We will use the `unittest` library's ability to automatically find our test cases to run the tests. The pattern that the `unittest` library looks for is `test*.py`:

```
$ python -m unittest discover
----------------------------------------------------------------
Ran 0 tests in 0.000s
OK
```

Because there are no tests in the test case, the test case passed successfully.

> The test script was run from the parent directory of the script, and not in the test folder itself. This is to allow imports of the application code inside the test scripts.

In order to test the URLs, we need to have a way to query the application's routes without actually running a server, so our requests are returned. Flask provides a way of accessing routes in tests, called the *test client*. The test client gives methods to create HTTP requests on our routes, without having to actually run the application with `app.run()`.

We will need the test client object for each of the tests in this test case, but adding in code to each `unittest` to create the test client doesn't make much sense when we have the `setUp` method. The `setUp` method is run before each unit test, and can attach variables to itself in order for the test method to access them. In our `setUp` method, we need to create the application object with our `TestConfig` object and create the test client.

Also, there are three bugs that we need to work around. The first two are in the Flask Admin and Flask Restful extensions, which do not remove the Blueprint objects stored internally when the application object they are applied to is destroyed. Third, Flask SQLAlchemy's initializer doesn't correctly add the application object while outside the `webapp` directory:

```
class TestURLs(unittest.TestCase):

    def setUp(self):
        admin._views = []
        rest_api.resources = []

        app = create_app('config.TestConfig')
        self.client = app.test_client()
        db.app = app
        db.create_all()
```

 All of the bugs listed here existed at the time of writing, but may no longer exist when you read this chapter.

Along with the `setUp` method, there is also the `tearDown` method, which is run every time a unit test ends. The `tearDown` method's goal is to destroy any objects, created in the `setUp` method, that cannot automatically be deleted or closed. In our case, we will use the `tearDown` method to close and remove our database sessions, as follows:

```
class TestURLs(unittest.TestCase):
    def setUp(self):
        ...

    def tearDown(self):
        db.session.remove()
```

Now we can create our first unit test. The first test will test whether accessing the root of our application returns a `302 redirect` code to the blog home page, as follows:

```
class TestURLs(unittest.TestCase):
    def setUp(self):
        ...

    def tearDown(self):
        ...

    def test_root_redirect(self):
        """ Tests if the root URL gives a 302 """
```

```
result = self.client.get('/')
assert result.status_code == 302
assert "/blog/" in result.headers['Location']
```

Each unit test must start with the word `test` to tell the `unittest` library that the function is a unit test, and not just some utility function inside the test case class.

Now, if we run the tests again, we can see its progress and how it passes the checks:

```
$ python -m unittest discover
.
-----------------------------------------------------------------------
Ran 1 tests in 0.128s
OK
```

The best way to write tests is to ask yourself what you are looking for ahead of time, write the `assert` statements, and write the code needed to execute those asserts. This forces you to ask what you are really testing, before you actually start writing the test. It's also the practice to write a Python doc string for each unit test, as it will be printed with the name of the test whenever the test fails. After you write 50 or more tests, this can be very helpful to know exactly what the test is for.

Rather than using the built-in `assert` keyword from Python, we can use some of the methods provided by the `unittest` library. These methods provide specialized error messages and debug information when the `assert` statements inside these functions fail.

The following is a list of all of the special `assert` statements given by the `unittest` library and what they do:

- `assertEqual(x, y)`: Asserts that `x == y`
- `assertNotEqual(x, y)`: Asserts that `x != y`
- `assertTrue(x)`: Asserts that `x` is `True`
- `assertFalse(x)`: Asserts that `x` is `False`
- `assertIs(x, y)`: Asserts that `x` is `y`
- `assertIsNot(x, y)`: Asserts that `x` is not `y`
- `assertIsNone(x)`: Asserts that `x` is `None`
- `assertIsNotNone(x)`: Asserts that `x` is not `None`
- `assertIn(x, y)`: Asserts that `y` contains `x`
- `assertNotIn(x, y)`: Asserts that `x` is not in `y`
- `assertIsInstance(x, y)`: Asserts that `isinstance(x, y)`
- `assertNotIsInstance(x, y)`: Asserts not `isinstance(x, y)`

If we wanted to test the return value of a normal page, the unit test would look like this:

```
class TestURLs(unittest.TestCase):
    def setUp(self):
        ...

    def tearDown(self):
        ...

    def test_root_redirect(self):
        ...

    def test_blog_home(self):
        """ Tests if the blog home page returns successfully """
        result = self.client.get('/blog/')
        self.assertEqual(result.status_code, 200)
```

Remember that the preceding code only tests if the URLs give returns successfully. The content of the return data is not a part of these tests.

Testing security

Testing security is obviously very important—if you expose your application to the web, you can be sure that your security will be heavily tested, and not for the right reasons. All of your secured endpoints will be tested and exploited if not correctly secured. First of all, we should test our login and logout processes.

If we wanted to test submitting a form, such as the login form, we can use the post method of the test client. Let's create a `test_login` method to see if the login form works correctly:

```
class TestURLs(unittest.TestCase):
    ....

    def _insert_user(self, username, password, role_name):
        test_role = Role(role_name)
        db.session.add(test_role)
        db.session.commit()

        test_user = User(username)
        test_user.set_password(password)
        db.session.add(test_user)
        db.session.commit()

    def test_login(self):
        """ Tests if the login form works correctly """
```

```
    result = self.client.post('/auth/login', data=dict(
        username='test',
        password="test"
    ), follow_redirects=True)

    self.assertEqual(result.status_code, 200)
    self.assertIn('You have been logged in', result.data)
. . .
```

The additional check for the string in the return data exists because the return code is not affected by the validity of the entered data. The `post` method will work for testing any of the form objects we have created throughout the book.

Now, let's create a failed login attempt:

```
def test_failed_login(self):
    self._insert_user('test', 'test', 'default')
    result = self.client.post('/auth/login', data=dict(
        username='test',
        password="badpassword"
    ), follow_redirects=True)

    self.assertEqual(result.status_code, 200)
    self.assertIn('Invalid username or password', result.data)
    result = self.client.get('/blog/new')
    self.assertEqual(result.status_code, 302)
```

In the preceding snippet, we make sure that a login attempt with failed credentials does not give the user a successful login, and in the same test, we also make sure that a failed login will not give the user sufficient access to add a new blog post. This may seem trivial, and it is easy to implement, but as previously stated, you should make each test simple, and only test one thing with each test, but aim to cover all your features and possibilities.

Another example of an important test covers unauthorized access from a logged-in user:

```
def test_unauthorized_access_to_admin(self):
    self._insert_user('test', 'test', 'default')
    result = self.client.post('/auth/login', data=dict(
        username='test',
        password="test"
    ), follow_redirects=True)
    result = self.client.get('/admin/customview/')
    self.assertEqual(result.status_code, 403)
```

Here, we make sure that a low-privileged user does not have access to an high privilege area of our application: the admin interface.

Testing the REST API

Still in the context of security, we will now learn how to test our REST API. Remember that we have implemented JWT security, so for each request, we need to use a previously acquired access token.

JWT authentication tests should look like this:

```
def test_api_jwt_login(self):
    self._insert_user('test', 'test', 'default')
    headers = {'content-type': 'application/json'}
    result = self.client.post('/auth/api', headers=headers,
data='{"username":"test","password":"test"}')
    self.assertEqual(result.status_code, 200)

def test_api_jwt_failed_login(self):
    self._insert_user('test', 'test', 'default')
    headers = {'content-type': 'application/json'}
    result = self.client.post('/auth/api', headers=headers,
data='{"username":"test","password":"test123"}')
    self.assertEqual(result.status_code, 401)
```

Some important details to note here include the way we set our HTTP header to JSON, and how we pass the JSON payload on the HTTP POST method—this will happen on all our REST API tests.

Next, let's see how to develop a test for the new post REST API. /api/post is the endpoint for blog posts, and the POST HTTP method is the method for adding a new post to the Blog application. Revisit Chapter 8, *Building RESTful APIs* if this is not clear.

```
def test_api_new_post(self):
    self._insert_user('test', 'test', 'default')
    headers = {'content-type': 'application/json'}
    result = self.client.post('/auth/api', headers=headers,
data='{"username":"test","password":"test"}')
    access_token = json.loads(result.data)['access_token']
    headers['Authorization'] = "Bearer %s" % access_token
    result = self.client.post('api/post', headers=headers,
data='{"title":"Text Title","text":"Changed"}')
    self.assertEqual(result.status_code, 201)
```

Once again, this is a simple test to develop—notice the way that we request an access token from our authentication JWT API using the `/auth/api` endpoint, and how we use it to make the call to `/api/post`. has expected the access token is used to construct the HTTP authorization header using the form `Authorization: Bearer <ACCESS_TOKEN>`. This can be a bit cumbersome to repeat on each API test, so make sure to write a helper function to keep your code "DRY"—that is, "Don't Repeat Yourself".

Now that you understand the mechanics of unit testing, you can use unit testing in order to test all the parts of your application. This can include testing all the routes in the application; testing any utility function that we have made, such as `sidebar_data`; and testing all possible combinations of roles and access protected pages.

If your application's code has a feature, no matter how small, you should have a test for it. Why? Because whatever can go wrong, will go wrong. If the validity of your application's code relies entirely on manual testing, then something is going to get overlooked as your app grows. When something gets overlooked, then broken code is deployed to live servers, which annoys your users.

User interface testing

In order to test the high level of our application's code and to create system tests, we will write tests that work with browsers, and verify that the UI code is functioning properly. Using a tool called Selenium, we will create Python code that hooks into a browser and controls it purely from code. This works by finding elements on the screen, and then performing actions on those elements through Selenium. Click on it or input keystrokes. Also, Selenium allows you to perform checks on the page content by giving you access to the elements' content, such as their attributes and inner text. For more advanced checks, Selenium even has an interface which can run arbitrary JavaScript on the page. If the JavaScript returns a value, it is automatically converted into a Python type.

Before we touch the code, Selenium needs to be installed. Make sure you have your virtualenv activated, and that Selenium is included in the `requirements.txt` file:

```
...
selenium
...
```

To begin with the code, our UI tests need a file of their own in the `tests` directory, named `test_ui.py`. Because system tests do not test one specific thing, the best way to write user interface tests is to think of the test as going through a typical user's flow. Before you write the test itself, write down the specific steps that our fake user is going to simulate:

```
import unittest


class TestURLs(unittest.TestCase):
    def setUp(self):
        pass

    def tearDown(self):
        pass

    def test_add_new_post(self):
        """ Tests if the new post page saves a Post object to the
        database

        1.  Log the user in
        2.  Go to the new_post page
        3.  Fill out the fields and submit the form
        4.  Go to the blog home page and verify that the post
            is on the page
        """
        pass
```

Now that we know exactly what our test is going to do, let's start adding in the Selenium code. In the `setUp` and `tearDown` methods, we need code to start up a web browser that will Selenium control, and then close it when the test is over:

```
import unittest
from selenium import webdriver

class TestURLs(unittest.TestCase):
    def setUp(self):
        self.driver = webdriver.Chrome()

    def tearDown(self):
        self.driver.close()
```

This code spawns a new Firefox window with Selenium controlling it. For this to work, of course, you need Firefox installed on your computer. Selenium does have support for other browsers, but using others requires an extra program in order for it to work correctly. Firefox thus has the best support out of all the browsers.

Before we write the code for the test, let's explore the Selenium API as follows:

```
$ python
>>> from selenium import webdriver
>>> driver = webdriver.Chrome()
# load the Google homepage
>>> driver.get("http://www.google.com")
# find a element by its class
>>> search_field = driver.find_element_by_class_name("gsfi")
# find a element by its name
>>> search_field = driver.find_element_by_name("q")
# find an element by its id
>>> search_field = driver.find_element_by_id("lst-ib")
# find an element with JavaScript
>>> search_field = driver.execute_script(
    "return document.querySelector('#lst-ib')"
)
# search for flask
>>> search_field.send_keys("flask")
>>> search_button = driver.find_element_by_name("btnK")
>>> search_button.click()
```

These are the main functions from Selenium that we will be using, but there are many other ways to find and interact with elements on the web page.

For the full list of available features, refer to the Selenium-Python documentation at http://selenium-python.readthedocs.org.

There are two gotchas in Selenium that need to be kept in mind while writing your tests, or you will run into very odd bugs that are almost impossible to debug from their error messages:

- Selenium is designed to work as if there is an actual person controlling the browser. This means that, if an element cannot be seen on the page, Selenium cannot interact with it. For example, if an element covers another element that you wish to click on—say, a modal window is in front of a button—then the button cannot be pushed. If the element's CSS has its display set to none, or its visibility set to hidden, the results will be the same.
- All of the variables that point toward elements on the screen are stored as pointers to those elements in the browser, meaning they are not stored in Python's memory. If the page changes without using the get method, such as when a link is clicked and a new element pointer is created, then the test will crash. This happens because the driver will continuously be looking for the elements on the previous page, and not finding them on the new one. The get method of the driver clears out all those references.

In the preceding tests, we used the test client in order to simulate a request to the application object. However, because we are now using something that needs to directly interface with the application through a web browser, we need an actual server to be running. This server needs to be run in a separate Terminal window before the user interface tests are run, so that the latter have something to request. To do this, we need a separate Python file in order to run the server with our test configuration, as well as needing to set up some models for our UI tests to use. At the root of the project directory, in a new file named run_test_server.py, add the following:

```
from webapp import create_app
from webapp.models import db, User, Role

app = create_app('config.TestConfig')

db.app = app
db.create_all()

default = Role("default")
poster = Role("poster")
db.session.add(default)
db.session.add(poster)
db.session.commit()

test_user = User("test")
test_user.set_password("test")
test_user.roles.append(poster)
```

```
db.session.add(test_user)
db.session.commit()

app.run()
```

Now that we have both the test server script and some knowledge of Selenium's API, we can finally write the code for our test:

```python
import time
import unittest
from selenium import webdriver


class TestURLs(unittest.TestCase):
    def setUp(self):
        self.driver = webdriver.Chrome()

    def tearDown(self):
        self.driver.close()

    def test_add_new_post(self):
        """ Tests if the new post page saves a Post object to the
            database

            1. Log the user in
            2. Go to the new_post page
            3. Fill out the fields and submit the form
            4. Go to the blog home page and verify that the post is
               on the page
        """
        # login
        self.driver.get("http://localhost:5000/auth/login")

        username_field = self.driver.find_element_by_name("username")
        username_field.send_keys("test")

        password_field = self.driver.find_element_by_name("password")
        password_field.send_keys("test")

        login_button = self.driver.find_element_by_id("login_button")
        login_button.click()

        # fill out the form
        self.driver.get("http://localhost:5000/blog/new")

        title_field = self.driver.find_element_by_name("title")
        title_field.send_keys("Test Title")
```

```
        #Locate the CKEditor iframe
        time.sleep(3)
        basic_page_body_xpath = "//div[contains(@id,
'cke_1_contents')]/iframe"
        ckeditor_frame =
self.driver.find_element_by_xpath(basic_page_body_xpath)

        #Switch to iframe
        self.driver.switch_to.frame(ckeditor_frame)
        editor_body = self.driver.find_element_by_xpath("//body")
        editor_body.send_keys("Test content")
        self.driver.switch_to.default_content()

        post_button = self.driver.find_element_by_class_name("btn-primary")
        post_button.click()

        # verify the post was created
        self.driver.get("http://localhost:5000/blog")
        self.assertIn("Test Title", self.driver.page_source)
        self.assertIn("Test content", self.driver.page_source)


if __name__ == "__main__":
    unittest.main()
```

Most of this test uses the methods that we introduced earlier. However, there is a new method in this test, named `switch_to`. The `switch_to` method is the context of the driver that allows the selection of elements inside an `iframe` element. Normally, it's impossible for the parent window to select any elements inside an `iframe` element using JavaScript, but because we are directly interfacing with the browser itself, we can access an `iframe` element's contents. We need to switch contacts like these, because the WYSIWYG editor inside the post creation page uses `iframe` in order to create itself. After we are done with selecting elements within the `iframe`, we need to switch back to the parent context using the `parent_frame` method.

You now have the tools that you need to completely test both your server code and your user interface code. For the rest of the chapter, we will focus on tools and methodologies, in order to make your testing even more effective in ensuring your application's correctness.

Test coverage

Now that our tests have been written, we have to know whether our code is sufficiently tested. The concept of **test coverage**, also known as **code coverage**, was invented to solve this issue. In any project, the test coverage represents what percentage of the code in the project was executed when the tests were run, and which lines were never run. This gives an idea of what parts of the project aren't being tested by our unit tests. To add coverage reports to our project, install the coverage library with `pip`, and make sure it's included in the `requirements.txt`:

```
(venv)$ pip install coverage
```

The coverage library can be run as a command-line program that will run your test suite, and take its measurements while the tests are running:

```
$ coverage run --source webapp --branch -m unittest discover
```

The `--source` flag tells `coverage` to only report on the test coverage for the files in the `webapp` directory. If that weren't included, the percentages for all the libraries used in the app would be included as well. By default, if any code in an `if` statement is executed, the entire `if` statement is said to have executed. The `--branch` flag tells `coverage` to disable this, and measure everything.

After `coverage` runs our tests and takes its measurements, we can see a report of its findings in two ways. The first is to see a printout of each file's coverage percentage on the command line:

```
$ coverage report
...
# You will get a full detailed report of your test coverage, breakdown by
python file name coverage, and with the line numbers missed by your test
...

TOTAL 729 312 118 10 56%
```

The second way to see the report is to use the HTML generating ability of `coverage` to see a detailed breakdown of each file in the browser, using the following command:

```
$ coverage html
```

The preceding command creates a directory named `htmlcov`. When the `index.html` file is opened in the browser, each file name can be clicked on to reveal the breakdown of which lines were run, and which were not, during the tests:

```
54
55  @blog_blueprint.route('/new', methods=['GET', 'POST'])
56  @login_required
57  @has_role('poster')
58  def new_post():
59      form = PostForm()
60      if form.validate_on_submit():
61          new_post = Post()
62          new_post.title = form.title.data
63          new_post.user_id = current_user.id
64          new_post.text = form.text.data
65          new_post.youtube_id = form.youtube_id.data
66          new_post.publish_date = datetime.datetime.now()
67          db.session.add(new_post)
68          db.session.commit()
69          flash('Post added', 'info')
70          return redirect(url_for('.post', post_id=new_post.id))
71      return render_template('new.html', form=form)
72
73
74  @blog_blueprint.route('/edit/<int:id>', methods=['GET', 'POST'])
75  @login_required
76  def edit_post(id):
77      post = Post.query.get_or_404(id)
78      # We want admins to be able to edit any post
79      if current_user.id == post.user.id:
80          form = PostForm()
81          if form.validate_on_submit():
82              post.title = form.title.data
83              post.youtube_id = form.youtube_id.data
84              post.text = form.text.data
85              post.publish_date = datetime.datetime.now()
86              db.session.add(post)
87              db.session.commit()
88              flash('Post edited', 'info')
89              return redirect(url_for('.post', post_id=post.id))
90          form.title.data = post.title
91          form.youtube_id.data = post.youtube_id
92          form.text.data = post.text
93          return render_template('edit.html', form=form, post=post)
94      abort(403)
```

In the preceding screenshot, the blog/controllers.py file was opened, and the coverage report clearly shows that the post route was never executed. However, this also gives some false negatives. As the user interface tests are not testing code that is being run by the coverage program, it doesn't count toward our coverage report. In order to fix this, just to make sure that you have tests in your test cases for each individual function that would have been tested in the user interface tests.

In most projects, the percentage to aim for is around 90% code coverage. It's very rare that a project will have 100% of its code testable, and this possibility decreases as the size of the project increases.

Test-driven development

Now that we have our tests written, how can they be integrated into the development process? Currently, we are using our tests in order to ensure code correctness after we create a feature. But, what if we flipped the order and used tests in order to create correct code from the beginning? This is what **test-driven development** (**TDD**) advocates.

TDD follows a simple loop to write the code of a new feature in your application:

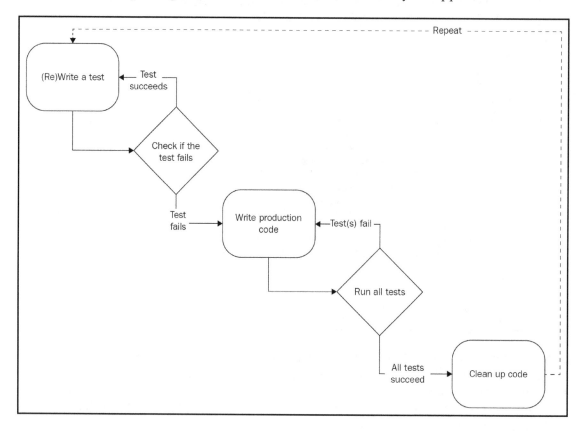

In a project that uses TDD, the first thing that you write, before any of the code that controls what you are actually building, is the tests. What this forces the programmers on the project to do is to plan out the project's scope, design, and requirements before writing any code. While designing APIs, it also forces the programmer to design the interface (or contract) of the API from a consumer's perspective, rather than design the interface after all the backend code has been written.

In TDD, tests are designed to fail the first time that you run them. There is a saying in TDD, that if your tests don't fail the first time that you run them, you're not really testing anything. What this means is that you are most likely testing to the tested unit's function, rather than how it should function while writing tests after the fact.

After your tests fail the first time, you then continuously write code until all the tests pass. This process is repeated for each new feature.

Once all of the original tests pass and the code is refactored, TDD tells you to stop writing code. By only writing code until the tests pass, TDD also enforces the **You Aren't Going To Need It (YAGNI)** philosophy, which states that programmers should only implement what they actually need, rather than what they perceive they will need. A huge amount of wasted effort is made during development when programmers try to preemptively add functionality when no-one needed it.

TDD also promotes the idea of **Keep It Simple, Stupid (KISS)**, which dictates that simplicity should be a design goal from the beginning. TDD promotes KISS because it requires small, testable units of code that can be separated from each other and don't rely on a shared global state.

Also, in projects that follow TDD, there is an always-current documentation throughout the tests. One of the axioms of programming is that with any sufficiently large program, the documentation will always be out of date. This is because the documentation is one of the last things on the mind of the programmer when they are changing the code. However, with tests, there are clear examples of each piece of functionality in the project (if the project has a large code coverage percentage). The tests are updated all the time, and therefore, show good examples of how the functions and API of the program should work.

Now that you understand Flask's functionality and how to write tests for Flask, the next project that you create in Flask can be made entirely with TDD.

Summary

Now that you understand testing and what it can do for your application, you can create applications that are guaranteed to be less bug-ridden. You will spend less time fixing bugs, and more time adding features that are requested by your users.

As a final challenge to the reader, before moving onto the next chapter, try to get your code coverage over 95%.

In the next chapter, we will finish the book by going over the ways by which you can deploy your application into a production environment on a server.

13
Deploying Flask Apps

Now that we have reached the last chapter of the book, and have a fully functioning web app made in Flask, the final step in our development cycle is to make the app available for the world. There are many different approaches for hosting your Flask app, each of them with its own pros and cons. This chapter will cover the best solutions and guide you through situations in which you should choose one over the other.

In this chapter, we will cover the following:

- A brief introduction to the most commonly used web servers and gateway interfaces
- How to deploy on various cloud services
- How to build Docker images
- How to describe services using Docker compose
- How to describe your infrastructure using AWS CloudFormation (IaC)
- How to set up and work with a CI/CD system to easily build, test, review, and deploy our application

Web servers and gateway interfaces

In this section, we will make a quick introduction to the most commonly used web servers and **Web Server Gateway Interfaces** (**WSGI**), and their differences and configuration. A WSGI is an application-agnostic layer between the web server and the python application itself.

Gevent

The simplest option to get a web server up and running is to use a Python library, named gevent, to host your application. Gevent is a Python library that adds an alternative way of doing concurrent programming,called co-routines, outside of the Python threading library. Gevent has an interface to run WSGI applications that is both simple and has good performance. A simple gevent server can easily handle hundreds of concurrent users, which is 99% more than the users of websites on the internet will ever have. The downside to this option is that its simplicity means a lack of configuration options. There is no way, for example, to add rate limiting to the server, or to add HTTPS traffic. This deployment option is purely for sites that you don't expect to receive a huge amount of traffic. Remember YAGNI: only upgrade to a different web server if you really need to.

 Co-routines are a bit outside of the scope of this book, but a good explanation can be found at https://en.wikipedia.org/wiki/Coroutine.

To install gevent, we will use pip with the following command:

```
$ pip install gevent
```

In the root of the project directory, in a new file named gserver.py, add the following:

```
from gevent.wsgi import WSGIServer
from webapp import create_app
app = create_app('webapp.config.ProdConfig')
server = WSGIServer(('', 80), app)
server.serve_forever()
```

To run the server with supervisor, just change the command value to the following:

```
[program:webapp]
command=python gserver.py
directory=/home/deploy/webapp
user=deploy
```

Now when you deploy, gevent will automatically be installed for you by running your requirements.txt on every deployment; that is, if you are properly pip freezing after every new dependency is added.

Tornado

Tornado is another very simple way to deploy WSGI apps purely with Python. Tornado is a web server that is designed to handle thousands of simultaneous connections. If your application needs real-time data, Tornado also supports WebSockets for continuous, long-lived connections to the server.

 Do not use Tornado in production on a Windows server. The Windows version of Tornado is not only slower—it is also considered beta-stage quality software.

To use Tornado with our application, we will use Tornado's WSGIContainer in order to wrap the application object to make it Tornado-compatible. Then, Tornado will start to listen on port *80* for requests until the process is terminated. In a new file, named tserver.py, add the following:

```
from tornado.wsgi import WSGIContainer
from tornado.httpserver import HTTPServer
from tornado.ioloop import IOLoop
from webapp import create_app
app = WSGIContainer(create_app("webapp.config.ProdConfig"))
http_server = HTTPServer(app)
http_server.listen(80)
IOLoop.instance().start()
```

To run the Tornado with supervisor privileges, just change the command value to the following:

```
[program:webapp]
command=python tserver.py
directory=/home/deploy/webapp
user=deploy
```

Nginx and uWSGI

If you need better performance or more options for customization, the most popular way to deploy a Python web application is to use a Nginx web server as a frontend for the WSGI-based uWSGI server by using a reverse proxy. A *reverse proxy* is a program in networks that retrieves contents for a client from a server, as if it returned from the proxy itself. This process is shown in the following diagram:

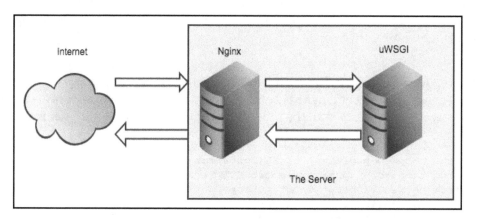

Nginx and **uWSGI** are used like this, because this way, we get the power of the Nginx frontend, while having the customization of uWSGI.

Nginx is a very powerful web server that became popular by providing the best combination of speed and customization. Nginx is consistently faster than other web severs, such as Apache's httpd, and has native support for WSGI applications. It achieves this speed thanks to the developers taking several good architecture decisions, as well as not going to try to cover a large amount of use cases, as Apache does. The latter point here was a decision taken early on in development of Nginx. Having a smaller feature set makes it much easier to maintain and optimize the code. From a programmer's perspective, it is also much easier to configure Nginx, as there is no giant default configuration file (`httpd.conf`) that can be overridden with `.htaccess` files in each of your project directories.

uWSGI is a web server that supports several different types of server interfaces, including WSGI. uWSGI handles the severing of the application content, as well as things such as the load balancing of traffic across several different processes and threads.

To install uWSGI, we will use a `pip` command, as follows:

```
$ pip install uwsgi
```

In order to run our application, uWSGI needs a file with an accessible WSGI application. In a file named `wsgi.py` in the top level of the project directory.

To test uWSGI, we can run it from the **command-line interface** (**CLI**) with the following commands:

```
$ uwsgi --socket 127.0.0.1:8080
--wsgi-file wsgi.py
--callable app
--processes 4
--threads 2
```

If you are running this on your server, you should be able to access port 8080 and see your app (if you don't have a firewall, that is).

What this command does is load the app object from the `wsgi.py` file, and make it accessible from `localhost` on port *8080*. It also spawns four different processes with two threads each, which are automatically load balanced by a master process. This amount of processes is overkill for the vast majority of websites. To start off, use a single process with two threads and scale up from there.

Instead of adding all of the configuration options on the CLI, we can create a text file to hold our configuration, which gives us the same benefits for configuration that were listed in the *Gevent* section, about supervisor. In the root of the project directory, create a file named `uwsgi.ini` and add the following code:

```
[uwsgi]
socket = 127.0.0.1:8080
wsgi-file = wsgi.py
callable = app
processes = 4
threads = 2
```

 uWSGI supports hundreds of configuration options, as well as several official and unofficial plugins. To leverage the full power of uWSGI, you can explore the documentation at `http://uwsgi-docs.readthedocs.org/`.

Let's now run the server from supervisor:

```
[program:webapp]
command=uwsgi uwsgi.ini
directory=/home/deploy/webapp
user=deploy
```

Because we are installing Nginx from the OS's package manager, the OS will handle the running of Nginx for us.

 At the time of writing, the Nginx version in the official Debian package manager is several years old. To install the most recent version, follow the instructions available at `http://wiki.nginx.org/Install`.

Next, we need to create an Nginx configuration file, and then, when we push the code, we need to copy the configuration file to the `/etc/nginx/sites-available/` directory. In the root of the project directory, create a new file named `nginx.conf`, and add the following:

```
server {
    listen 80;
    server_name your_domain_name;

    location / {
        include uwsgi_params;
        uwsgi_pass 127.0.0.1:8080;
    }
    location /static {
        alias /home/deploy/webapp/webapp/static;
    }
}
```

What this configuration file does is tells Nginx to listen for incoming requests on port *80*, and forwards all requests to the WSGI application that is listening on port *8080*. Also, it makes an exception for any requests for static files, and instead sends those requests directly to the file system. Bypassing uWSGI for static files gives a great boost to performance, as Nginx is really good at serving static files quickly.

Apache and uWSGI

Using Apache httpd with uWSGI mostly requires the same setup. First off, we need an Apache configuration file, so let's create a new file, named `apache.conf`, in the root of our project directory, and add the following code:

```
<VirtualHost *:80>
    <Location />
        ProxyPass / uwsgi://127.0.0.1:8080/
    </Location>
</VirtualHost>
```

This file simply tells Apache to pass all requests on port *80* to the uWSGI web server listening on port *8080*. However, this functionality requires an extra Apache plugin from uWSGI, named `mod-proxy-uwsgi`.

Next, we will cover several solutions for deploying our application on **Platform as a Service (PaaS)** and **Infrastructure as a Service (IaaS)** utilities. You will learn how to create several types of environments and make our example Blog application available to the world.

Deploying on Heroku

Heroku is the first of the **Platform as a Service (PaaS)** providers that this chapter will cover. PaaS is a service given to web developers that allows them to host their websites on a platform that is controlled and maintained by someone else. At the cost of some freedom, you gain assurances that your website will automatically scale with the number of users your site has, with no extra work on your part. Using PaaS utilities may, however, tend to be more expensive than running your own servers.

Heroku is a PaaS utility that aims to provide ease of use to web developers by hooking into already existing tools, and not requiring any large changes in the app. Heroku works by reading a file named `Procfile`, which contains commands that your Heroku dyno (basically a virtual machine sitting on a server) will run. Before we begin, you will need a Heroku account. If you wish to just experiment, there is a free account available.

In the root of the directory, in a new file named `Procfile`, we have the following:

```
web: uwsgi heroku-uwsgi.ini
```

This tells Heroku that we have a process named `web`, which will run the uWSGI command and pass the `uwsgi.ini` file. Heroku also needs a file named `runtime.txt`, which will tell Heroku what Python runtime you wish to use—at the time of writing, the latest Python release is 3.7.0:

```
python-3.7.0
```

Next, make sure that **uwsgi** is present in the `requirements.txt` file.

Finally, we need to make some modifications to the `uwsgi.ini` file that we made earlier:

```
[uwsgi]
http-socket = :$(PORT)
die-on-term = true
wsgi-file = wsgi.py
```

```
callable = app
processes = 4
threads = 2
```

We set the port on which uWSGI listens to the environment variable port, because Heroku does not directly expose the dyno to the internet. Instead, it has a very complicated load balancer and reverse proxy system, so we need to have uWSGI listening on the port that Heroku needs us to listen on. Also, we set **die-on-term** to true, so that uWSGI listens for a signal termination event from the OS correctly.

To work with Heroku's command-line tools, we first need to install them, which can be done from `https://toolbelt.heroku.com`.

Next, you need to log in to your account:

```
$ heroku login
```

We can test our setup to make sure that it will work on Heroku before we deploy it, by using the `foreman` command:

```
$ foreman start web
```

The `foreman` command simulates the same production environment that Heroku uses to run our app. To create the dyno, which will run the application on Heroku's servers, we will use the `create` command. Then, we can push Heroku to the remote branch on our Git repository to have Heroku servers automatically pull down our changes:

```
$ heroku create
$ git push heroku master
```

If everything went well, you should now have a working application on your new Heroku dyno. You can open a new tab to your new web application with the following command:

```
$ heroku open
```

To see the app in action in a Heroku deployment, visit `https://mastering-flask.herokuapp.com/`.

Using Heroku Postgres

Maintaining a database properly is a full-time job. Thankfully, we can use one of Heroku's built-in features in order to automate this process for us. Heroku Postgres offers a database that is maintained and hosted entirely by Heroku. Because we are using SQLAlchemy, using Heroku Postgres is trivial. In your dyno's dashboard, there is a link to your **Heroku Postgres** information. By clicking on it, you will be taken to a page similar to the following screenshot:

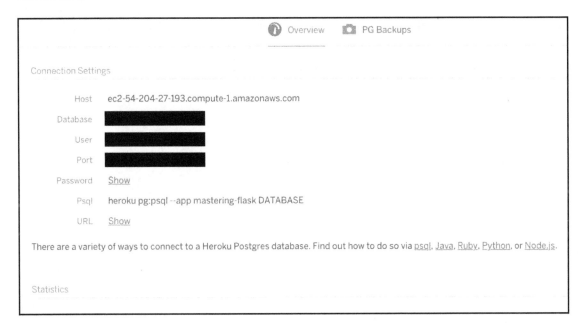

By clicking on the **URL** field, you will be given an SQLAlchemy URL, which you can copy directly to your production configuration object.

Using Celery on Heroku

We have our production web server and database set up, but we still need to set up Celery. Using one of Heroku's many plugins, we can host a RabbitMQ instance in the cloud, while running the Celery worker on the dyno. The first step is to tell Heroku to run your Celery worker in `Procfile`:

```
web: uwsgi heroku-uwsgi.ini celery: celery worker -A celery_runner
```

Next, to install the Heroku RabbitMQ plugin with the free plan (the `lemur` plan), use the following command:

```
$  heroku addons:create cloudamqp:lemur
```

 To get the full list of Heroku add-ons, go to
`https://elements.heroku.com/addons`.

At the same location on the dashboard where Heroku Postgres was listed, you will now find **CloudAMQP**:

Clicking on **CloudAMQP** will also give you a screen with a URL, which you can copy and paste into your production configuration:

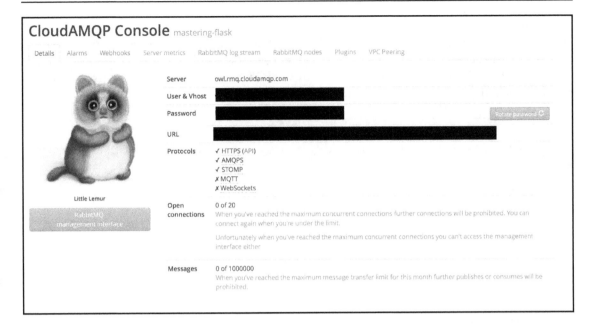

Deploying on Amazon Web Services

Amazon Web Services (**AWS**) is a collection of services maintained by Amazon, and built on top of the same infrastructure that runs Amazon.com. To deploy our Flask code, we will be using Amazon Elastic Beanstalk in this section, while the database will be hosted on Amazon's **Relational Database Service** (**RDS**), and our messaging queue for Celery will be hosted on Amazon's **Simple Queue Service** (**SQS**).

Using Flask on Amazon Elastic Beanstalk

Elastic Beanstalk is a platform for web applications that offers many powerful features for developers, so they don't have to worry about maintaining servers. For example, your Elastic Beanstalk application will automatically scale by utilizing more and more servers as the number of people using your app at once grows. For Python apps, Elastic Beanstalk uses Apache, in combination with `mod_wsgi`, to connect to WSGI applications—if your deployment is simple with mid-to-low load, there is no extra configuration needed.

Before we begin, you will need an Amazon.com account to log in to the console. Next, you need to install **awscli** and configure it with your credentials—you must generate an AWS access key and secret: go to the AWS console, choose IAM service, choose your user, then choose the **Security Credentials** tab, and click on the **Create access key**. Next, we need to install awsebcli to manage Elastic Beanstalk from the CLI:

```
$ pip install awsebcli --upgrade --user
```

Next, from the root directory of our project, we are going to configure the CLI and create a new Elastic Beanstalk application:

```
$ eb init

Enter Application Name
(default is "Chapter-13"): myblog
Application myblog has been created.

It appears you are using Python. Is this correct?
(Y/n): Y

Select a platform version.
1) Python 3.6
2) Python 3.4
3) Python 3.4 (Preconfigured - Docker)
4) Python 2.7
5) Python
(default is 1): 1
Cannot setup CodeCommit because there is no Source Control setup,
continuing with initialization
Do you want to set up SSH for your instances?
(Y/n): Y

Select a keypair.
1) aws-sshkey
2) [ Create new KeyPair ]
(default is 1): 1
```

Elastic Beanstalk looks for a file named `application.py` in your project directory, and it expects to find a WSGI application, named `application`, in that file:

```
import os
from webapp import create_app
from webapp.cli import register

env = os.environ.get('WEBAPP_ENV', 'dev')
application = create_app('config.%sConfig' % env.capitalize())
register(application)
```

Next, we are going to create a development environment. Each Elastic Beanstalk application can contain one or many environments. But as things currently stand, our application will fail—we need to tell Elastic Beanstalk how to install Flask-YouTube on Python's virtual environment and initialize the database. To do this, we need to extend the default setup.

In the root directory, we need a directory named `.ebextensions`. This is where we create a lot of extra configuration and setup scripts. In `.ebextensions`, we create two shell scripts that will run in the post-deploy phase. So, in the `.ebextensions/10_post_deploy.config` file, add the following code:

```
files:
"/opt/elasticbeanstalk/hooks/appdeploy/post/01_install_flask_youtube.sh":
        mode: "000755"
        owner: root
        group: root
        content: |
            #!/usr/bin/env bash

            cd /opt/python/current/app
            . /opt/python/current/env
            source /opt/python/run/venv/bin/activate
            sh install_flask_youtube.sh

    "/opt/elasticbeanstalk/hooks/appdeploy/post/02_migrate_database.sh":
        mode: "000755"
        owner: root
        group: root
        content: |
            #!/usr/bin/env bash
...
```

Using YAML notation here, we tell Elastic Beanstalk to create two shell scripts to install Flask-YouTube and create or migrate the database. The location of these files is special—`/opt/elasticbeanstalk/hooks/appdeploy/post` is where we can drop scripts to be executed after deploying. These scripts are executed in alphabetic order. Also, take note of the following locations:

- `/opt/python/current/app`: This is the deploy location of the application.
- `/opt/python/current/env`: This is a file containing defined environment variables on Elastic Beanstalk.
- `/opt/python/run/venv`: This is python's `virtualenv`, and is where Elastic Beanstalk installed all our defined dependencies.

Now, for our environment creation, run the following commands:

```
$ eb create myblog-dev
$ # Setup this environment variable
$ eb setenv WEBAPP_ENV=Dev
```

Finally, after the environment has finished provisioning the infrastructure and deployment, we can check out our application using the following command:

```
$ eb open
```

To deploy new versions of our application, we just have to run this command:

```
$ eb deploy
```

Note that our development environment uses SQLite, so the database is on a file on the web server itself. On each deployment or instance recreation, this database is recreated.

Using Amazon RDS

Amazon RDS is a database-hosting platform in the cloud that automatically manages several things, such as recovery on node failure, scheduled backups, and master/slave setups.

To use RDS, go to the **Services** tab on the AWS console and click on **Relational Database Service**.

Now, create and configure a new database—make sure that on the **Publicly accessible** option, you choose **No**. Choose the same VPC as the instances, and register your admin credentials carefully. Now, wait a few minutes for the instance creation. After that, choose your instance, go to the details configuration, and find the field for the **endpoint**—it should look something like myblog.c7pdwgffmbqdm.eu-central-1.rds.amazonaws.com. Our production configuration uses system environment variables to set up the database URI, so we have to configure Elastic Beanstalk to set the DB_URI environment variable.

To use these environment variables, we need to change our blog's config.py file to use the actual OS environment variables, as follows:

```
class ProdConfig(Config):
    SQLALCHEMY_TRACK_MODIFICATIONS = False
    SQLALCHEMY_DATABASE_URI = os.environ.get('DB_URI', '')

    CELERY_BROKER_URL = os.environ.get('CELERY_BROKER_URL', '')
```

```
CELERY_RESULT_BACKEND = os.environ.get('CELERY_BROKER_URL', '')

CACHE_TYPE = 'redis'
CACHE_REDIS_HOST = os.environ.get('REDIS_HOST', '')
CACHE_REDIS_PORT = '6379'
CACHE_REDIS_PASSWORD = ''
CACHE_REDIS_DB = '0'
```

Make sure your instances can connect to the database. If you chose the security group default options and RDS creation, then the wizard will have created a security group for you (the default name is 'rds-launch-wizard'). On EC2, edit this security group and open port 3306 to your instances' VPC CIDR.

In .ebextensions, take a look at the 01_env.config—this is where we set our environment variables:

```
option_settings:
  aws:elasticbeanstalk:application:environment:
    WEBAPP_ENV: Prod
    DB_URI: mysql://admin:password@myblog.c4pdwhkmbyqm.eu-
central-1.rds.amazonaws.com:3306/myblog
    CELERY_BROKER_URL: sqs://sqs.us-east-1.amazonaws.com/arn:aws:sqs:eu-
central-1:633393569065:myblog-sqs/myblog-sqs
```

Finally, let's create the production environment with the following command:

```
$ eb create myblog-prod
```

Using Celery with Amazon SQS

In order to use Celery on AWS, we need to have our Elastic Beanstalk instance run our Celery worker in the background, as well as set up an SQS messaging queue. For Celery to support SQS, it needs to install a helper library from pip. Once more, verify that our requirements.txt file contains the **boto3** package. Elastic Beanstalk will look at this file and create a virtual environment from it.

Setting up a new messaging queue on SQS is very easy. Go to the **Services** tab and click on **Simple Queue Service** in the applications tab, then click on **Create New Queue.** After a very short configuration screen, you should see a screen much like the following:

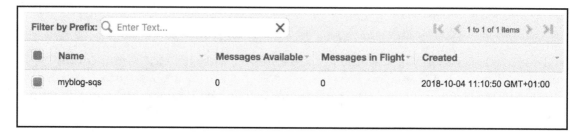

Next, we have to give our instances access to the newly created SQS. The easiest way to do this is editing the Elastic Beanstalk default instance profile (this is not recommended, however—you should create a separate instance profile and associate all your instances with it using .ebextensions option settings). The default IAM instance profile is named aws-elasticbeanstalk-ec2-role. Go to IAM service, then roles, then choose the aws-elasticbeanstalk-ec2-role role. Next, click on **Add inline policy** and follow the wizard to give access to the newly created SQS.

Now we have to change our CELERY_BROKER_URL to the new URL, which takes the following format:

```
$ eb setenv CELERY_BROKER_URL=sqs://sqs.us-
east-1.amazonaws.com/arn:aws:sqs:us-east-1:<AWS_ACCOUNT_ID>:myblog-
sqs/myblog-sqs
```

Change the AWS_ACCOUNT_ID value to your AWS account ID.

Finally, we need to tell Elastic Beanstalk to run a Celery worker in the background. Once more, we can do this in .ebextensions. Create a file named 11_celery_start.config, and insert the following code into it:

```
commands:
    celery_start:
        command: |
                #!/usr/bin/env bash
                cd /opt/python/current/app
                . /opt/python/current/env
                source /opt/python/run/venv/bin/activate
                celery multi start worker1 -A celery_runner
```

Note that this kind of Celery worker deployment lives on the web server (which is not recommended), and will also scale along with the web servers in line with demand. A better option would be to explore the worker feature from Elastic Beanstalk, but this would imply a complete rework of the feature, and we'd suffer from subsequent vendor lock-in.

Using Docker

Docker is a container-based technology created in 2013 by Docker, Inc. Container technology is not new, and has been around for some time on Unix OS, with chroot created in 1982, Solaris Zones in 2004, and WPAR available on AIX or OS400 systems (although WPAR is more of a virtualization technology than a container). Later, two important features were integrated on Linux: **namespaces**, which isolate OS function names, and **cgroups**, a collection of processes that are bound by configuration and resource limits. These new features gave birth to Linux containers, so why use Docker?

Mainly, because Docker made configuration definitions simple. Using a very easy-to-write Dockerfile, you can describe how to provision your container and create a new image with it. Each Dockerfile line will create a new FS layer using UnionFS, which makes changes very quick to apply, and it's equally easy to roll back and forward between changes. Also Docker, Inc. created an open image repository, where you can find quality images of almost any Linux software available . We have already used some of these for Redis and RabbitMQ in `Chapter 9`, *Creating Asynchronous Tasks with Celery*.

Docker has gained enormous traction and hype. Some of its best features are the following:

- Solving dependency issues from the OS: Since we are packing a thin OS with your container image, it is safe to assume that what runs on your laptop will run on production as well.
- Containers are very light, and users are able to run multiple containers on the same VM or hardware host, which can reduce operations costs and increase efficiency.
- Containers bootstrap very quickly, enabling your infrastructure to scale equally quickly, if, for example, you needed to address an increase in workload.
- Developers can easily share their application with other developers using containers.
- Docker supports DevOps principles: developers and operations can and should work together on the image and architecture definition, using Dockerfile or Docker Compose.

If we consider the differences in features on offer from Docker containers versus VMs, let's remember that containers share the same kernel and normally run a single process, while VMs run a fully featured guest OS:

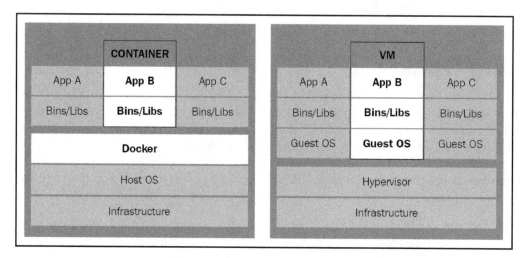

This architecture makes containers very lightweight and quick to spawn.

Creating Docker images

Throughout the previous chapters, our Blog application has grown from a simple three-tier architecture to a multi-tier one. We now need to address a web server, database, cache system, and queue. We are going to define each of these layers as Docker containers.

First, let's begin with our web server and Flask application. For this, we will be using an Nginx frontend, and a WSGI, called uWSGI, for the backend.

A Dockerfile is a text file that contains special instructions with which we use to specify our Docker image and how it should be run. The build process is going to execute the commands one by one, creating a new layer on each one. Some of the most used Dockerfile commands include the following:

- FROM: Specifies the base image that our new image is based upon. We can start from a really thin OS, such as Alpine, or directly from an RabbitMQ image.
- EXPOSE: Informs Docker that the container listens on a specified network port/protocol.
- ENV: Sets environment variables.

- `WORKDIR`: Establishes the base directory for the Dockerfile.
- `RUN`: Runs bash Linux commands on a new layer. This is normally used to install additional packages.
- `COPY`: Copies files or directories from local filesystem to the Docker image.
- `CMD`: There can be only one instance of CMD. It specifies how the container should be run.
- `ENTRYPOINT`: This has the same objective as CMD, but is a script in Docker.

For a full reference of Dockerfile commands, check out the documentation at `https://docs.docker.com/engine/reference/builder/#usage`.

Our directory structure for Docker deploy is going to be the following:

```
/
  deploy/
  docker/
    docker-compose.yml -> Compose file
    ecs-docker-compose.yml -> Specific compose file for AWS ECS
    Dockerfile_frontend -> Dockerfile for the frontends
    Dockerfile_worker -> Dockerfile for the workers
    prod.env -> Production environment variables
    worker_entrypoing.sh -> entrypoint for the celery worker
  supervisor_worker.sh -> Supervisor conf file for the celery worker
  uwsgi.ini -> Conf. file for uWSGI
```

The images we are going to create will be used with Docker Compose (more on this later in this chapter), so they will not work on a standalone basis. If you don't want to use Docker Compose, very few modification are needed for the images to work—you just have to change the `prod.env` file.

First, let's create a Dockerfile for our web server. We will use a previous image that already contains NGINX and uWSGI, saving us the work to install and configure them. Our `Dockerfile_frontend` is the Dockerfile containing the definition for creating frontend images:

```
FROM tiangolo/uwsgi-nginx:python3.6

# Create and set directory where the code will live
RUN mkdir /srv/app
WORKDIR /srv/app

# Copy our code
```

```
COPY . .
# Install all python packages required
RUN pip install -r requirements.txt
RUN sh install_flask_youtube.sh

# Setup NGINX and uWSGI
COPY ./deploy/uwsgi.ini /etc/uwsgi/uwsgi.ini
ENV NGINX_WORKER_OPEN_FILES 2048
ENV NGINX_WORKER_CONNECTIONS 2048
ENV LISTEN_PORT 80

EXPOSE 80
```

First, in the preceding snippet, we base our image on `uwsgi-nginx:python3.6`, which means we are going to use Python 3.6. Next, we create and set the directory where our application will live—this will be in `/srv/app`. Then we copy all our local content (myblog code) to the image itself using the `COPY . .`. Next, we copy the configuration file for our WSGI, finally configuring the number of workers that NGINX will use. At the end, we inform Docker that this image will be listening on port 80, using `EXPOSE 80`.

Next, let's take a look at our Celery worker Dockerfile:

```
FROM ubuntu
RUN  apt-get update && \
     apt-get install -y supervisor python3-pip python3-dev libmysqlclient-
dev mysql-client
RUN mkdir /srv/app
WORKDIR /srv/app
COPY . .
RUN pip3 install -r requirements.txt
RUN sh install_flask_youtube.sh

COPY ./deploy/supervisor_worker.conf
/etc/supervisor/conf.d/celery_worker.conf
COPY ./deploy/docker/worker_entrypoint.sh .
ENTRYPOINT ["sh", "./worker_entrypoint.sh"]
```

This time, our base image is going to be Ubuntu (in particular, a really thin Ubuntu version for Docker). We are going to use the **supervisor** Python package to monitor and launch our Celery process, so if Celery crashes for some reason, supervisor will restart it. So, at the OS level, we are installing the supervisor, Python 3, and MySQL client packages. Take a look at the `worker_entrypoint.sh` shell script in the preceding code block, where we are doing some interesting things:

- We are waiting for MySQL to become available. When using Docker Compose, we can define the order that each task (that is, each Docker container) is launched, but we don't have a way to know if the service is already available.
- Next, we use the Flask CLI and Alembic to create or migrate our database.
- Finally, we insert test data to our database (simply because it's nice to have for the readers), so that when you launch the app, it's in a workable state with some fake post data already present.

To build and create our images, execute the following Docker commands on the shell in the root directory of our project:

```
$ docker build -f deploy/docker/Dockerfile_frontend -t myblog:latest .
```

This will create an image named **myblog** with the tag **latest**. As part of production best practices, you should tag your images with your project version, also using a **git** tag. This way, we can always be sure what code is in which images; for example, what changed between `myblog:1.0` and `myblog:1.1`.

Finally, create the Celery worker image with the following command:

```
$ docker build -f deploy/docker/Dockerfile_worker -t myblog_worker:latest .
```

Now that we have our custom images created, we are ready to go to the next section, where we are going define our of all infrastructure and link the containers to each other.

Docker Compose

Docker Compose is a tool for defining our multi-layer application. This is where we define all the services needed to run our application, configure them, and link them together.

Docker Compose is based on YAML files, which is where all the definition happens, so let's dive right into it and take a look at the `deploy/docker/docker-compose.yaml` file:

```
version: '3'
services:
  db:
    image: mysql:5.7
    env_file:
      - prod.env
  rmq:
    image: rabbitmq:3-management
    env_file:
      - prod.env
    ports:
      - 15672:15672
  redis:
      image: redis
  worker:
    image: myblog_worker:latest
    depends_on:
      - db
      - rmq
    env_file:
      - prod.env
  frontend:
    image: myblog
    depends_on:
      - db
      - rmq
    env_file:
      - prod.env
    restart: always
    ports:
      - 80:80
```

In Docker Compose, we have defined the following services:

- **mysql**: This is based on the Docker Hub community image for MySQL 5.7. All the custom configuration happens with environment variables, as defined in the `prod.env` file.
- **rmq**: Rabbit MQ is based on the Docker Hub community image, customized by us to create user credentials, cookies, and VHOST. This will install the management interface as well, which can be accessed on `http://localhost:15672`.

- **redis**: This is the Redis service for our cache.
- **worker**: This uses our previously built `myblog_worker` Docker image.
- **frontend**: This uses our previously built `myblog_worker` Docker image.

This is a very simple composer definition. Note `depends_on`, where we define which services depend on other services. So, for example, our frontend service is going to depend on the database and Rabbit MQ. The `ports` key is a list of exposed ports; in this case, the frontend port 80 is going to be exposed by the Docker host on port 80 also. This way, we can access our application on the Docker host IP port 80, or by using a load balancer in front of the Docker hosts. On your machine with Docker already installed, you can access the application on `http://localhost`.

The use of the `prod.env` file is important, because this way, we can define different configurations for different environments and still use the same compose file. Using the same compose file across environments obeys another Twelve-Factor App rule about making the infrastructure components the same across all environments.

Let's take a look at the `prod.env` file:

```
WEBAPP_ENV=Prod
DB_HOST=db
DB_URI=mysql://myblog:password@db:3306/myblog
CELERY_BROKER_URL=amqp://rabbitmq:rabbitmq@rmq//
REDIS_HOST=redis
MYSQL_ROOT_PASSWORD=rootpassword
MYSQL_DATABASE=myblog
MYSQL_USER=myblog
MYSQL_PASSWORD=password
RABBITMQ_ERLANG_COOKIE=SWQOKODSQALRPCLNMEQG
RABBITMQ_DEFAULT_USER=rabbitmq
RABBITMQ_DEFAULT_PASS=rabbitmq
RABBITMQ_DEFAULT_VHOST=/
```

This file environment variables will set actual OS-level environment variables so that it's simple to use them on the configuration file for our application. This will comply with another of the Twelve-Factor App rules from `https://12factor.net/`.

At the top, we set our application environment for production configuration using `WEBAPP_ENV=Prod`.

The `MYSQL_*` variables is where we configure the MySQL 5.7 container. We set the root password and an initial database to create (if necessary) a user and password for this database.

It's important to note that the `REDIS_HOST`, `DB_URI`, `CELERY_BROKER_URL` variables are using the actual host names that each container will use to communicate with the other containers. By default, these are the service names, which makes everything pretty simple. So, the frontend container accesses the database using the `db` network hostname.

Finally, let's start our application:

```
$ docker-compose -f deploy/docker/docker-compose.yml up
```

Wait for all the containers to start up, then open your browser and go to `http://localhost`.

Deploying Docker containers on AWS

To deploy on AWS, we are going to use the **Amazon Elastic Container Service** (**ECS**). ECS is a service that provides a scalable cluster for Docker, without the need to install any software to orchestrate your containers. It's based on **AWS Auto Scaling Groups** (**ASG**), which scale instances up or down with Docker installed. This scaling is triggered by monitoring metrics, such as CPU usage or network load. ECS also migrates all containers from an instance that, for some reason, terminates, or gets its service impaired. ECS thus acts as a cluster. After this, the ASG will spawn a new instance to replace the faulty one.

CloudFormation Basics

AWS provides many services, each of which has many configuration options. You also need to wire these services up. To effectively and reliably create, configure, update, or destroy these services, we are going to show you how to use an **IaC** (**Infrastructure as code**) technology from AWS, called CloudFormation. **CloudFormation** is not a complex technology, but follows the extension of all AWS services and configuration options. The details and operation of CloudFormation could be subject to a book on its own.

CloudFormation is an extended data structure that you write using JSON or YAML. I say extended, because it's possible to use references, functions, and conditions. A CloudFormation file is composed of the following sections:

```
AWSTemplateFormatVersion: "version date"
Description: "Some description about the stack"
Parameters: Input parameters to configure the stack
Metadata: Aditional data about the template, also useful to group
parameters on the UI
Mappings: Data mappings definitions
Conditions: Setup conditions to setup resources or configuration
```

```
Transform: Mainly used for AWS serverless
Resources: Resource definitions, this is the only required section
Output: Section to output data, you can use it return the DNS name to
access the created application
```

Let's take a quick look at the provided CloudFormation file
in `./deploy/docker/cfn_myblog.yml`. We are going to follow all the CloudFormation
sections, one be one. First, let's examine the **Parameters** section:

```
...
Parameters:
  ApplicationName:
    Description: The application name
    Type: String
    Default: ecs001
  Environment:
    Description: Application environment that will use the Stack
    Type: String
    Default: prod
    AllowedValues:
    - dev
    - stg
    - prod
  InstanceType:
    Description: Which instance type should we use to build the ECS
cluster?
    Type: String
    Default: t2.medium
...
```

Without going into much detail, in this file, an input parameter is defined by a name, and
may contain a description, a type, a default value, and rules for accepted values. All these
values will be referenced later when configuring our infrastructure. These values are going
to be filled when deploying or updating the CloudFormation stack.

Next, look at the **Mappings** section:

```
...
Mappings:
  AWSRegionToAMI:
    us-east-2:
      AMI: ami-b86a5ddd
    us-east-1:
      AMI: ami-a7a242da
    us-west-2:
      AMI: ami-92e06fea
...
```

This is simply a convenient data structure for mapping AWS regions into AMIs. An AMI is a base OS image that we are using for our Docker VMs. Each AMI has a different identification in each region, so we need to map them out to make our stack deployable on any AWS region. On our case, we will be using Amazon ECS-optimized Linux.

Now, let's consider the **Metadata** section:

```
...
Metadata:
  AWS::CloudFormation::Interface:
    ParameterGroups:
    - Label:
        default: System Information (Tags)
      Parameters:
      - Environment
      - ApplicationName
    - Label:
        default: Networking
      Parameters:
      - VPC
      - Subnets
...
```

Here, we are declaring an `Interface` to group our parameters. This is just to make the parameters display in a nicer way to whomever is going to deploy the stack. Remember that the parameters section is a dictionary, and that dictionary keys have no order.

The main, and more important section is **Resources**. We are not going to go into full detail on this, rather, we'll just quickly highlight the main infrastructure resources we are going to create and how they are wired. First, for the database, we are going to use another AWS service, called **RDS**, and create a MySQL server:

```
Resources:
...
DB:
  Type: AWS::RDS::DBInstance
  Properties:
    AllocatedStorage: "30"
    DBInstanceClass: "db.t2.medium"
    Engine: "MariaDB"
    EngineVersion: "10.2.11"
    MasterUsername: !Ref DBUsername
    MasterUserPassword: !Ref DBPassword
    DBSubnetGroupName: !Ref DBSubnetGroup
    VPCSecurityGroups:
      - Ref: DBSecurityGroup
```

Each resource has a type. For RDS, this is `AWS::RDS:DBInstance`. Each type has its own specific set of properties. Also, notice how `!Ref` declares values that are references from other resources or parameters. `DBUsername` and `DBPassword` are parameters, but `DBSubnetGroup` and `DBSecurityGroup` are resources created by CloudFormation to set up the network ACL and subnet placement for our database.

The ECS cluster resource declaration is as follows:

```
ECSCluster:
  Type: "AWS::ECS::Cluster"
  Properties:
    ClusterName: !Sub ${Environment}-${ApplicationName}

ECSAutoScalingGroup:
  Type: AWS::AutoScaling::AutoScalingGroup
  Properties:
...

ECSLaunchConfiguration:
  Type: AWS::AutoScaling::LaunchConfiguration
  Properties:
...

ECSRole:
  Type: AWS::IAM::Role
  Properties:
...
ECSInstanceProfile:
  Type: AWS::IAM::InstanceProfile
  Properties:
...
ECSServiceRole:
  Type: AWS::IAM::Role
  Properties:
...
```

All these definitions belong to the ECS cluster. This cluster can be used to provision many different applications, so it would make sense to declare these definitions on a separate CloudFormation file, or use nested stacks. To simplify the deployment, we will use a single file to create our application. First, we create the ECS cluster, and set its name to be a concatenation with the `Environment` and `ApplicationName` parameters. This is done using the `!Sub` CloudFormation function.

Next, we declare the **Auto Scaling Group** (**ASG**) for our cluster, and set up the way AWS is going to provision each instance that belongs to this ASG. These are the `ECSAutoScalingGroup` and `ECSLaunchConfiguration` resources. Finally, `ECSRole`, `ECSInstanceProfile`, and `ECSServiceRole` are used to set up the security permissions needed for the ECS cluster to fetch Docker images, work with AWS load balancers (ELB), S3, and so on. These permissions are the standard used by AWS as an example, and can be most certainly be downgraded.

Now, for our application, we are going to define ECS services and ECS task definitions. A task definition is where we define one or more container definitions that reference the Docker image to use, along with environment variables. Then, the ECS service references an ECS task definition, and may tie it up with a load balancer and set up deployment configuration options, such as performance limits and auto scaling options (yes, the ECS cluster can scale up or down on load shifts, but our containers may scale up or down independently as well):

```
FrontEndTask:
  DependsOn: WorkerTask
  Type: "AWS::ECS::TaskDefinition"
  Properties:
    ContainerDefinitions:
      -
        Name: "frontend"
        Image: !Ref DockerFrontEndImageArn
        Cpu: "10"
        Memory: "500"
        PortMappings:
          -
            ContainerPort: "80"
            HostPort: "80"
        Environment:
          -
            Name: "WEBAPP_ENV"
            Value: !Ref Environment
          -
            Name: "CELERY_BROKER_URL"
            Value: !Sub
"amqp://${RMQUsername}:${RMQPassword}@${ELBRMQ.DNSName}:5672//"
          -
            Name: "DB_URI"
            Value: !Sub
"mysql://${DBUsername}:${DBPassword}@${DB.Endpoint.Address}:3306/myblog"
          -
            Name: "REDIS_HOST"
            Value: !Sub ${ELBRedis.DNSName}
```

This is the task definition for our frontend containers. You may notice that this is the CloudFormation version of the Docker Compose service that we've already seen. We declare a name for our container, `Name: "frontend"`, that will later be referenced in the load balancers. Next, the image: `!Ref DockerFrontEndImageArn` is a reference to an input parameter. This will allow us to easily deploy new versions of our blog application. The port mappings for Docker are declared in `PortMappings`. This is a list of key values, repeating the keys for `ContainerPort` and `HostPort`. The environment is, once again, a list of key values, and here we make the "wiring" for DB, RMQ, and Redis from other resources we are creating. For example, here is how we use `DB_URI`:

```
-
      Name: "DB_URI"
      Value: !Sub
"mysql://${DBUsername}:${DBPassword}@${DB.Endpoint.Address}:3306/myblog"
```

This `Value` is where we construct the URI for the database, using our already known `!Sub` function and a reference for `DBUsername` and `DBPassword`. The `DB.Endpoint.Address` is how we can reference the DNS name that AWS created for our newly created MySQL server.

In the service definition, we tie our container to an AWS Elastic Load Balancer, and make some deployment configuration:

```
MyBlogFrontendService:
  Type: "AWS::ECS::Service"
  Properties:
    Cluster: !Ref ECSCluster
    DeploymentConfiguration:
      MaximumPercent: 200
      MinimumHealthyPercent: 50
    DesiredCount: 2
    TaskDefinition: !Ref FrontEndTask
    LoadBalancers:
      -
        ContainerName: 'frontend'
        ContainerPort: 80
        LoadBalancerName: !Ref ELBFrontEnd
  DependsOn:
    - ECSServiceRole
    - FrontEndTask
```

First, we declare that this service will run on our newly created ECS cluster, using `Cluster: !Ref ECSCluster`. Then, using the `DeploymentConfiguration` and `DesiredCount`, we say that this service will start with two containers (for high availability) and allow it to scale up and down between 4 and 1. This obeys the following formulas:

- The maximum number of containers = DesiredCount * (MaximumPercent / 100)
- The minimum number of containers = DesiredCount * (MinimumPercent / 100)

So, applying the formulas to our case gives us the following:

- 4 = 2 * (200/100)
- 1 = 2 * (50/100)

With `TaskDefinition: !RefFrontEndTask`, we say that this service uses our previous frontend task definition. And finally, with the `LoadBalancers` key property, we tie our service with a load balancer. This means that our two newly created containers will evenly receive requests from the users, and new containers will automatically be registered on the load balancer as they are created, as well.

Finally, let's look at the load balancer definition:

```
ELBFrontEnd:
  Type: AWS::ElasticLoadBalancing::LoadBalancer
  Properties:
    SecurityGroups:
    - Fn::GetAtt:
      - ELBFrontEndSecurityGroup
      - GroupId
    Subnets:
      Ref: Subnets
    Scheme: internet-facing
    CrossZone: true
    Listeners:
    - LoadBalancerPort: '80'
      InstancePort: '80'
      Protocol: HTTP
      InstanceProtocol: HTTP
    HealthCheck:
      Target: TCP:80
      HealthyThreshold: '2'
      UnhealthyThreshold: '3'
      Interval: '10'
      Timeout: '5'
```

This is an AWS classic ELB definition, where we associate the ELB with a network security group, which serves more or less like a firewall. This is done with the `SecurityGroups` key property. Next, we define in which subnets the ELB is going to serve. Each subnet is created in a different AWS availability zone, each of which represent a data center in an AWS region (each region contains two or more data centers, or availability zones). Then, we define that this ELB is going to be exposed to the internet using `Scheme:` `internet-facing`. For `Listeners`, we say that port 80 of the ELB is mapped to port 80 of the Docker host. And finally, we define a health check for the service, and the period for which this will occur.

> Check out more details on ELB CloudFormation definitions at `https://` `docs.aws.amazon.com/AWSCloudFormation/latest/UserGuide/aws-` `properties-ec2-elb.html`.

We further create the following resources in the `./deploy/docker/cfn_myblog.yml` YAML file provided by CloudFormation:

- Several security groups for ELBs and Docker hosts
- Task definition and the respective service for our myblog Celery workers
- Task definition and the respective service for our RabbitMQ container
- Task definition and the respective service for our Redis container
- Load balancer for the Redis container
- Load balancer for RabbitMQ

Using a load balancer for RabbitMQ is a cheap way to get service discovery functionality—it's strange to balance load on a single instance, but if the Docker host, located where our RabbitMQ is, crashes for some reason, then the RabbitMQ container is going to be created on another Docker host, and the application needs to be able to find it dynamically.

Create and update a CloudFormation stack

We can create and deploy our CloudFormation stack using the console or the CLI. To create it using the console, choose the AWS CloudFormation service, and then click on the **Create Stack** button. You will see the following form:

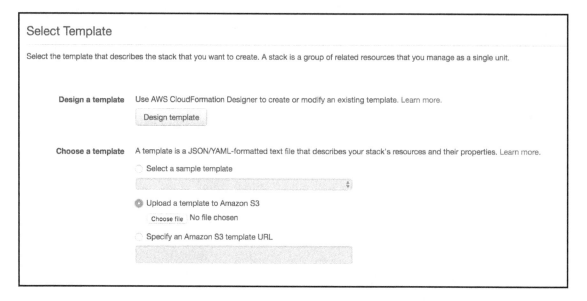

Choose the **Upload a template to Amazon S3** option, then choose the `deploy/docker/cfn_myblog.yaml` file from the provided code, and click **Next**. Now, we need to fill the stack parameters as follows:

- **Stack Name**: Provide a name to identify this stack; use whatever you want.
- **Environment**: Choose the environment of this stack for production, staging, and development.
- **ApplicationName**: Here, use whatever you want to identify the ECS cluster.
- **VPC**: Choose an AWS VPC.
- **Subnets**: From the drop-down menu, choose all the subnets that belong to the VPC (if you have public and private subnets, choose only public subnets, remember that the ELB's are internet facing).
- **ClusterSize**: This is the ECS cluster size; leave the default setting of 2 here.
- **InstanceType**: This is the AWS instance type for the Docker hosts.

- **KeyName**: This is the AWS key pair, and needs to be one that we created previously. We can use the private key to SSH to the Docker hosts.
- **DockerFrontEndImageArn**: This is the ARN of the ECR repository to which we uploaded our Docker image for the frontend.
- **DockerWorkerImageArn**: This is the ARN of the ECR repository to which we uploaded our Docker image for the worker.
- **DBUsername, DBPassword, RMQUsername**, and **RMQPassword**: These are all the credentials for the database and RabbitMQ; choose whatever values you want.

After filing all the parameters, click **Next**. An Options form is presented—just click **Next** again. A review page is presented with our parameters and possible stack changes. Here, we need to check the **I acknowledge that AWS CloudFormation might create IAM resources with custom names.** option, and click **Create**. The creation of all the resources is going to take a few minutes—wait for the **CREATE_COMPLETED** state. To check out our application, just go to the **Output** tab and click on the URL.

Now, let's see how easily we can develop and deploy a code change. First, make a simple code change. For example, in the `webapp/templates/head.html` file, find the following line:

```
...
<h1><a class="text-white" href="{{ url_for('blog.home') }}">My
Blog</a></h1>
...
```

Now, change the preceding line to the following:

```
...
<h1><a class="text-white" href="{{ url_for('blog.home') }}">My Blog
v2</a></h1>
...
```

Then create a new Docker image, and tag it with `v2`, as shown here:

```
$ docker build -f deploy/docker/Dockerfile_frontend -t myblog:v2 .
```

Next, push this image to AWS ECR using the following command:

```
$ ecs-cli push myblog:v2
```

Then, go to AWS console and choose our previously created stack. On **Actions**, choose **Update Stack**. On the first form, choose **Use current template**. Then, in the input parameters, we need to change `DockerFrontEndImageArn`—update it with the new tag, and postfix it with `:v2`. The new ARN should look something like this: `XXXXXXXX.dkr.ecr.eu-central-1.amazonaws.com/myblog:v2`. Then, click **Next**, and on the **Options** forms click **Next** again. On the preview form, notice how, in the **Preview your Changes** section, the updater identifies exactly what needs to be updated. In this case, `FrontEndTask` and `MyBlogFrontendService` are selected for updates, so let's update them. While we wait for the **UPDATE_COMPLETE** state, just keep using the application—notice how no downtime occurs. After one to two minutes. notice how our Blog displays the main title as **My Blog v2**.

In the next section, we will see how to integrate this approach with a modern CI/CD system to build, run tests, check code quality, and deploy on different environments.

Building and deploying highly available applications readily

Whether our web app is on the cloud or in a data center, we should aim for reliability. Reliability can impact the user is various ways, either by downtime, data loss, application error, response time degradation, or even on user deploy delay. Next, we are going to cover some aspects to help you think about architecture and reliability, to help you plan ahead to handle issues, such as failures or increased load. First of all, we will cover the necessary steps for you to deploy rapidly and, of course, reliably.

Building and deploying reliably

With today's demanding markets, we need to build and deploy easily and quickly. But the speed of our deployment must also deliver reliability. One of the steps needed to achieve this is to use automation via scripts, or with CI/CD tools.

To help us set up the entire process, we should use a CI/CD tool, such as Jenkins, Bamboo, TeamCity, or Travis. First, what exactly is CI/CD?

CI stands for **Continuous Integration**, and is the process defined for integrating software changes, made by many developers, into a main repository—and, of course, doing so quickly and reliably. Let's enumerate what we need, from bottom to top:

- First, it is imperative to use a source control and versioning system, such as Git, along with a well established and internally defined branching model, such as **GitFlow**. This will give us a clear view of code changes, along with the ability to accept and test them, at either feature or hotfix level. This will also make it easy to rollback to a previous version.
- Before approving any merges proposed by pull requests, make sure to set up automated triggering of tests and reviewing of code. Pull-request reviewers can then make more informed decisions before approving a merge. Failed tests are certainly a warning sign that we want to see before merging code that will end up on production. Fail fast, and don't be afraid to fail often.

As was said previously, we have several tools to automate this process. One easy way to do this is to use GitHub with Travis and landscape.io. You can freely create an account on all three of them and try them out. After this, just create the following two files on your repository.

Create a `.travis.yml` file, which should contain the following:

```
language: python
python:
    - "3.6"
    - "3.3"
    - "2.7"
install:
    - "pip install --upgrade"
    - "pip -V"
    - "pip install -r requirements.txt"
    - "pip install coveralls"
script:
    - coverage run --source webapp --branch -m unittest discover
after_success:
    coveralls
```

This is all we need to have automated tests running on every commit. Also, our tests will run independently using Python versions 3.6, 3.3, and 2.7. GitHub and Travis integration will also give us the result of these tests on every pull request.

For code quality control, landscape.io is very easy to use with GitHub (other tools include flake8, Sonarqube, and Codacy, for example).

To set up landscape.io, we just have to create the following `.landscape.yml` file at the root of our project:

```
ignore-paths:
  - migrations
  - deploy
  - babel
```

Further automation can be achieved by merging every branch automatically to the develop branch, for example, but we need a third tool to automate this process on GitHub.

CD stands for **Continuous Delivery**, and is based on reduced cycles of development and the actual delivery of changes. This must be done quickly and reliably, and rollback should always be accounted for. To help us define and execute this process, we can use **Jenkins/Blue Ocean pipelines.**

Using Jenkins pipelines, we can define the entire pipeline process, from build to deployment. This process is defined using a `Jenkinsfile` at the root of our project. First, let's create and start our Jenkins CI server from the CLI, as follows:

```
docker run \
  --rm \
  -u root \
  -p 8080:8080 \
  -v jenkins-data:/var/jenkins_home \
  -v /var/run/docker.sock:/var/run/docker.sock \
  -v "$HOME":/home \
  jenkinsci/blueocean
```

On start, the Docker output will show the following:

```
...
INFO: Pre-instantiating singletons in
org.springframework.beans.factory.support.DefaultListableBeanFactory@340c82
8a: defining beans [filter,legacy]; root of factory hierarchy
Sep 16, 2018 11:39:39 AM jenkins.install.SetupWizard init
INFO:

*************************************************************
*************************************************************
*************************************************************

Jenkins initial setup is required. An admin user has been created and a
password generated.
Please use the following password to proceed to installation:
```

```
476c3b81f2gf4n30a7f9325568dec9f7
```

This may also be found at: /var/jenkins_home/secrets/initialAdminPassword

```
*************************************************************
*************************************************************
*************************************************************
```

Copy the password from your output and open Jenkins in your browser by going to http://localhost:8080. On startup, Jenkins will ask for a one-time password—paste in the password provided by the Docker output. Next, Jenkins will ask you for some initial configuration. This consists of creating an Admin user, and installing plugins (for our example, you can simply accept the suggested plugins).

To set up an automated approach to build and deploy our Docker images to AWS ECR, we need an extra plugin called **Amazon ECR**. To install this plugin, go to **Manage Jenkins**, then choose **Manage Plugins**, and click on the **Available** Tab for a list of available and not-yet-installed plugins. From this list, choose the **Amazon ECR** plugin, and finally click on the **Install without restart** option.

Next, we must configure a set of credentials, so that Jenkins can authenticate on AWS and push our newly built Docker images. For this, on the left-hand menu, choose **Credentials**, then choose **Jenkins credential scope** and **Global credentials**. Now, on the left-hand panel, choose **Add credentials** and fill the form with the following info:

- **Kind**: AWS Credentials
- **Scope**: Global
- **ID**: ecr-credentials
- **Description**: ecr-credentials
- **Access Key ID**: Use the AWS Access Key ID that you already created in the previous section for pushing your Docker images
- **Secret Access key**: Use the AWS Secret Access Key that you already created in the previous section for pushing your Docker images

For security reasons, it's better to choose the IAM role approach. However, for the sake of simplicity, we are using AWS keys here. If you still want to use AWS keys, remember to never use your personal keys on automation processes—instead, create a specific user for the process with contained and managed privileges.

Now we are ready to create our first CI/CD pipeline. Follow these steps:

1. On the main page, choose the **Create new Jobs** link
2. On the input box for "**nter an item name**, write `myblog`
3. Choose the **Multibranch pipeline** option. Then click **Ok**

On the Jobs configuration, you need to fill in the following fields:

- **Branch Sources**: Create new Jenkins' credentials for your GitHub account, or set up using your own credentials from your private Git repository. Then, choose the GitHub repository for this book, or use your private repository URL.
- Then, for now, remove all behaviors except "**Discover branches**", as shown here:

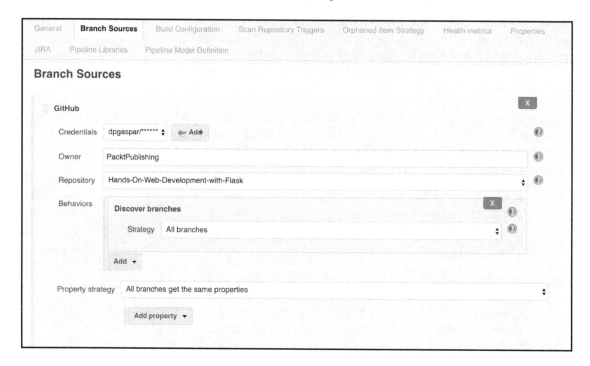

On the "Build Configuration" job section, change the "Script Path" to `Chapter-13/Jenkinsfile` if you're using this book's GitHub repository. This is required because the repository is organised by chapters, and the `Jenkinsfile` is not at the root of the repository.

This is all it takes, because the heavy lifting is done using the `Jenkinsfile` pipeline definition. Let's take a look at this file:

```
pipeline {
    agent any

    parameters {
        string(description: 'Your AWS ECR URL: http://<AWS ACCOUNT
NUMBER>.dkr.ecr.<REGION>.amazonaws.com', name: 'ecrURL')
    }

    environment {
        CHAPTER = 'Chapter-13'
        ECRURL = "${params.ecrURL}"
        ECRCRED = 'ecr:eu-central-1:ecr-credentials'
    }
...
```

> The Jenkins pipeline definition gives you a huge amount of configuration options. We can even use Groovy scripts embedded in it. Please take a look at the documentation for more details, available at `https://jenkins.io/doc/book/pipeline/jenkinsfile/`.

On the `pipeline` main section, we have created a manual parameter for you to fill out the AWS ECR URL to which the images should be pushed. This section also configures some necessary environment variable to make our stages more dynamic.

Next, let's take a look at the pipeline stages section:

```
....
stages {
    stage('Build') {
        steps {
            echo "Building"
            checkout scm
        }
    }
    stage('Style') {
        agent {
            docker 'python:3'
        }

        steps {
            sh '''
                #!/bin/bash

                cd "${CHAPTER}"
                python -m pip install -r requirements.txt
                cd Flask-YouTube
                python setup.py build
```

```
                    python setup.py install
                    cd ..
                    python -m pip install flake8
                    flake8 --max-line-length 120 webapp
                '''
            }
        }
    ...
```

The `stages` section will hold all the stages necessary to build, test, check, and deploy our application. The build declared with `stage('Build')` just executes a checkout of our repository using `checkout scm`.

In the *Style* stage, we will check the code style using **flake8**. We are assuming that a critical style problem is enough to make the pipeline fail, and never deploy the application. To run it, we tell Jenkins to run a Docker container with Python 3 by using the `docker 'python:3'` command, and inside, we install all the necessary dependencies and run **flake8** against our code.

Next you will find a *Test* stage, which very similar to the *Style* stage. Notice that we can easily define tests for Python 3 and 2.7 using specific Docker containers to run it.

The Docker build stage is as follows:

```
stage('Build docker images') {
    agent any
    steps {
        echo 'Creating new images...'
        script {
            def frontend = docker.build("myblog:${env.BUILD_ID}", "-f
${CHAPTER}/deploy/docker/Dockerfile_frontend ${CHAPTER}")
            def worker = docker.build("myblog_worker:${env.BUILD_ID}", "-f
${CHAPTER}/deploy/docker/Dockerfile_worker ${CHAPTER}")
        }
    }
}
```

In this stage, we use Groovy to build our images for the frontend and Celery workers. The images will be produced and tagged with the Jenkins build identification, which we can use as an `env.BUILD_ID` environment variable.

In the final stage, we push the newly created images to the AWS ECR Docker image repository as follows:

```
stage('Publish Docker Image') {
    agent any
```

```
steps {
    echo 'Publishing new images...'
    script {
        docker.withRegistry(ECRURL, ECRCRED)
        {
            docker.image("myblog:${env.BUILD_ID}").push()
            docker.image("myblog_worker:${env.BUILD_ID}").push()
        }
    }
}
}
```

Finally, to run our job, choose the "myblog" job, then "master," and on the left panel, choose "Build with parameters." Fill in your AWS ECR URL (this URL takes the form `http://<ACCOUNT_NUMBER>.dkr.ecr.<REGION>.amazonaws.com`), and then click **Build**. After the build is done, we just have to update our CloudFormation with the newly created Docker images.

A great final stage would be to update the previously deployed CloudFormation, scripting the process with what we've already tested in this book, in the previous *Create and Update a CloudFormation Stack* section. For this, we could use the "pipeline: AWS steps" plugin.

Creating highly available applications that scale

High availability (**HA**) and scalability is an ever more important subject. It should be taken into consideration from the development phase, all the way up to the release stage. Monolithic architectures, where all the features and services that comprise your application can't be separated or are installed on one single instance, will not resist failure, and won't scale either. Vertical scaling will only go so far, and in case of failure, will increase recovery times, as well as the impact on the user. This is an important and complex subject and, as you may have guessed, there is no single solution to solve it.

To think about HA, we have to be pessimistic. Remember—failure can't be eliminated, but failure points can be identified, and recovery plans should be put in place so that downtime takes seconds or minutes, instead of hours or even days.

First, let's think about all the components that our Blog application has, and identify the stateless ones:

- **Frontend**: Webserver and uWSGI – stateless
- **Celery workers**: Celery – stateless
- **Message queue**: RabbitMQ or AWS SQS – state

- **Cache**: Redis – state
- **Database**: SQL or NoSQL – state

Our first goal is to identify all the **Single Points of Failure (SPOF)** in our application, and try to eliminate them. For this, we have to think about redundancy:

- **Frontend**: This is a stateless service that receives direct requests from the users. We can balance these requests using a load balancer, and by always having at least two instances. If one fails, the other immediately starts receiving all the load. Looks good? Maybe, but can a single instance support all the load? Huge response times are a failure too, so think about it—maybe you need at least three instances. Next, can your load balancer fail too? This is not a problem when using some sort of cloud-based load balancer, such as AWS ELB or ALB, but if you aren't using these, then set up redundancy on this layer as well.
- **Celery workers**: Workers are stateless, and a complete failure does not have an immediate impact on users. You can have at least one instance, as long as recovery is done automatically, or failure can be easily identified and a failed instance can rapidly be replaced with a new one.
- **Message queue**: If using AWS SQS or CloudMQ, failure is already accounted for. If not, a clustered RabbitMQ can be an option, or you can make sure that message loss is an option, and that RabbitMQ replacement is automatic, or can at least be rapidly executed.
- **Cache:** Make sure you have more then one memcached instance (using cluster key sharding), or your application can gracefully account for failure. Remember that a memcached replacement comes with a cold cache, which can have a huge impact on the database, depending on your load.
- **Database**: Make sure you have an SQL or NoSQL slave/cluster in place, ready to replace writes from the failed master.

Layers that contain state are more problematic, and a small failure (seconds or milliseconds) may be inevitable. Hot standbys or cold standbys should be accounted for. It's very useful to test system failures of all your services while load testing. Redundancy is like a software feature—if not tested, it's probably broken.

Scaling can be verified with load tests. It's a very good idea to include it somewhere along the way in your production pipeline release. **Locust** is an excellent Python tool to implement highly configurable load tests that can scale to any load level you want. These kinds of tests are a great opportunity to verify your high availability setup. Take down instances while simulating your expected load, and load test until you break your stack. This way you will know your limits—knowing what will break first *before* it breaks on production will help you test performance tuning.

Locust python package documentation is available at `https://docs.locust.io/en/stable/`.

Scaling using cloud infrastructure, such as AWS, Azure, and GCP, is all about automation. You need to set up your instances automatically, so that monitoring metrics can automatically trigger the creation of new VMs or Dockers containers.

Finally, please make sure you backup your database periodically. The delta time between backups is a point of possible data loss, so identify it and report back. Also, it's very important to restore your production backups—again, if not tested, then they're probably broken.

Monitoring and collecting logs

Monitor all your systems and components, collect OS level metrics, and produce application metrics. You have great tools for doing this, including DataDog; NewRelic; a combination of StatsD, Graphana, InfluxDB, and Prometheus; and ELK.

Set up alarms on failures based on metric thresholds. It's very important not to go overboard on the amount of alarms you create—make sure that a critical alarm really implies that the system is down or severely impaired. Set up time charts so that you can identify issues or upscale necessities early.

Collect logs from OS, applications, and cloud services. Parsing, structuring, and adding metadata to your logs enriches your data, and enables proper log aggregation, filtering, and charting. Being able to easily filter all of your logs relative to a specific user, IP, or country is a step forward.

Log collection has become more critical on the cloudc and even more so on containers, because they are short-lived and break your applications down into microservices, so that by the time something happens, your logs may no longer exist, or you may have to manually go through dozens, if not thousands, of log files to find out what was and is happening. This is increasingly becoming impossible to do. There are many good solutions out there, however: you can use ELK (ElasticSearch, logstash, and Kibana) or EFK (ElasticSearch, Fluentd, and Kibana) stacks, Sumo logic, or DataDog.

Summary

As this chapter explained, there are many different options for hosting your application, each with their own pros and cons. Deciding on one depends on the amount of time and money you are willing to spend, as well as the total number of users you expect.

Now, we have reached the conclusion of the book. I hope that this book was helpful in building your understanding of Flask, and how it can be used to create applications of any degree of complexity with both ease and simple maintainability.

Web application development is a fast paced area that touches different technologies and concepts. Don't stop here—keep improving your Python skills, read about UX design, improve your knowledge on CSS and HTML, master SQL and query performance, and develop a single page application using Flask and Javascript. Each chapter of this book is an invitation for further knowledge.

Other Books You May Enjoy

If you enjoyed this book, you may be interested in these other books by Packt:

Python Testing Cookbook - Second Edition
Greg L. Turnquist

ISBN: 9781787122529

- Run test cases from the command line with increased verbosity
- Write a Nose extension to pick tests based on regular expressions
- Create testable documentation using doctest
- Use Selenium to test the Web User Interface
- Write a testable story with Voidspace Mock and Nose
- Configure TeamCity to run Python tests on commit
- Update project-level scripts to provide coverage reports

Building Django 2.0 Web Applications
Tom Aratyn

ISBN: 9781787286214

- Build new projects from scratch using Django 2.0
- Provide full-text searching using ElasticSearch and Django 2.0
- Learn Django 2.0 security best practices and how they're applied
- Deploy a full Django 2.0 app almost anywhere with mod_wsgi
- Deploy a full Django 2.0 app to AWS's PaaS Elastic Beanstalk
- Deploy a full Django 2.0 app with Docker
- Deploy a full Django 2.0 app with NGINX and uWSGI

Leave a review - let other readers know what you think

Please share your thoughts on this book with others by leaving a review on the site that you bought it from. If you purchased the book from Amazon, please leave us an honest review on this book's Amazon page. This is vital so that other potential readers can see and use your unbiased opinion to make purchasing decisions, we can understand what our customers think about our products, and our authors can see your feedback on the title that they have worked with Packt to create. It will only take a few minutes of your time, but is valuable to other potential customers, our authors, and Packt. Thank you!

Index

with scalability feature, creating 305

I

IaC (Infrastructure as code) 288
identity providers 101
IIS integrated windows authentication 97
indexing 41
Infrastructure as a Service (IaaS) 271
integration testing 246

J

Jenkins 19
Jenkins pipeline
  reference 303
Jinja2 55
Jinja
  comments 55
  filters 50
  Flask-specific variables and functions 57
  if statements, using 55
  loops 55
  macros 57
  syntax 49
JSON Web Token (JWT)
  authentication 171, 173

K

Keep It Simple, Stupid (KISS) 263
key-value NoSQL database
  Amazon DynamoDB 128
  Redis 128
  Riak 128

L

LDAP (lightweight directory access protocol) 98
LDAP services
  Microsoft Active Directory 98
  OpenLDAP 98
links 132
Locust python package
  reference 306
loops 49

M

many-to-many relationship 39, 40
message queue 186
minification 218
Model View Controller (MVC) 77
model, creating
  about 27
  user table, creating 30
models
  creating 31
  detecting 35
  queries, filtering 33
  reading 31
  relationships 35
  updating 35
modular application
  about 87
  code, refactoring 89, 90
MongoDB
  about 140
  CRUD 147
  documents, defining 142
  executing 140
  installation link 140
  MongoEngine, setting up 141
MongoEngine
  setting up 141

N

Network File System (NFS) 162
NGINX configuration
  reference 96
Nginx
  about 268
  installation link 270
node 132
NoSQL
  leveraging 155, 159
  relationships 152
Not Only SQL (NoSQL) database
  about 127
  column family stores 130
  document stores 129
  graph databases 132

CPSIA information can be obtained
at www.ICGtesting.com
Printed in the USA
BVHW012003030419
544516BV00008B/121/P